Penn Greek Drama Series

Series Editors
David R. Slavitt
Palmer Bovie

The Penn Greek Drama Series presents fresh literary translations of the entire corpus of classical Greek drama: tragedies, comedies, and satyr plays. The only contemporary
series of all the surviving work of Aeschylus, Sophocles,
Euripides, Aristophanes, and Menander, this collection
brings together men and women of literary distinction
whose versions of the plays in contemporary English poetry
can be acted on the stage or in the individual reader's theater of the mind.

The aim of the series is to make this cultural treasure acces-
sible, restoring as faithfully as possible the original luster of
the plays and offering in living verse a view of what talented
contemporary poets have seen in their readings of these
works so fundamental a part of Western civilization.

Euripides, 2

Hippolytus, Suppliant Women,
Helen, Electra, Cyclops

Edited by
David R. Slavitt and Palmer Bovie

PENN

University of Pennsylvania Press
Philadelphia

Copyright © 1998 University of Pennsylvania Press
Printed in the United States of America on acid-free paper

10 9 8 7 6 5 4 3 2 1

Published by
University of Pennsylvania Press
Philadelphia, Pennsylvania 19104-4011

Library of Congress Cataloging-in-Publication Data

Euripides.
    [Works. English. 1997]
    Euripides / edited by David R. Slavitt and Palmer Bovie.
        p.   cm.—(Penn Greek drama series)
    Contents: 1. Medea. Hecuba. Andromache. The Bacchae—
2. Hippolytus. Suppliant women. Helen. Electra. Cyclops
    ISBN 0-8122-3415-4 (v. 1 : cloth : alk. paper).—ISBN 0-8122-1626-1
(v. 1 : pbk. : alk. paper).—ISBN 0-8122-3421-9 (v. 2 : cloth : alk. paper).—
ISBN 0-8122-1629-6 (v. 2 : pbk. : alk. paper)
    1. Euripides—Translations into English.   2. Greek drama (Tragedy)—
Translations into English.   3. Mythology, Greek—Drama.   I. Series.
PA3975.A1   1997
882'.01—dc21   97-28892
                                                                    CIP

Contents

Introduction

Palmer Bovie

Classical Greek tragedy, which flourished in Athens during the fifth century B.C., grew out of country festivals originating a century earlier. Three different celebrations in honor of Dionysus, known as the rural Dionysia, occurred during the winter months. One of these, the Lenaea, was also observed at Athens in the sanctuary of Dionysus. In addition to song it offered ecstatic dances and comedy. Another, the Anthesteria, lasted for three days as a carnival time of revelry and wine drinking. It also included a remembrance of the dead and was believed to be connected with Orestes' mythical return to Athens purged of guilt for killing his mother Clytemnestra.

The rural Dionysia were communal holidays observed to honor Dionysus, the god of wine, of growth and fertility, and of lightning. Free-spirited processions to an altar of Dionysus were crowned by lyrical odes to the god sung by large choruses of men and boys chanting responsively under the direction of their leader. The ritual included the sacrifice of a goat at the god's altar, from which the term "tragedy," meaning goat-song, may derive. Gradually themes of a more serious nature gained ground over the joyful, exuberant addresses to the liberating god, legends of familiar heroes, and mythological tales of divine retribution. But the undercurrent of the driving Dionysiac spirit was seldom absent, even in the sophisticated artistry of the masterful tragic poets of the fifth century.

Initially the musical texts were antiphonal exchanges between the chorus and its leader. Thespis, who won the prize of a goat for tragedy at Athens in 534 B.C., is traditionally said to have been the first to appear as an actor, separate from the chorus, speaking a prologue and making set speeches, with his face variously disguised by a linen mask. A fourth festival, the City Dionysia or the Great Dionysia, was instituted by the ruler Peisistratus, also in 534, and nine years later Aeschylus was born. It seems that the major area of Greek tragic art was destined to begin.

The Great Dionysia, an annual occasion for dramatic competitions in tragedy and comedy, was held in honor of Dionysus Eleutheros. Its five-day celebration began with a procession in which the statue of Dionysus was carried to the nearby village of Eleutherai (the site of the Eleusinian Mysteries) and then back, in a parade by torchlight, to Athens and the precincts of Dionysus on the lower slopes of the Acropolis. In the processional ranks were city officials, young men of military age leading a bull, foreign residents of Athens wearing scarlet robes, and participants in the dramatic contests, including the producers (*choregoi*), resplendent in colorful costumes. The ceremonies ended with the sacrificial slaughter of the bull and the installation of Dionysus' statue on his altar at the center of the orchestra.

For three days each of the poets chosen for the competition presented his work, three tragedies and one satyr play (a farcical comedy performed in the afternoon after an interval following the staging of tragedies). In the late afternoon comedies were offered. The other two days were marked by dithyrambic competitions, five boys' choruses on one day, five men's on the other. The dithyramb, earlier an excited dramatic dance, became in the Athenian phase a quieter performance, sung by a chorus of fifty and offering little movement.

The theater of Dionysus at Athens was an outdoor space on the southern slope of the Acropolis. A semicircular auditorium was created on the hillside from stone or marble slabs, or shaped from the natural rock with wooden seats added. Narrow stepways gave access to the seats, the front row of which could be fitted out with marble chairs for official or distinguished members of the audience. From sites visible today at Athens, Delphi, Epidaurus, and elsewhere, it is evident that the sloping amphitheater had excellent acoustic properties and that the voices of the actors and the chorus were readily heard.

The acting area began with an *orchestra*, a circular space some sixty feet in diameter where the chorus performed its dance movements, voiced its commentaries, and engaged in dialogue with the actors. In the center of the orchestra was an altar of Dionysus, and on it a statue of the god. Behind the orchestra several steps led to a stage platform in front of the *skene*, a wooden building with a central door and doors at each end and a flat roof. The actors could enter and exit through these doors or one of the sides, retiring to assume different masks and costumes for a change of role. They could also appear on the roof for special effects, as in Euripides' *Orestes* where at the end Orestes and Pylades appear, menacing Helen with death, before she is whisked away from them by Apollo. The skene's facade represented a palace or temple and could have an altar in front of it. Stage properties included the *eccyclema*, a wheeled platform that was rolled out from the central door or the side of the skene to display an interior setting or a tableau, as at the end of Aeschylus' *Agamemnon* where the murdered bodies of Agamemnon and Cassandra are proudly displayed by Clytemnestra.

Another piece of equipment occasionally brought into play was the *mechane*, a tall crane that could lift an actor or heavy objects (e.g., Medea in her chariot) high above the principals' heads. This device, also known as the *deus ex machina*, was favored by Euripides who, in the climactic scene of *Orestes* shows Apollo protecting Helen in the air high above Orestes and Pylades on the roof. Or a deity may appear above the stage to resolve a final conflict and bring the plot to a successful conclusion, as the figure of Athena does at the end of Euripides' *Iphigenia in Tauris*. Sections of background at each end of the stage could be revolved to indicate a change of scene. These *periaktoi*, triangular in shape, could be shown to the audience to indicate a change of place or, together with thunder and lightning machines, could announce the appearance of a god.

The actors wore masks that characterized their roles and could be changed offstage to allow one person to play several different parts in the same drama. In the earliest period tragedy was performed by only one actor in counterpoint with the chorus, as could be managed, for example, in Aeschylus' *Suppliants*. But Aeschylus himself introduced the role of a second actor, simultaneously present on the stage, Sophocles made use of a third, and he and Euripides probably a fourth. From such simple elements (the orchestra space for the chorus, the slightly raised stage and its scene front, the minimal cast of actors) was created the astonishingly powerful poetic drama of the fifth-century Athenian poets.

What we can read and see today is but a small fraction of the work produced by the three major poets and a host of fellow artists who presented plays in the dramatic competitions. Texts of tragedies of Aeschylus, Sophocles, and Euripides were copied and stored in public archives at

Athens, along with Aristophanes' comedies. At some later point a selection was made of the surviving plays, seven by Aeschylus, seven by Sophocles, nine by Euripides, and ten others of his discovered by chance. In the late third and early second centuries B.C., this collection of thirty-three plays was conveyed to the great library of Alexandria, where scholarly commentaries, *scholia*, formed part of the canon, to be copied and transmitted to students and readers in the Greco-Roman cultural world.

Euripides (485–406 B.C.) was born near Athens, the son of prosperous middle-class parents. He spent most of his life in study and in writing his poetry "in a cave by the sea in Salamis." At Athens his associates included Archelaus, a pupil of the philosopher Anaxagoras, Protagoras, Prodicus, and Socrates. Such acquaintances, cited by early biographers, are well worth considering in view of Euripides' flair for weaving philosophical debates into many dramatic dialogues, or marshaling logical principles in set speeches. During the oppressive decades of the Peloponnesian War, Euripides may have incurred the hostility of his fellow citizens by his denunciation of war and its havoc, a recurrent theme in many of his plays. For whatever reason, he withdrew into retirement, living a rather unsociable existence. For his conventional treatment of mythological figures and situations he was mercilessly mocked by the comic poets, especially Aristophanes. And his skeptical approach to standard religious conceptions may have disturbed many of his listeners. Late in life, three or four years before his death, Euripides left Athens for residence, first, in Magnesia and then in Macedon at the court of King Archelaus, where he was received with great honor. There he continued writing plays, his last work being *The Bacchae*, a dramatic limning of the dire consequences of abandoning belief in Dionysus.

Euripides differs from his fellow playwrights in several ways. He adopts unusual versions from the repertory of myth, and his plots and characters are often so realistically developed as to seem new and modern rather than classical. Often we see his principals escape from their predicaments. Fate turns out to be the unexpected. The chorus may interact with the players or its lyrics may form a descant on themes quite separate from the action in progress. In the fluent and quick-witted play of ideas, skepticism can override belief and logic and challenge simple convictions.

His *Electra* varies from the versions of Aeschylus and Sophocles in its astonishing recharacterization of Electra as now married to a peasant farmer who treats her with respect and honors her chastity. Their simple country hut becomes the scene of Clytemnestra's murder. Electra summons her mother on the pretext of having borne a child and wanting her there to perform the ritual of cleansing. With this ironic, macabre embellishment on the conventional murder scene, Euripides seems to be actually increasing the guilt felt by the children. But until this point Electra's conduct as the humble helpmeet of a husband with a heart of gold outclasses her mourning. She smolders with resentment but bides her time, waiting for Orestes, hoping. That Euripides sees her in a different light is also signaled in his refuting the others' recognition tokens. A lock of hair, a scrap of child's clothing, footprints? Absurd to think of such things as clues to Orestes' identity! What he can be known by is the scar on his forehead, "on his brow— where he was cut in a fall, chasing a fawn with you in his father's courtyard" (ll. 568–69). So tangible and realistic a memory convinces Electra. The fact is that Orestes is scarred for life. His identification was not just a clever bit of literary criticism.

Brother and sister are, at the end of the *Electra*, brought to the depth of sorrow by the realization of what they have done. But they are lifted out of despair by the timely appearance of their divine relatives Castor and Polydeuces, *ex machina*. The Dioscuri, the heavenly Twins, have paused as they "speed to seas off Sicily, to protect the ships in danger there" (ll. 1335–36). Athens had sent an expedition to the aid of the fleet in Sicily in 413, so it appears that Euripides is being historical as well as mythical here. Electra is to leave Argos and marry Pylades, to live in exile. Orestes must go to Athens and await trial at the Areopagus. The children's generation, marked by the ancient curse of violence on their house, has nevertheless emerged to survive. The Dioscuri (Castor and Polydeuces were the divine brothers of Helen and Clytemnestra) also report, almost casually, that Menelaus and Helen will attend to the burial rites for Clytemnestra and Aegisthus. They explain that Menelaus and Helen have recently arrived from Egypt. She, Helen, never went to Troy, they add laconically.

The year 412 saw the production of Euripides' drama *Helen*, which offers the counter-myth that Hermes had spirited Helen away to Egypt, substituting for her at Troy a phantom image. In Egypt she enjoyed the protection of the king, Proteus, during the ten years of the Trojan war, but after his death his son holds her hostage and wants to make her his wife. She fends him off by maintaining a constant vigil at Proteus' tomb, a sacred refuge. This story line, sketched in by Helen in the prologue in her play, was suggested earlier by an episode in Book II, the Egyptian book, of Herodotus' *Histories*, and poems in praise of Helen by Stesichorus and other sixth-century lyric poets in Euripides' combination. He has seized the opportunity to dramatize Helen's rescue, starting with her joyful reunion with Menelaus, who has been shipwrecked with his crew and the phantom Helen on these shores. Her meeting with him surely constitutes the most appealing recognition scene of any in the Greek drama we know, and Euripides weaves a spell of exciting suspense as husband and wife devise the strategy for eluding their Egyptian captor. Plans are made and discarded until finally Helen hits on the right tactics, saying (almost under her breath) that even a woman might have "a good suggestion" (l. 1086). Their daring plan enables husband and wife to escape from impending doom, and Helen from captivity and slander.

Another Euripidean heroine to escape from peril is found in *Iphigenia in Tauris*. Orestes and Pylades join forces with Iphigenia in devising a plan to outwit the barbarous king of Thrace and sail away to Athens. The men supply the force, the woman the strategic plan. Men may be forceful, Euripides implies, but women are more resourceful. In other female figures, like Ion's mother in the *Ion* and Alcestis in the *Alcestis*, women are rescued from tragedy. Alcestis, indeed, is wrested from the arms of Death by Heracles and restored to her husband's embrace.

Euripides explores the complex dimensions of female character from many angles. In plays from the Trojan War cycle, women are towering figures of tragic sorrow as they voice the grief that descends on the victims of war. Swept up in the grotesque futility of war, the Trojan women endure further humiliation in the senseless murders of their children in the war's catastrophic aftermath. Small wonder that we should weep for Hecuba. A later representation of Andromache finds her married to Neoptolemus, Achilles' son, and having borne a son to him. As if this irony were not insult added to injury, Andromache is now threatened with murder by the new mistress who has replaced her. She is protected by Peleus (a Trojan Woman saved by a Trojan Man), but Menelaus and Hermione, the new mistress, are still bent on doing her in. At the melodramatic moment, Orestes arrives on the scene and will despatch Neoptolemus, taking Hermione as his bride. Here Euripides has ingeniously rescued two women from imminent destruction, one Trojan and one Greek, Hermione being the daughter of Helen. He evidently found such figures as the poignant Andromache and the jealousy-ridden rival Hermione well worth close attention.

The poet's fascinating portraits of celebrated women drawn from the mythological traditions rises to the level of Aeschylean or Sophoclean theatricality. While he may not invoke the grandeur of Aeschylus' vision or the nobility of Sophocles' unerring judgment, Euripides offers his audience real life human beings, natural characters under, at times, supernatural pressures. His memorable women Medea and Phaedra become avenging forces and are demonically driven to destroy the source of their happiness. They do not gain wisdom through suffering, but plunge into darkness. Medea may fly off to Athens in a chariot drawn by dragons, but in reality her burden is her murdered children and all she and Jason once cherished. Her husband is ruined: she, almost worse, is deluded. What she said of herself turns out to be true: "My will is stronger than my reason." Phaedra's psychological burden in the *Hippolytus* is shame and guilt. Her lust humiliates her and compels her to bring disgrace on the innocent young hero. His devotion to Artemis conflicts with her subjection to Aphrodite: both Hippolytus and Phaedra are destroyed in the clash of wills. Tragedy is, of course, the truth realized too late: and too late Theseus discovers his son's innocence and his wife's aberration.

From a terrifying view of women driven to a demonic state we find, in *The Bacchae*, Euripides' last play, what can be considered a misogynist stance. But on the whole this brutal drama chiefly brings to mind the peril of denying an underlying neutral power, the life force that of necessity controls all beings. That is, Dionysus, whose cosmic energy animates life and whose passionate powers motivate the "drama," the forward motion registered by Greek tragedy.

Toward men as heroes Euripides' attitude is sometimes disparaging. The men in *Iphigenia at Aulis* are hardly impressive as they assemble to sail against Troy. Only Achilles achieves some stature, and all are far below the unblemished radiance of Iphigenia, their victim. And Orestes, in the tragedy named after him, is frantic, haunted by his guilty conscience; he plunges wildly into futile gestures of revenge. Heracles can be driven mad and returns to his senses, chastened but none the wiser. In the first play of which we have a record, the *Alcestis*, produced at Athens in 438 B.C. and winner of second prize in the contest at the Great Dionysia, Euripides plays woman against man, wife against husband. The drama itself was in fact the fourth of the group offered, in place of a satyr play. But it does not function as a satyr play; rather, it sets the stage for a reconciliation of an ordinary man and his extraordinary wife. Alcestis has offered to die in her husband's stead, and it is only when Death leads her off the stage that her husband Admetus realizes what he has lost by his wrongminded acceptance of Alcestis' sacrificial gesture. Luckily, Heracles has come to visit his friend Admetus, who, in his characteristically hospitable manner, receives him cordially and hides his knowledge of Alcestis' death. But Heracles learns the truth and it is not too late: he strides off to confront Death, wrests Alcestis from the fatal grasp, and leads back a veiled female figure. He places her in Admetus' hands, instructing his host not to raise the veil until three days have passed. The bulky hero leaves. The play ends. We realize that this well-intentioned but blundering man and his somber, self-denying wife were well worth being saved from their tragic destiny, as the chorus exits, singing:

> The powers take on many shapes;
> the gods accomplish miracles.
> What was predicted fails to happen,
> then gods reveal their hidden design.
> —and this was what took place.

Hippolytus

Translated by
Richard Moore

Translator's Preface

A word is due about my interpretation of *Hippolytus*. This is one of Euripides' greatest plays and, for a modern audience, one of his most confusing. Aristotle's prescription that a tragedy be the imitation of an action "single, complete, and of a certain magnitude" seems to be violated. There seem to be two such actions: first, Phaedra's suffering and death; and second, its consequences, the quarrel of Theseus and Hippolytus and its resolution in the young man's death. For David Grene in his essay on the play[1] and for many others, the real action concerns Phaedra and her torn emotions; the rest is anticlimax. In this view the men do not qualify as tragic: Theseus because he is a mere dupe and Hippolytus because he is a fanatical prig with whom it is impossible to sympathize. Clearly male chastity is a difficult concept for modern culture. (In Racine's version of the play, Phèdre is clearly the main character and Hippolyte is a much more "normal" young man who is in love with another woman. Racine also disposes of the incest problem by having Phèdre avow her love only after she believes that her husband, Hippolyte's father, is dead.)

I too have difficulty sympathizing with the likes of Hippolytus, but it seems to me that the difficulties of not doing so are even greater. It is not easy to assign the final half of the play (46 percent by line count) to anticlimax; and its title is, after all, not *Phaedra*, as in Racine, but *Hippolytus*. Aphrodite's prologue clearly states that the central action is going to be her revenge on Hippolytus for his arrogant refusal to honor her, and her presence is kept very much alive in the dialogue and the choral odes throughout the play. From her point of view, at least, Phaedra's suffering is incidental— sad and moving, no doubt, but in the end, beside the point. Hippolytus is the first mortal to enter, and his death ends the play. Phaedra does indeed become the center of attention in the first half, but even as she dies

---

1. Grene, "Hippolytus," in *Greek Plays in Modern Translation*, ed. Dudley Fitts (New York: Dial Press, 1947), pp. 561–72.

Euripides dissipates the pathos with one of his famous jokes about the theatrical customs of his day. Macabre comedy threatens when the nurse's voice within calls for help from the chorus. The dancers cannot give it because the formalities of the drama require that they stay in their dance area, removed from the action. Their debate about what they should do and its foregone conclusion remind us that we are, after all, only watching a play: it is an essentially comic "distancing" effect. Euripides knows that Phaedra's death must be quickly dismissed from the audience's consciousness so that the tragedy can deepen: she, like Aphrodite herself, is beyond mortal life now, removed from its human feelings. The depiction of Phaedra's wild suffering and the stiffening of her resolve to die show us Euripides at his sophisticated best, but so do the wonderful touches that follow: the hints, for example, of jealousy between the father and the son, whose lifestyles are so different, and the way those differences are resolved in the ecstatic reconciliation with which the play ends.

We first see Hippolytus in an act of devotion, consecrating his wreath "from an untouched meadow" to Artemis. In his sexual chastity and rejection of Aphrodite, he is untouched like the meadow—which I might also have translated as "an uncontaminated, undefiled place of moisture [life]." Excluded from this scene of primal blessedness are "men who have learned things, dominant sure ones"—men like his beloved father, Theseus, who gave him life by raping an Amazon. In this one little speech, we are brought face-to-face with that distrust of technology and meddling with nature which runs through all Classical civilization (even Archimedes, the great inventor of war machines, scorned his own inventions and professed to value only the pure serenity of his geometric theorems). Perhaps we have reached the point in our own civilization, surrounded by our conquests of nature and our pollutions of it, which is just right for an appreciation of Euripides' main character. There is something downright New Age about him. The dialogue makes it perfectly clear that others understand him and he understands himself to be a holy man (or, for Theseus at first, the pretense of one). If his pride and proneness to anger seem unsaintly to us, we should remember that the tradition of the Christian saints hasn't begun yet, and that for the Greeks nearness to the divine—as in Achilles and in Oedipus at Colonus—includes a disposition to rage and impatience with mere mortal frailties.

But viewed from another angle these qualities also constitute a serious fault in Hippolytus, as the little scene with his old servant in the beginning points out: the fault, as always in Greek tragedy, of hubris. The ancient word means many things, among them the very wanton arrogance—and lewdness even—that Hippolytus has consecrated his life as a holy man to subduing in himself. But more particularly, hubris is that wanton arrogance—so awesome, so admirable even—which leads a man to set himself up as an equal and to compete with the gods. There is no escape for man: the urge to subdue hubris is itself a form of hubris. Artemis may admire it in her detached way, but Aphrodite will punish it.

After these first two telling glimpses, Hippolytus drops out of sight, and in our fascination with Phaedra's agonies we almost forget him—until he reappears in his famous scene with the nurse. The culmination of that, his bitter diatribe against women, is what most establishes him in modern consciousness as a prig. I think we tend to forget the horror of the nurse's proposal in this age when parents are routinely desecrated by their children, who ruin themselves in the process. Hippolytus is genuinely horrified, as any Greek would have thought he should be. He is also young, impulsive, and overflowing with energy; and the prospect of incest clearly unnerves him. In his violent reaction and almost comic denunciation of women, surely we sense that he himself feels threatened by his own animal nature. His old lecher of a father has, after all, found himself a wife who is young and beautiful.

For its ancient Greek audience, which awarded it the first prize, the play's most moving part must have been its last, in which the young man grows to a tragic understanding and joyous acceptance of his horrible fate and the father and son transcend their deep contrasts and nagging suspicions and in their awe of each other are reconciled. The divine detachment of Artemis sets off this human suffering and ecstasy with terrifying clarity. In its stark, almost Homeric ironies, the death of Hippolytus—on stage, be it noted—is surely one of the great moments in Greek drama.

Cast

APHRODITE, goddess of love, also called Cypris
ARTEMIS, virgin goddess of hunting
HIPPOLYTUS, son of Theseus
HUNTSMEN
MESSENGER
NURSE of Phaedra
PHAEDRA, wife of Theseus, stepmother of Hippolytus
SERVANT
THESEUS, king of Athens and Troezen
CHORUS of Troezen women

*(Statue of Aphrodite, left; statue of Artemis, right; palace door,
center. Choral space between audience and stage. Aphrodite
enters from her image.)*

APHRODITE
　Everyone knows me. I'm Cypris, the goddess.
　Sex and desire, my specialties, draw men
　helpless from Pontus to Heracles' Pillars.
　Those that delight in me, I can reward them;
　those that detest me will harvest my hatred.
　Even immortals get caught in my soft snares.
　Goddesses love it when worshipers gather.
　Listen: I'll prove that this very hour.
　There is a fellow, King Theseus' young son,
　huntsman Hippolytus, lover of horses,　　　　　　　　　　10
　born of an Amazon lady in Athens.
　Grandfather Pittheus raised the boy here in
　Troezen because of his unmarried mother.
　Hates me, this fellow. The thought of me sickens.
　Hates love's bed, scorns pleasures of marriage,
　worships instead prim Artemis, huntress,

Phoebus' sister and Zeus' proud daughter;
says she's the sacredest thing in the heavens.
Never can leave her, adores her, his maiden.
There with his dogs hunts beasts in the forest,   20
he and his she-spirit blessing each other.
Why should that bother me? Why should I mind that?
Well, my Hippolytus, you shall pay dear, dear.
All is prepared, and the path lies open.
Not that I'll work very hard at it, mind you.
Oh, it was years ago now when it started.
Theseus, bringing a sexy new consort,
Phaedra dear, home to his kingdom in Athens,
thought: now what of Hippolytus, young boy
got on that Amazon lady I mentioned?   30
That's when he sent him to grandfather Pittheus
here to be raised as the ruler of Troezen.
But, as it happened, he went back to Athens
once, to take part in the mysteries held there.
Phaedra caught sight of him, heart in her throbbing
shamefully: she was the wife of his father,
she, proud ladyship, gripped in a raging
criminal lust for him. That was my doing.
Then, before coming to Troezen herself, she
built me a shrine on a storm-lashed headland,   40
visible here in the city, and called it,
"Love from afar," for Hippolytus: wishes.
("Goddess, be seated!" our aftertimes call it.)
Meanwhile Theseus, dealing with uncles,
shed much blood, so he took a vacation,
hoping for calm, and he moved his young family
here, where Hippolytus lives. Here Phaedra
wastes away, stung by her furious longings,
dies of them, agonized; dares, though, no word
breathe of it, guiltily hoarding her sickness.   50
Terrified servants in wonderment whisper.
Ah, but the truth of it's sure to get out soon,

Theseus hear of it . . . that I will see to.
Oh then loudly he'll cry to Poseidon,
call down curses the Sea God promised,
down on that hateful Hippolytus, sweep him
deep under earth . . . poor Phaedra, devoted . . .
Oh, what a pity! for she will die also,
nevertheless with her name unsullied;
still, she must die. How else can my proud foes   60
learn that it's most unwise to insult me?

Look there: Theseus' boy is approaching,
beautiful man, and his hunting is over,
lordly Hippolytus. Best that I leave now.
Followers come with him, raising their clamor,
filling the day with his Artemis ditties.
Hasn't a clue that the Underworld's waiting.
This day's light won't end till it ends him.
(*Exit. Enter Hippolytus and huntsmen.*)

HIPPOLYTUS
Sing of her, sing of her,
sing of sweet Artemis,   70
Zeus' great daughter
cares for us ever.

HUNTSMEN
Lady, lady, most holy,
Zeus' great daughter,
joy to you, joy to you,
daughter of Zeus and of Leto,
fairest of maidens
high in the heavenly
courts of your father
glittering, golden,   80
fairest of all on Olympus.

HIPPOLYTUS

> Lady, this wreath from an untouched meadow,
> picked for you, woven with my own fingers,
> where no shepherded flocks, no farmer's
> plow has invaded, but only the bees in the springtime
> frequented, spirit of reverence tilled it,
> coaxed from the nearby stream sweet waters:
> men who have learned things, dominant sure ones,
> they have been left out, they have no place here.
> Untaught modesty gathers your flowers,   90
> leaving those impure spirits excluded.
> Queen of my being, accept this wreath now,
> meant for your glorious hair, all golden.
> I among mortals alone, great goddess,
> speak with you, hear you alone in the darkness,
> never have seen you, nor do I hope to.
> Let life end for me as you began it!

SERVANT

> Only the gods have the title of master:
> would you consider a piece of advice, Prince?

HIPPOLYTUS

> Fool I would be, good friend, if I wouldn't.   100

SERVANT

> One great rule for us mortals—you know it?

HIPPOLYTUS

> Know what? I don't understand what you're saying.

SERVANT

> Men can get full of themselves, lack friendship.

HIPPOLYTUS

> Right. People full of themselves will deserve that.

SERVANT
  And your relaxed ones tend to be charming?

HIPPOLYTUS
  Definitely, and it costs them nothing.

SERVANT *(pointing to the sky)*
  There among gods, things also are like that?

HIPPOLYTUS
  Doubtless. We copy immortals, so yes, friend.

SERVANT
  Furious goddesses, Prince, we should placate?

HIPPOLYTUS
  Which goddess? Tell me, and watch what you're saying.   110

SERVANT *(pointing to the statue of Aphrodite)*
  This goddess standing right here now, Cypris.

HIPPOLYTUS
  That one chastely I greet from a distance.

SERVANT
  Still, though, terrible, glorious is she.

HIPPOLYTUS
  Bedtime goddesses, friend, you can keep them.

SERVANT
  Honor all goddesses, or you'll regret it.

HIPPOLYTUS
  Some choose one goddess, others another.

SERVANT
>Luck to you, Prince, I'm afraid you may need it.

HIPPOLYTUS
>Inside, followers! Look to our supper!
>After a good hunt, eating's a pleasure.
>You there, rub down my horses, and when we've   120
>eaten our fill, we'll go chariot riding.
>I say, Joy to you, Cypris, stay far off.

(Exit.)

SERVANT
>We say, young fools need not be mimicked.
>We who must serve in humility, humbly
>worship you, Cypris, and beg of you, dear one,
>try to forgive youth's follies, forgive him.
>Goddesses ought to be wiser than mortals.

(Exeunt. Enter Chorus of Troezen women.)

CHORUS
>Cliff in the mountains,
>flowing with water
>far from the ocean,   130
>fair to be scooped up,
>filling our pitchers,
>there a companion,
>washing our garments,
>spread them for drying,
>warm on the rock face—
>there I heard news of my Queen.

>Lying afflicted,
>feverish, sickened
>there in her bedroom   140
>three long days now,
>nothing to nourish
>poor wracked body,

golden hair shrouded:
what secret grieving
drives her life's voyage,
soon to be harbored in death?

Is it the wildness of forests
deeply invades you,
oh my suffering queen?   150
Hecate's spirit or Pan's,
mad Corybantian revels,
honoring mountain-born Cybele?
Have you sinned against Artemis,
queen of all hunters?
Dear, are you tainted?
Is it the Lakelady
lost in the eddying surf?

Maybe your husband,
nobly born ruler of Athens,   160
ruled by his passions,
finds other women,
here in the palace perhaps
makes love far from your bed.
Maybe some sailor from Crete
new to our harbor has just brought
terrible news to our queen,
binding her fast to her bed,
lost in misfortunes.

Nature in woman lacks harmony.   170
Helpless she dwells among dangers,
helplessness ever in all things.
Birth's hard suffering wracks her,
her own great foolishness also.
Into my womb pierced birth pangs.
Artemis, hearing me calling,

came to me, quietly soothing.
Her I shall worship forever.

Look! It's her mistress' nurse in the doorway,
and she is bringing the queen into daylight.   180
Look there, look at her face all clouded!
Sweet sad body so ravaged, so altered!
Somehow, if we could just comprehend this . . .

NURSE
Oh, these wretched diseases that plague us!
What shall I do for you? What shall I not do?
Darling, there's light here, I've brought out your sickbed
just as you asked. Will you find some contentment
clear of the house? "Take me out!" you kept calling.
Now that you're out here, you still cry, find no
constancy anywhere. What do you *want*, dear?   190
Nothing, apparently, gives any pleasure.
Anything present displeases you, *not* there's
wished for. Better be sick than this nurse work!
Sickness is miserable, yes, and I know that.
That's just *one* thing. Nursing is *two* things:
feeling the trouble and hard labor also.
Nothing but misery, life for us mortals!
Oh, is there anything better beyond this?
All is in darkness, the poor sad light here
all that we have, this light that we cling to,   200
knowing not anything better behind it.
Stories we tell of it, nothing but stories.

PHAEDRA
Lift me up! Hold up my head! All my muscles
loosened and feeble, my beautiful arms, look!
Off with this hat! Can't bear it. It's heavy.
Off with it! Free my hair to my shoulders!

NURSE

Easy, my dear one! Don't toss about so!
Sickness is easier, dear, when you're patient.
Think of your dignity! People can see you.
Suffering goes with mortality. Bear it!   210

PHAEDRA

Bring me to fresh springs high in the mountains.
Let me drink cool fresh water and lie there,
glad in the untouched meadows.

NURSE

Child, this is madness; those people will hear you,
shocked that their queen's gone out of her senses.

PHAEDRA

Mountains! I must to the mountains. The pine groves
wait for me, hounds of the huntsmen, the wild beasts,
stags and the dog pack hurrying after,
huntsmen shouting, the javelin cocked back
right at my gold-haired ear, steel-pointed.   220

NURSE

What strange feverishness, wild madness?
Hunting? And you such a delicate lady?
Fresh springs? Right by the city wall, flowing.
Drink there, dearie—as much as you thirst for.

PHAEDRA

Artemis, there in the salt lake splashing,
mistress of echoing hoofs, you must help me.
Oh, I shall run with you, taming wild horses.

NURSE

Gyrating words, wild frenzy and madness.
Off to the hunt in the mountains, then horses

suddenly breaking in—where? By the seashore?   230
Dearie, my dearie, what god, what diviner
is there to tell us what fury has gripped you?

PHAEDRA

Miserable! Oh, I'm so miserable! Help me!
What have I done? Gone out of my senses.
Madness, some goddess has maddened me, helpless.
I'm so ashamed. Quick! Cover me quickly,
hide me away again, Oh, so unhappy.
Tears on my cheeks, I can feel them. They scald me,
torture me, tell what I lack . . . moderation.
Bitter to know that, bitter to feel it.   240
Better to die, know no more ever.

NURSE

There now, I've covered you. My old body,
may deep death soon cover that also.
(turns to the audience and Chorus)
This long living can teach many lessons.
Friendship, the feeling of one for another,
sweet wine mixed with the evenings—
not to be mixed too strong. Sweet affection—
never allow it to touch to the marrow.
Let such fetters be easily broken,
easily tightened and easily loosened.   250
It is not good that a bond pull deep as
mine for this woman, and many have said it:
thoughts too constant, too pure, can destroy us.
Men must attend to their health, must remember,
love may be sweet; moderation preserves us.

CHORUS

Gray-haired nurse to the queen, we can see poor
Phaedra's affliction, but don't understand it.
Kindly inform us. We wait for your answer.

NURSE
Nothing to tell you; she'll tell *me* nothing.

CHORUS
Not one hint of her trouble's beginning?   260

NURSE
Nothing, I tell you; obstinate silence.

CHORUS
Look at her body, though, agonized, wasted.

NURSE
Three whole days not a morsel has eaten.

CHORUS
Then . . . is it madness, her longing for death, then?

NURSE
Yes, undoubtedly that's where she's headed.

CHORUS
Well, does her husband know anything of this?

NURSE
No, she denies it, her sickness conceals it.

CHORUS
But he would guess with a glance at her wracked face.

NURSE
He's not here. He's away from the city.

CHORUS
Well, you must force her, must press her to tell you   270
clearly what's making her poor wits wander.

NURSE

> Look, I've tried everything; nothing unlocks her.
> Well, even now, though, I won't stop trying.
> Judge me, you women; I have always been faithful,
> haven't I, fighting my master's afflictions?

(to Phaedra)

> So, noble lady, dear child, let's be gracious,
> kind; and let's soften that glowering at me.
> Granted, I've not sympathetically listened
> always before. So we'll try something new now.
> If you are ill with a secret, some illness,   280
> women are standing right here who can help you
> if you will let them and tell them your troubles.
> Say, so a doctor can make a pronouncement.
> Nothing, dear? Can't you say anything, lady?
> This grim silence is getting us nowhere.
> Either I'm wrong and you can correct me,
> or I am right and you should obey me.
> Say something! Look at me! . . . Oh, it's hopeless.
> Woman, I've tried, I have labored, belabored . . .

(to the Chorus)

> We are as far from all knowledge as ever.   290
> Now it's the same as before. Unmelted,
> stiff she remains and refuses to hear me.

(to Phaedra)

> Queen, you should know this, though to my reasons
> obstinate still as the circling ocean:
> Dying is murderous, murders your children.
> They, if you die, lose out in your kingdom.
> One, by the Amazon rider who bore him,
> bastard in birth, but a prince in his own mind,
> one you know well, dear, Hippolytus—

PHAEDRA

> No, no!

NURSE

So, that's touched you.

PHAEDRA

O nurse, don't kill me.   300

Oh, don't mention that man to me ever.

NURSE

Well then; you've come to your senses . . . and still you

don't mind killing yourself and your children?

PHAEDRA

Children? I love them. Other storms wrench me.

NURSE

Is there a stain on your hands? Are they bloody?

PHAEDRA

Clean! It's my heart that is stained, blood-sodden.

NURSE

Sorcery, then, from some enemy taints you?

PHAEDRA

Loved one! Ruins me! Neither one wills it.

NURSE

Master? Has *he* done something against you?

PHAEDRA

Gods! Keep me guiltless in that man's presence!   310

NURSE

What is this strange thing driving you deathward?

PHAEDRA
> Leave me my wrongs. You're not wronged by them, are you?

NURSE *(on her knees, clasping Phaedra)*
> Why are you doing this, driving me from you?

PHAEDRA
> Why are you grasping me, grasping my hands now?

NURSE
> Knees too grasping. I won't let you go, dear.

PHAEDRA
> Sorrowful nurse! You will find out my secret.

NURSE
> Losing you, what more terrible sorrow?

PHAEDRA
> *And* you will kill me. My life is in silence.

NURSE
> Still you'll hide it, ignore my pleading?

PHAEDRA
> Here in my shame, dear, I will have honor.   320

NURSE
> If there's honor here, let words tell it!

PHAEDRA
> Oh, by the gods, let go of me, go, go!

NURSE
> Not till you tell me, not till I hear it.

PHAEDRA
> Spoken! Your suppliant arms have compelled me.

NURSE

I'll say no more; yours is the word now.

PHAEDRA

Miserable mother, your lust . . . what horror!

NURSE

That she adored that bull, even mated . . .

PHAEDRA

Sister as well; Dionysus seduced her.

NURSE

Why these tales of your relatives, darling?

PHAEDRA

I am the third who miserably perish.   330

NURSE

Frightening words, where, where are they leading?

PHAEDRA

It's an inherited curse, not recent.

NURSE

What's not recent? I *still* have heard *nothing*.

PHAEDRA

Oh can't you *say* them, the words? Do I *have* to?

NURSE

Am I a prophet, to guess hidden secrets?

PHAEDRA

What is it? Poor men label it, *passion*.

NURSE

Pleasure it brings, pain, braided together.

PHAEDRA

Pain, yes; that I have known, and I know it.

NURSE

Ah! You're in love, child! Who is the man, then?

PHAEDRA

There is a man . . . with an Amazon mother . . .   340

NURSE

Meaning . . . Hippolytus!

PHAEDRA

                              You said it, not I.

NURSE

What do you say, child? This will be *my* death.
No, woman; no one's alive who can bear this.
I . . . live? Die rather, cursing the daylight,
cursing the bright hot sun there above us,
throw myself from a cliff, fall headlong.
I will be rid of life somehow, somehow
say to you all, Farewell!—and be ended.
(goes to the statue of Aphrodite)
Chaste people don't love vice, now do they?
Oh, but they *do* love it. You are no goddess,   350
Cypris; you're stronger than that, if it can be,
you who have ruined her, ruined this great house.
(Exit.)

CHORUS

Hear, did you hear it,
hear the queen crying

cries of disaster?
Ears oughtn't hear that.
Die I would rather,
rather then hear that.
Sorry I am for her,
cry for her troubles.   360
Troubles destroy her.
You are the dead one,
dragging your ruin
into our daylight.
Now what will happen,
now what waits in your
long life's ruin?
What new horror
comes to this house now?
Yes, we can see now   370
how it will all end,
miserable Crete girl,
victim of Cypris,
born of your dark and
bull-loving mother.

PHAEDRA *(distracted, trying to make sense)*
Listen to me, you women of Troezen,
watching me here on Hellas' headland:
often through night's long dark I've considered
how an existence like mine can be shattered.
Foolishness can't be the cause, for the victim's   380
often intelligent. Look at it this way:
Some know the good, apprehending it clearly,
just can't seem to achieve it, and others,
lazy perhaps, or they value some pleasure
other than honor . . . and woman's existence,
so full of pleasures—amusements and gossip—
leisure, that curse of us. Shame! How it plagues us!
Shame is of two kinds: one, quite harmless . . .

then, there's this other, this ruin of houses.
Can't I be clearer? I think so. I'll try to.   390
That one word, it has *two* different meanings.
Oh, have I said that? . . . Here's my opinion.
Nothing will change it, no spell, no elixir.
From the beginning I'll say how my thoughts went.
Then, when the rage first entered me, how best
bear it, I wondered? Conceal it in silence!
That is the best thing clearly, for tongues are
not to be trusted. They criticize, slander,
and to their owners they bring much trouble.
Second, I thought I could fight love's fury,   400
nobly endure it, subduing the madness,
brave, overpower her, Cypris . . . My failure
moved me at last to consider the third way.
Death is the best of all plans. Who disputes it?
Death leaves virtue intact. Let my good deeds
honor my memory, shames be forgotten.
Cursed be the deed and the passionate longing!
I am a woman, and men don't forgive that.
Vile to pollute it, the marital chamber,
bringing strange men there. Our high-born women   410
showed us the way. The nobility lead us;
they're the example. The lowly will follow.
Women who mouth chaste words, but in secret
revel in lechery—Oh, I detest that!
How can such guilty ones look at their husbands?
Answer me, Cypris! Oh, won't they in terror
hear in the darkness their roofbeams screaming?
Death will protect me from that, and my husband,
children. And may they have prosperous lifetimes,
nurtured in Athens, where free men flourish!   420
They will have strength from their much-honored mother.
How it enslaves stout men to remember
sins that their fathers and mothers committed!
One thing only in life gives mortals

strength to endure life: they have been decent.
Life shows, as to a girl in a mirror,
each of us, sooner or later, his vileness.
All must look at it. I shall not be there.

CHORUS
  Ah, ah! Everywhere chastity valued,
  felt to be beautiful. Isn't that lovely!   430
(Enter Nurse.)

NURSE
  Mistress, the terrible news that you gave me
  suddenly just now—dearie, it shocked me.
  Now I can see I was foolish. With mortals,
  second thoughts, now I can see, might be better.
  Really, they strike us a lot, to my thinking,
  passion-bolts flung by the Goddess. You love him.
  What's there to marvel at? Many are like you.
  Will you destroy your existence because love
  doesn't seem proper? What profit's in that, dear?
  Everyone loves, and it's nothing to die for.   440
  Cypris attacks us; she's rough when resisted,
  but when we yield, she becomes much milder.
  How she mistreats them, the haughty and proud ones!
  Flies through the air, then dips in the sea-wave.
  Everything's born of her, everything living.
  Hers is the urge and desire that brings forth
  all earth's creatures, and all are her children.
  Haven't you read in the books of the poets
  how once for Semele great Zeus lusted?
  Didn't the radiant Dawn once snatch up   450
  Cephalus? These have been driven by love, all.
  Think of them, happy up there in the heavens,
  glad, though they're gods, to be conquered by passion.
  Won't play along with this, will you? Your father
  should have begotten you under a contract

not to obey love's laws—under different
gods set apart from the rest of us. Tell me:
How many men, dear, seeing their wives in
bright day carrying on with a lover,
close their eyes and pretend to see nothing?   460
How many fathers have pandered for sons, dear?
Wise men can tell you: dishonor kept hidden's
perfectly honorable, and I ask you:
whence comes man's strange itch for perfection?
Even the roofs of his houses are sloping.
Lost on your life's deep storm-tossed ocean,
think about swimming to shore. And consider:
here in our state of mortality, when your
good deeds outweigh evil, you're lucky.
Dearie, get rid of your thoughts, of that proud old   470
urge to outdo the immortals, that madness.
Courage! Some deity wished this to happen.
Since you are sick, find something to cure you:
charms, incantations, who knows what might help you?
All those clever discoveries men make
wouldn't be made without women to help them.

CHORUS

Phaedra, the words that she utters are useful
in your predicament; praiseworthy, *your* words,
though they may sound to you much less pleasant:
kind to your name, not to you; yet I praise them.   480

PHAEDRA *(to the Nurse)*

Speeches like yours bring cities to ruin,
pleasant to hear, yet they dash down houses.
Words aren't needed to flatter and soothe me;
words are required that will save my honor.

NURSE

Fiddlesticks. High-flown rhetoric's *not* what's
needed. What's needed's a lover. It's high time

plain words entered and stripped the disguises,
spoke clear truth to you, desperate mistress.
Oh, if your life didn't hang in the balance,
or if you weren't too weak to resist love's   490
fury, I wouldn't be pandering like this.
Life's to be saved, and I'm fighting to save it.

PHAEDRA

Speaker of horrors, for once will you keep still?
Lock up your words! They are wicked and shameful.

NURSE

Shameful, no doubt; but they're beautiful for you,
saving your life as they do. And your good name?
Proud words bring you, my dear, to destruction.

PHAEDRA

Oh, gods . . . these sweet words . . . are disgusting.
Go no further! I'm schooled. I am ready.
I can endure love's fate. Won't you let me?   500
Oh, I am trapped in the shame I would flee from!

NURSE

That's how you feel? Stick closer to virtue!
Next best thing is to do what I tell you.
I can provide you with medicine, love-cures,
there in the house, that I just now thought of.

Nothing to frighten you, nothing to shame you,
but it will lull you; you mustn't be timid.
Yes! We must get from the loved man something—
maybe a word, or his hair, or a piece of
clothing, to knit you two firmly together.   510

PHAEDRA

What is it, then—salve, ointment, or potion?

NURSE
> Never mind! Go for the benefit, dearie.

PHAEDRA
> Nurse, I'm frightened. You're getting too clever.

NURSE
> Everything frightens you, doesn't it, poor dear?

PHAEDRA
> Promise me Theseus' son won't hear this.

NURSE
> Perish the thought! Just leave the arranging
> wholly to me! . . .
> *(to the statue of Aphrodite)*
> > You, born of the sea foam,
> Cypris, consider us, Goddess, and help me!
> *(to Phaedra)*
> Friends in the house will help me as well, dear.
> *(Exit.)*

CHORUS
> Eros, Eros,   520
> son of the thunder,
> in whom men's eyes
> swim with enchantment,
> ruined with pleasure:
> wild, wild love-touch,
> come not ever to me:
> not in your wildness,
> only in measure,
> son of the thunder,
> stronger than daylight,   530
> longer than star-beams,
> offspring of Cypris.

Makers of sacrifice
singing aloud by
Alpheus' banks or in
Phoebus' Pythian home:
honor him carefully,
children of Hellas,
honor him: Eros,   540
ruin of mortals,
mankind's despot.
Lying alone in
Cypris' chambers,
all shall adore him.

Remember poor Iole,
Oechalia's daughter,
taken by Heracles
out of her city's
plunder and flames:
Remember her love-day,   550
conqueror-tasting,
palace roof, smoking,
death-shrieks for love-hymns,
Cypris' present to
her blood-soaked darling.

Thebes, in your ramparts
where Dirce's rough river
pours to the sea,
you have been witness
to the Love-Queen's coming   560
where the lost girl slumbered,
Dionysus' mother.
Cypris, the terrible,
flies in the garden,
everywhere stinging,
wide as the murmuring bee-swarm.

PHAEDRA

Quiet, you women! Oh, gods, I am finished!

CHORUS

What is it, Phaedra? What's happening in there?

PHAEDRA

Quiet! I hear them inside, their voices.

CHORUS

Quiet, yes; quietly evil is coming.   570

PHAEDRA

Oh! Oh! Aie!
Miserable! How my agonies heap up!

CHORUS

What are you telling us? What are you shrieking?
Into your heart what crying and terror?

PHAEDRA

Oh, I am finished. Just stand at the door here,
listen and hear that clamoring in there.

CHORUS

Phaedra, you're right there. Household matters
ought to concern you only.
Tell me, though, what are you hearing, what awful . . .

PHAEDRA

Oh, it's Hippolytus, son of that horse-proud   580
Amazon, horribly cursing my poor nurse.

CHORUS

Voices? I do hear voices, but not too clearly.
Shouting in there, in the doorway,
anger and fury, but what are they *saying*?

PHAEDRA

> Clear! A lascivious pander, he calls her,
> traitress, polluting the bed of her master.

CHORUS

> Woe, woe, hidden things tipped into daylight!
> You've been betrayed, dear, your secret—
> what can I tell you?—toppled and torn down.

PHAEDRA

> Aie! Oh! Oh!

CHORUS

> The loved one! *She* was the traitor!   590

PHAEDRA

> Oh, she has told him, told what afflicts me,
> dear nurse, shaming me, hoping to heal me.

CHORUS

> What will you do, poor desperate lady?

PHAEDRA

> Only one way now, straightway die now.
> Only one cure for the sickness that grips me.
> *(Phaedra rushes to the side. Enter Hippolytus from the palace, followed
> by the Nurse. Phaedra overhears the following.)*

HIPPOLYTUS

> Earth mother! Sunlight's sick revelations!
> What unspeakable speeches, what noisome . . .

NURSE

> Hush, hush, dear boy; someone may hear you.

HIPPOLYTUS

> What do I care about that? What horrors!

NURSE *(on her knees)*
Oh, sir, I beg you; clasping you, beg you.   600

HIPPOLYTUS
Hands off me! Don't dare touch my clothes!

NURSE
Prince, I beg of you, do not destroy us.

HIPPOLYTUS *(nastily)*
But you have *said* you have said nothing *evil*.

NURSE
No, but it wasn't for everyone's hearing.

HIPPOLYTUS
Nice pretty tales should have everyone hear them.

NURSE
Dear boy, do you remember your promise?

HIPPOLYTUS
It was my tongue that promised it, not I.

NURSE
Child, your dear ones—will you destroy us?

HIPPOLYTUS
I have no criminals honored as "dear ones."

NURSE
Son, we are human, forgive us our frailties.   610

HIPPOLYTUS
Great Zeus, why on this earth is there room for
women, that counterfeit version of mankind?

Why, if you needed to propagate people,
couldn't we go to your temples and buy them?
Why must we labor and sweat upon females?
We could pay pieces of gold or of silver,
bronze, lead, iron to pay for our offspring,
charging the poor dads less than the rich ones,
everyone happily dwelling in houses
blissfully free of detestable females.   620
Now, as it is, what happens? The banes come
home with us, burdening, costing us dearly.
Positive proof that women are baneful's
this: that the father who got one and raised her
pays out *more* money, pays out a *dowry*,
just to be *free* of her after his trouble.
Then, think of *him*, the poor husband, who takes this
growing catastrophe into his household,
drapes her in finery, miserable creature,
spills out the wealth of his house into garments.   630
Either good relatives come with a scarecrow,
or he gets beauty, related to rotters.
Best that your woman be totally brainless,
empty of any philosophy, knowledge,
notions of justice. Of course, they're a bother,
uselessly sitting there all day. Yes, but
clever ones, Oh, they are totally loathsome.
Lusts make mischief in clever ones daily.
Witlessness gives the dears perfect discretion.
Slaves ought never be trusted to women.   640
Give them instead beasts, toothy and speechless,
for their companions, and let them converse with
no one, hatching their plots inside that
servants will execute out in the city.
That's how you've come now, detestable person,
soiling the sanctified bed of my father.
Into my ears I shall pour running water,
woman, to wash out your filthy proposals.

How could you think me so ghastly a traitor
when the mere *sound* of it makes me feel dirty?   650
Well! I will tell you plainly what saves you:
piety—mine. Oh, had you not tricked me,
got me to swear you an oath to say nothing,
father would hear about this. As it is now,
Theseus out of the city . . . I also . . .
I shall leave too, and my mouth shall be locked shut.
When he returns, I shall see how you greet him,
you and your lady. I know you so well now.
I am so nicely experienced—curse you!
Why do I keep going on about women?   660
Well, then! Let women either be chaste or
let me trample upon them forever.
(Exit.)

NURSE
    Dark, dark doom here
    fallen on women!
    Oh, I have failed her,
    failed her, my darling.
    Now what pleading
    ever can save us,
    undo the knot that
    words have tied for us?   670
    Yes, I deserve this!
    Earth full of sunlight,
    where shall I hide now,
    where hide the terrible deed?
    God or kind mortal,
    sit by my side now,
    share my injustice!
    Suffering's limit,
    Oh, I have reached it,
    I, most luckless of women.   680
(Phaedra comes forward.)

CHORUS

So, it is done now, and nothing's succeeded.
Queen, it is over now, dreadfully over.

PHAEDRA *(to the Nurse)*

Hateful! Of those you loved the destroyer.
Now you have ruined me. Zeus, father, help me!
Strike her with thunderbolts, blast her to cinders!
Didn't I tell you? Oh, didn't I warn you?
Didn't I caution you not to disgrace me?
You, you, you wouldn't listen . . . and I won't . . .
die without shame now. Now . . .
(a new thought strikes her)

is there something? 690

He with his wits fine-honed by his anger
soon will be slashing me, first to his father,
then to his guardian, then to the wide world,
each fine bit of your stupid proposal
retailing . . . curses on you and on all who
ruin their friends by attempting to help them.

NURSE

Mistress, of course you have reason to blame me,
bitten by sorrow that masters your judgment.
If you will listen, I'll make you an answer.
Didn't I nurture you, guide you through childhood?
Didn't I grieve for your malady, seek out   700
cures for it? Yes, they were wrong, I confess it.
Had they been right, I'm sure you'd forgive me.
Plans that are lucky seem perfect in wisdom.

PHAEDRA

So, that's enough for me—deftly to stab me,
pull out the dagger, and tell me you're sorry?

NURSE

Don't waste words! I admit I was stupid.
But there is hope still, hope for escape, dear . . .

PHAEDRA

Finish the talk! Your advice was dishonor,
mischief, and shame; yes, those you have brought me.
Leave me now therefore. Look to yourself now.   710
(Exit Nurse.)
You now, nobly born daughters of Troezen,
there's a request that I hope you will grant me:
plunge into silence whatever you've heard here.

CHORUS

Artemis, daughter of Zeus, be our witness:
we won't reveal any hint of your troubles.

PHAEDRA

Well said. Now, let me add one thing more:
I have discovered a curious blessing
in this debacle: my sons shall have honor
still, and my homeland no shame in my ruin.
Nor will I need face Theseus ever.   720
One poor life will be what this costs me.

CHORUS

Then it's the dread, the incurable ill deed . . .

PHAEDRA

Death; but the means I have still to consider.

CHORUS

No, no!

PHAEDRA

No? Well, give me advice, then! . . .
This grim day will give pleasure to Cypris,
who with this sickness, this passion, destroyed me,

and I shall gladden her, leaving the daylight.
But there is someone living for whom my
death will be painful, who will not triumph
over me, feel no arrogant joy, but   730
in his misery learn moderation.
(Exit.)

CHORUS
Oh, let me flee to the cliffs of the mountains,
riding on wings there,
feathered and flying,
lost among flocks of my kind;
soar over shorelines,
deep Eridanus,
river of dying.
Girls there are singing,
weep for lost Phaethon,   740
and shed their amber tears.

Or to the apple-tree coasts of the far north
bear me on wings where
deep lordly Ocean
fixes the boundaries of Earth,
Atlas upholds the
pillars of Heaven.
There flow the fountains,
there father Zeus lay.
Earth felt his vigor,   750
the source of every good.

White-sailed vessel from Crete shores
bearing my lady
out of her glory of girlhood
into her marriage's
miseries waiting;
ill-omens beckon
in the beginning

and in the ending:
Crete, great island,   760
glorious Athens;
and they threw their ropes to the mainland.

Soul-wrenched, maddened, and lovesick,
Cypris' victim,
under the burden she sinks down,
fastens the noose to the
beam in her chamber,
fitting her white neck,
slender and graceful,
ready to die now,   770
eager for good name,
now she will do it,
and she frees her soul from her sick love.

NURSE *(in the palace, screaming)*
> Help, help, run to her, rescue her, neighbors!
> Loosen this rope at her neck. She's strangling.

CHORUS
> Ai, Ai, done, then! She's finished; it's over.
> Queen of our city, she swings from a rafter.

NURSE
> Hurry, for god's sake! Bring us a good sharp
> dagger to cut this noose and release her!

CHORUS
> What should we do, friends, go inside and   780
> loosen the queen from her strangling neckpiece?

CHORUS (2)
> Why, when our place is out here on the dance floor,
> meddle? There ought to be servingmen in there.

NURSE
Lay her out carefully, poor tortured body.
Theseus may not be pleased with the help here.

CHORUS
Dear! Evidently she's dead, as I judge from
noises inside. Have they laid out her body?
(Enter Theseus.)

THESEUS
What's going on here? What's the commotion?
Shrieks in the distance, and wails, and I find now
doors of my own house bolted against me, 790
back from the oracle, coming with good news.
What can have happened? A death? Is it Pittheus?
Father is old. We're prepared for his death soon.
Nevertheless, it will bring great sorrow.

CHORUS
Not to the aged one comes the misfortune.
It's the destruction of youth that will grieve you.

THESEUS
Heavens! My sons? Is a child's life taken?

CHORUS
They are alive. For the mother you'll sorrow.

THESEUS
What do you say? Dear wife . . . dead? How, then?

CHORUS
Rope noose, tied by her own hand, strangled. 800

THESEUS
Was she aggrieved? About what? What reason?

CHORUS

> That's all we know. We have only come lately,
> Theseus, over the hill paths to mourn her.

THESEUS

> Why with these leaves did I crown my forehead,
> celebrate, since I return to this horror?
> Unlock doors, unbar the great portal,
> loosen all fastenings, servants, and let me
> see her, who with her death has destroyed me.
> (*The doors are opened. Phaedra's body is revealed.*)

CHORUS

> Unlucky woman, you endured;
> your life, a dynasty's destruction;   810
> your death, a deed unsanctified.
> You wrestled with yourself and lost.
> We gaze, and do we see in you
> the divine power that brought this darkness?

THESEUS

> Misery's mine, and suffering.
> This is the hugest of my sorrows.
> Heavy it falls upon me now,
> weighs on my hearth and lineage.
> Lost woman, now in a wide sea
> I swim. There's no shore anywhere   820
> that I can reach, nor even glimpse,
> no respite from this flood of sorrows.
> There is no name for it, no end.
> Light as a bird you fly away,
> and you take with you the whole world
> in one swift flitting into Hades.
> Why is it now, this suffering?
> Stroke of what god? Whose sin before me
> lost in the endless gloom of time?

CHORUS
Lord, it is not to you only, such deep grief.   830
Others have had their dear wives taken.

THESEUS
Under earth, darkened, I would lie
removed from luck and joy and hope
who have no fortune any more
nor ever, dear, with you sweet words.
You give worse death than you have suffered.
What brutal stroke brought you to this?
Will no one tell me what has happened?
Or do I keep the flock of you
for nothing? Misery, Oh, I . . .   840
No, it is more than I can utter.
My house dead, children motherless.
O my darling wife, you're gone, gone!
You were the best on whom the sun's
light looked, the all-beholding sun,
the whole night full of watching stars.

CHORUS
Suffering man, house stricken with evils,
into my eyes, when I hear you, the tears come,
fear in my heart for the evils approaching.

THESEUS
Ah!   850
What's this tablet attached to her hand here?
Dear, have you something to tell me, some last thing,
oh poor miserable one, to request me,
pleading—our living together, our children?
Have no fear, dear. No other woman
ever shall enter my bed, rule these halls.
Look! It's her signet ring's symbol in wax there.
Now I shall break it, the seal, and discover
what words come still, out of her silence.

CHORUS
> Misery, misery, oh, I can feel it,   860
> riding on wings that the gods have provided.
> How my heart stirs with a gloomy foreboding!
> Gods, if it's possible, hear my entreaty:
> not to this house—not utter destruction!

THESEUS
> Sorrow on sorrow,
> speech cannot hold it,
> passes endurance!

CHORUS
> What is it? Tell us.
> If it's permitted,
> say what you read there.   870

THESEUS
> Loudly it sings out,
> death in its singing.

CHORUS
> Singing our ruin . . .

THESEUS
> Heart cannot hold it,
> secret imprisoned.
> Out of my mouth's gates
> cry, let the truth out.
> City of Athens,
> hear it, the horror.
> Oh, my dear wife! Hip-   880
> polytus . . . raped her!
> He has dishonored
> God's holy sunlight.
> Father Poseidon,

god of the ocean,
you who once gave me
curses to utter—
three—and you'd do them;
now, for the first one:
kill him!—my dear son,   890
not to escape you,
now, before sunset,
do it! You promised.

CHORUS
Call back your curses!
King, call them back now!
Quick! You will learn your
terrible error.
Trust me! Believe me!

THESEUS
Never! And now I make this addition:
he shall be banished . . . from Athens . . . our city.   900
That way, he will be stricken, in one way
or in another, and either Poseidon,
true to his word, God's word, strikes him,
or he will wander, miserable beggar,
drain to the dregs his goblet of sorrow.

CHORUS
Look there, king! It's Hippolytus coming—
timely arrival! But Theseus, hear me!
Think of your house now, swallow your anger.
(Enter Hippolytus.)

HIPPOLYTUS
Terrible cries from you, Father, that bring me
hastily—what could have moved you to shout so,   910
what can have caused . . . Ah! Phaedra! She's dead, then?

No, it's impossible! Hardly a moment—
then—when I left her—and she was so young still,
beautiful . . . How can this *be*, this happen?
What can have brought her to this? . . . You are silent.
Won't you explain to me, Father? Your silence—
that's no way to endure great sorrow.
Telling your troubles will ease them, and ease me.
It's not right to keep secrets from dear ones.
I am your son, Father, more than a dear one.   920

THESEUS

Men are such fools! Work, labor—for what, then?
Numberless crafts that they teach each other;
twist and invent and discover; but one thing
always, it seems, will elude them, the cure for
all these clever accomplishments: wisdom.

HIPPOLYTUS

Cleverly, Father, you speak; and I wish you
good luck, herding the witless to wisdom!
Such speculations, however, seem ill-timed:
grief-stricken ravings, a tongue near-maddened.

THESEUS

Men should possess a reliable test, boy,   930
how to determine a friend, that he's honest;
how to be sure that he'll never betray you.
Every man ought to have two clear voices
speaking inside him. The first shall be justice.
As for the other—whatever it chances.
Then, let the just voice silence the false one!
Let it reveal all hypocrites, traitors!

HIPPOLYTUS

What? Can it *be* I'm the object of slander?
I who have *done* nothing? Do you condemn me—

I am astonished—for what, then? Such strange 940
words, unconnected with meaning, bewilder.

THESEUS
Man's mind, where will it march to in boldness,
past what boundary next? Generations
watch it advancing, in each new age, new
summits of villainy . . . Finally, with no room
left for the new populations, the gods shall
build a new world for us criminals, cutthroats.
Look at this man. He has come from my own flesh,
yet he dishonored my own bed. Clearly!
She who is dead here testifies to it. 950
(Hippolytus turns away.)
No, boy, show your face. Let me *see* you!
Foul one, look at your father! O you, who
walked with the gods in your purity—said so,
boasted about it—are gods so demented
they would consort with a villain? . . . And do you—
Oh, such a delicate specimen!—banquet
only on pure foods, vegetables only?
Delicate Orpheus, he is your king now,
tootling tunes in the woods, from your study
fluting and fluttering out of your scroll-books? 960
Oh, I have caught you, will warn all men of
hypocrites like you, who hunt souls, praising
purity, steeping themselves in corruption.
That she is dead, you suppose that saves you.
That is what most, foul villain, convicts you.
What protestations would ever, boy, ward off
this, this message from her, the departed?
I know: stepmothers hate all stepsons;
bastards despised, and they're thrust into shadows.
What strange bargain was that, then, trading 970
life for a poor little morsel of vengeance?
There's no folly in *men*, you will say, just

women? The men—as lascivious, trust me,
once dread Cypris invades them, the young ones,
even though male resolution can save them.
Why am I uttering all this nonsense?
This dead flesh speaks louder than voices.
Out with you, out into exile, and quickly!
Never again let me see you in Athens,
city raised up by the gods, nor where my   980
sharp spear governs. If I should sit here
meekly enduring this deed you have dealt me,
Sinis, the brigand, would shriek that he's living,
cry that I only pretended to kill him,
and the Skyronian rocks and their breakers
claim that I'm kind to the doers of evil.

CHORUS
How can I dare call any man happy?
All that is noblest collapses in ruin.

HIPPOLYTUS
Father, your deep-felt hurt and your anger,
Oh, they are fearful! But if you consider   990
carefully, calmly the charges against me,
you will be forced to concede their unfairness.
I am not skillful, haranguing a large crowd,
but to the few, the select, I am cogent.
This I believe to be right, to be proper
since there are many, not known for their wisdom,
who are inspired when addressing the masses.
But in disaster, my tongue must be loosened.
Let me begin at that point where, to crush me,
you have supposed what can't be refuted;   1000
but I refute it. Observe it, this daylight,
shining on no heart purer than mine is,
though you deny it. I know too how to
honor the gods and to choose for companions

those who will revel in innocence, justice,
scruple to give, or accept, base orders.
I never mock: I respect those around me,
who are the same to me, absent or present.
One thing finally, Father: you think me
vulnerable to your scorn and your mocking   1010
when you imply that my chastity's falsehood.
Now, to this day, has my body remained, Sir,
clean in its bed: unknown all those things
people will do there. Of course, there are paintings.
I can forgo them, preferring my freedom.
Granted, my purity fails to convince you,
still, you should show how I came to be tempted.
Maybe her deep irresistible beauty,
greater than all other women's, subdued me.
Maybe I hoped to inherit your kingdom   1020
since, after all, your queen was the heiress.
What a great fool, far gone in my madness,
that would have made me! To lust for corruption!
"Thirsting for power corrupts even chaste men,"
you will reply and presume that I faltered.
Kingship corrupts, Sir, *all* who have held it!
No, in the Games let me rather be victor
known as an athlete throughout Hellas,
happy with second place here in my city,
wise and relaxed in my genuine friendships.   1030
Therein lies true scope for my actions.
Safety is sweeter than sovereignty, Father!
Well, then! Those are my counterpleas . . . One more:
If I could call that woman to witness,
honestly face my accuser, who knows all,
then there would be for the guilty, the wicked,
questions to answer . . . but now, in the silence,
great Zeus, keeper of oaths, be my witness:
Never, Sir, once have I touched your dear wife,
nor have I wished it, nor ever once dreamt it.   1040

Great God, grant that I perish in exile,
cityless vagabond, unknown, nameless;
earth and deep ocean forbid to receive my
poor dead bones, if I did this vileness.
Whether in fear or in fury she perished,
I cannot tell, lest my high oath perish.
Honor dishonorably she has guarded;
guarding my honor has brought me to ruin.

CHORUS

Adequately you've rebutted the charges.
Oaths like yours to the gods—I respect them.   1050

THESEUS

Doesn't he juggle his phrases so nicely!
Thinking his unperturbed calm is his bulwark,
deftly he charms, and dishonors, his father.

HIPPOLYTUS

Father, I marvel at you and your sentence.
Had you been *my* son, I, Sir, your father,
I would have killed you, not eased you to exile,
had you performed such acts upon *my* wife.

THESEUS

Well said! *That's* not how you will die, though.
That's not for you, that death you have chosen,
easy quick end, much favored by wretches.   1060
Yours shall be lingering, wandering, cast out,
tasting a strange soil's bitterness, driven;
that is the penalty apt for the impious.

HIPPOLYTUS

What do you mean? Oh . . . Will you not even
let time testify? Banish this instant?

THESEUS

    Far beyond Pontus, the Pillars of Atlas,
    were it but possible! *So* far I loathe you.

HIPPOLYTUS

    No divination, no oracles questioned,
    now, right now, without trial to be sent out?

THESEUS

    No divination is needed. This tablet   1070
    clearly accuses you, *and* I believe it.
    Ominous birds there, joy to you, winged ones!

HIPPOLYTUS

    Great Gods, why do I suffer in silence
    when the respect I have shown you destroys me?
    No; clear evidence wouldn't convince him.
    I would have broken my oath to no purpose.

THESEUS

    All this muttering sanctity, how it
    sickens me! Out of the fatherland! Out now!

HIPPOLYTUS

    Miserable! Where will I go? What friendly
    house will receive me, for *that* crime banished?   1080

THESEUS

    Someone, no doubt, who can relish those guests who'll
    diddle their wives, stout plotters of incest.

HIPPOLYTUS

    That strikes home, Father, that you believe that.
    Let me shed tears now, that you so think me.

THESEUS

    Moans and forebodings, boy, would have been better
    spent before raping her—wife of your father.

HIPPOLYTUS

    Halls of this house, Oh, won't you witness,
    not say whether or not I am wicked?

THESEUS

    That's right, keep your witnesses speechless.
    (pointing to Phaedra's body)
    This can't speak, but declares you a monster.   1090

HIPPOLYTUS

    Would I were not just me, but another
    able to see me here, what I suffer!

THESEUS

    Always you looked at yourself, your perfections
    honoring more then you honored your parents.

HIPPOLYTUS

    Mother of misery, why did you bear me?
    Of my companions, may none be a bastard!

THESEUS

    Seize him, my servants! Remove this person!
    Haven't you heard me declare him an outcast?

HIPPOLYTUS

    Any who touch me will rue that they did so.
    Do it yourself! Can you bear to, my father?   1100

THESEUS

    That's what I'll do if you fail to obey me.
    Seeing you driven out rouses no pity.
    (Exit.)

HIPPOLYTUS

So, it is fixed, clear. Luckless, I set out,
knowing the truth, knowing not how to tell it.
Dearest of deities, daughter of Leto,
Artemis, long my companion, my huntress,
look at me, lashed out of Athens, an exile!
Farewell, my city, the land of Erechtheus;
forests of Troezen, the glories you brought me,
blessing my youth, farewell now forever!   1110
Come, my companions, we'll say our goodbyes now.
Give me your company out to the border.
Friends, you will never find chaster than I am
anyone, no, though my father denies it.

(Exit.)

CHORUS

It is helpful to worship the gods
if a mortal can only believe;
for it makes a man happy
to suppose there is something:
that there's wisdom and form in his days.
Yet all my thoughts grow dim   1120
when I observe man's life:
injustice, chaos, wildly shifting currents.

For the fortune in life that I seek
and I pray to the gods I may have:
let me never know sorrow,
be a stranger to anguish;
let me relish existence in peace.
Nor yet sincere, nor false,
I'd lightly change my ways
and change myself for every new tomorrow.   1130

But now my mind feels thoughtless peace no more:
things unexpected wound it.

The brightest star in Hellas
is driven out of Athens.
Stung by his father's anger,
he wanders hopeless through the world.
Sands of the seashore,
mountainside thicket,
beasts out of hiding
drove he, the hunter,   1140
the goddess Artemis his company.

He'll speed behind Venetian mares no more.
Their hoofbeats all are silent;
and silent now the music
upon his sleepless lyre
beneath his flying fingers.
That's finished in your father's house.
Haunts of the Goddess
deep in the forest
silent now, empty;   1150
music all ended
and rivalry of maidens for your love.

But I shall not let sorrow die.
I'll tend it carefully with tears
and let the whole world hear of it.
Sad mother, futile that you bore.
I am not happy with the gods.
Why do you, Graces, not help him,
alone, bearing his father's curse,
guiltless himself of all ill deeds?   1160

Look! It's Hippolytus' servant I see there
comes now running. He looks so gloomy.

MESSENGER
Where do I go to find Theseus, king here?
Say, women, where, if you know—in the palace?

CHORUS

There he is, just coming out, as it happens.

(Enter Theseus.)

MESSENGER

Theseus, sorrowful words I must bring you,
you and the citizens here in the city,
people of Troezen and far-off Athens.

THESEUS

What now? Has some other disaster
fallen on these two once-happy cities?   1170

MESSENGER

Yes, to Hippolytus, slaughtered—or almost.
Stricken and bloody, he clings to the light still.

THESEUS

Who did it? Someone, perhaps, in a quarrel—
someone whose wife, as his father's, he'd outraged?

MESSENGER

Chariot horses of his have destroyed him—
they and the curses your loud voice called, Sir,
down on your son from your father, the Sea Lord.

THESEUS

Mighty Poseidon, indeed you're my father!
Oh, and you heard me! You heeded my curses!
How did he die, then? Tell me how justice   1180
snapped in its trap my dishonorer! Tell me!

MESSENGER

There on the beach not far from the breakers
rolling ashore, we were combing the horses'
manes; we were crying; for someone had just then
come with the news that Hippolytus, master

dear to us all, had been cruelly banished—
yours, Sir, the edict—would leave us forever.
Then he appeared there himself, and he told us.
That brought tears again. Many companions
came there as well, all men of his own age,   1190
all of them weeping. He paused; then he cried out,
"Why do I moan like this? I am exiled.
There is the end of it. Father, you ordered;
I shall obey. Friends, ready the horses.
Harness them. This is no longer my city."
Everyone hastened. Before you could say it,
there was the chariot, ready for master.
Mounting, he fitted his feet in the footlocks,
gathered the reins, looked up at the sky and
cried out, stretching his hands to a dark cloud,   1200
"Great Zeus, kill me if I am a villain.
Let my father discover he wronged me—
when I'm in Hades, if not in the daylight."
Then with his quick whip lashed at the horses.
Forward they leapt with his servants beside them.
And we remained with him, followed our master
close, as the horse heads tossed, where the seaside
road seeks far Epidaurus and Argos.
Out into strange, uninhabited country
quickly we traveled to where, at the border,   1210
steeply the land slopes down to the seashore.
All of a sudden a terrible roaring
deep in the earth rose louder than thunder,
rolled on us, huge, and the horses could hear it,
neighing and tossing their heads; and we all gazed,
frightened, to see where the miracle came from.
It was a sea-wave, blotting the mountains
opposite, rose to the heavens, the Isthmus
veiling and even the crag of Asclepius.
Still swelling higher and higher, it spurt forth   1220
foaming and wind-blown spray in a cloud. As

all this lunged at the chariot horses,
suddenly out of the depths of that breaker
came a gigantic and bull-like monster,
bellowing, shaking the earth with its thunder,
echoing everywhere. No one could bear that
rage, and the four horses bolted in panic.
Oh, but Hippolytus, master of horses,
wholly in charge and maintaining his calmness,
reined them magnificently. As a sailor   1230
pulls on his oar, *he* pulled, leaning backward,
knowledge and strength counteracting their fury.
Onward they plunged, though; the fire-forged iron
clenched in their teeth and, ignoring their master,
heedless of harness or even the car's weight,
carried him helpless. Whenever he pulled them
out to the safe smooth ground, there the bull stood,
driving them back to the cliff and the rocks there.
There, on an outcropped boulder, a wheel-rim
snagged, and the horses went maddening on still,   1240
overturned chariot dragging behind them.
All was confusion of axle-pins, wheel-rims
leaping and smashing, the driver, the poor man,
tangled in harness—for who could untie him?—
smashing his head on the sharp rocks, leaving
flesh on them, Oh, and the things that he called out:
"Stay, horses! You that my mangers have nourished,
do not destroy me! Oh curse of my father!
Who will now stand by a good man and help him?"
Oh, there were many who wished. He outran us,   1250
slow feet falling behind; but at last he
fell from the reins (they were clean-cut from him,
god knows how), his remains, little breath left
in him. The horses had vanished, the great bull
too, all gone among rocks and the seashore.
Slave that I am in your house, good master,
never, Sir, will I believe that your son was

guilty—no, not though the whole great tribe of
females hang itself up from the rafters,
not though they fill with their scribbling more pine   1260
tablets than grow in the forests of Ida.
Theseus, he, your son, was a good man.

CHORUS

New and yet newer disasters! They plague us.
Destiny's blows . . . Ah! No one escapes them.

THESEUS

Hatred of him makes news of his hard death
pleasure to me, but I'm filled with an awe too,
awe for the gods—and for him, one once loved.
No pain, then, to be felt, and no pleasure.

MESSENGER

Well, Sir, what shall I do? Will you see your
son here? Tell us, Sir, how may we please you?   1270
Dare I advise you? Perhaps you should see him.
One so unfortunate ought to have kindness.

THESEUS

Bring him here; let me observe in his own face
him who polluted my marital chamber,
see how he answers the gods' clear judgment.

CHORUS

Cypris, you rule all;
mortal, immortal,
none can withstand you.
Flashing-winged Eros,
glitterer, quick-winged,   1280
over earth flying,
over the salt sea,
over the thunders,

into the frenzied
sending his arrows.
How you bewitch them,
flashing your gold wings!
Beasts of the mountain,
monsters of ocean,
all of them feel you,   1290
Cypris, our ruler;
beings that earth bears,
blazing sun looks on,
none can withstand you.
(Enter Artemis, as from her statue.)

ARTEMIS
Offspring of Aegeus,
Theseus, great one,
listen and hear me!
Artemis speaks now,
daughter of Leto.
Miserable mortal,   1300
impious, hateful,
how can you joy in
innocent blood spilled?
How could you kill your
son who was guiltless?
Oh, you *believed* things
secret and hidden,
deeds to which one dead
testified falsely.
Now you can *see* what   1310
ruin you've brought down,
death to your fortunes.
Why don't you hide your
face in the shadows
or, as a bird, fly
far from your horrors

since, among good men,
you have no place now.

Theseus, hear your summation of evils;
make yourself miserable; I can't help you.   1320
First I shall speak of your innocent son, who
now in his death should be properly honored,
then of your wife, who, though maddened with passion,
kept, in a manner of speaking, her honor.
She was afflicted by that great goddess
who by us all who delight in our pure thoughts
most is detested and, fixed on your young son,
languished. She struggled to conquer this. Cypris
entered her nurse who, hoping to help her,
plunged her in ruin: confessed to your son all;   1330
drew him first, with an oath, into silence.
He, as was proper, rejected this vileness,
yet, being pious, he clung to his silence.
Phaedra, afraid of enquiries looming,
shored up her honor with lies. You believed them;
and you permitted deceit to destroy him.

THESEUS
(an inarticulate cry of anguish)

ARTEMIS
Ah, so it hurts, then, Theseus, does it?
Quiet now! So you can hear what follows.
Then you can groan even more. You were given
excellent curses, the three from you father.   1340
One of these went, vile man, to destroy your
son, when it could have been used on a real foe.
Father Poseidon—of course he would keep his
promise, but still he detested this mad deed.
You, therefore, are detestable also,
both to your father and me, for you wouldn't
stay for a proof or the voice of a prophet,

make an enquiry, even allow time's
slow revelations, but rushing insanely,
called down that curse on your son and destroyed him.   1350

THESEUS

Goddess, destroy me!

ARTEMIS

Your deeds have been dreadful;
but it is possible we will forgive you.
Cypris has willed all these vile actions
spitefully. Gods have the following custom:
No god dares interfere with the actions
taken by others among the immortals.
All stand aside when a plot's undertaken.
You may be sure, had I not feared dread Zeus,
never would I have endured such shame: the
death of him dearest to me among mortals.   1360
Agony, forced to look on and do nothing!
So you were ignorant. That may excuse you.
It was impossible for you to test her,
and you believed. How troublesome death is!
So you have suffered . . . but I grieve also.
Death of the innocent brings no pleasure
to the immortals; we only delight in
wrecking the wicked, their houses, their children.

CHORUS

The suffering Hippolytus
comes, his smooth young limbs, golden head,   1370
battered. A wreck, his flesh. This house,
grief after grief come down upon it,
horribly down out of the heavens.

HIPPOLYTUS

Oh me, me! I am ruin.
Words of an unjust father
mutilate me. I am gone, gone.

Pains leap in my head, lightnings.
Spasms lash in me—horses!
Put me down! Let me rest!
Horses, I fed you, I stroked you.   1380
Why did you do this to me?
With my own hand, and you killed me.
Servants—Gods!—if you love me,
handle me gently.
How can I stand this?
Who's that standing there, there on the right?
Lift me up! Carefully!
Don't wrench me—wretch! My father did this.
Zeus, Father Zeus, do you see this?
I was the holy one, I revered you,   1390
I, chastest of men—Zeus, do you see this?—
thrust into Hades. It's death I see there.
All lost. All labors, all piety, pointless.

Oh, oh, the pain now,
pain comes over me.
Let the poor wretch go!
Death, be my healer.
Kill me, kill the wretch quickly!
Oh, let me taste it,
the two-edged blade   1400
cut me in two,
lay me to rest.
Curse of my father,
curse in the family,
bloodstained ancestors
breaking upon me.
Why won't it stop, then,
coming upon me?
Why when I'm guiltless?
Oh, oh,   1410
who am I? What, then?

Gods, get me clear now,
clear of this pain now,
clear of this horror.
Darkness, compulsion,
death's night take me,
lay me down, wretched!
Rest me, oh, rest me!

ARTEMIS
Miserable one, there, yoked to misfortune,
it's your nobility that has destroyed you.   1420

HIPPOLYTUS
What is that fragrance? Divinity breathing?
Goddess, I sense you, my agony lightened.
Oh, it is Artemis, she, she is near now.

ARTEMIS
Poor one, yes! Of the gods to you dearest.

HIPPOLYTUS
Lady, you see me? You see me here, stricken?

ARTEMIS
Yes, I can see you. But tears are forbidden.

HIPPOLYTUS
Gone are the hounds now, gone is your hunter.

ARTEMIS
Yet, though you die, mortal, still I can like you.

HIPPOLYTUS
No one to tend you, your horses, your image.

ARTEMIS
No, thus treacherous Cypris would have it.   1430

HIPPOLYTUS
Ah, so! That's it—the power that wrecked me.

ARTEMIS
She, feeling slighted, detested your splendor.

HIPPOLYTUS
That makes three of us Cypris has ruined.

ARTEMIS
Your poor father and you and his consort.

HIPPOLYTUS
My poor father I pity, so luckless.

ARTEMIS
He was deluded. A deity willed it.

HIPPOLYTUS *(turning to Theseus)*
What strange mischance ruined you, Father!

THESEUS
Yes, and destroyed all. Life has no joy left.

HIPPOLYTUS
More than for me, I weep for your sadness.

THESEUS
Oh, in your place, how gladly I'd die, child!   1440

HIPPOLYTUS
Gifts of your father, Poseidon, proved bitter.

THESEUS
How did it get in my mouth, that vile curse?

HIPPOLYTUS

That or some other way, you would have killed me.

THESEUS

Yes, for the gods had uprooted my senses.

HIPPOLYTUS

Horrible gods! Might men uproot *them*!

ARTEMIS

Hush now! You *will* have a lovely revenge,
dear, for the vile machinations of Cypris.
Plunged though you'll be in the Underworld's loathsome
darks, you will have that reward for your goodness.
Soon now, the very next mortal she fancies,   1450
him my errorless arrows will slaughter,
and she'll be punished. For you, poor hapless,
I shall decree, recompensing your sorrows,
wonderful honors in Troezen, where maidens
soon to be married will cut long strands of
hair for you. Down through the ages, you'll harvest
tears they have shed in their maidenhood's mourning.
Poetry sung by those talented virgins
yearly will honor your memory, Phaedra's
passion for you, your impeccable honor,   1460
both of you, proud names, famous forever.

Now, son of Aegeus, enfold him, your dear child,
close in your arms. Though you killed him, you're guiltless.
Terrible deeds that the gods may accomplish,
using you: no man's responsible for them.
Now, then . . . Hippolytus, turn to your father,
try to forgive. Blame destiny . . . Now, dears,
farewell! Viewing the dead is forbidden,
hearing the gasps of the dying pollutes us,
and I can see those evils begin now.   1470

HIPPOLYTUS

> Farewell, beautiful one, blest maiden,
> who can so easily leave a long friendship!
> Do you request it? My father's forgiven.
> Heretofore haven't I always obeyed you?
> Over my eyes it is falling, the darkness.
> Father, take hold of my body and raise me.

THESEUS

> Child, child, what do you do to your father?

HIPPOLYTUS

> Now I can see them, the gates; they are open.

THESEUS

> Ah, will you leave me, then, stained with your murder?

HIPPOLYTUS

> No, Father! Now, of my death, I acquit you.   1480

THESEUS

> What? Oh, can you? My dear son, can you?

HIPPOLYTUS

> Dread-bowed Artemis, you be my witness!

THESEUS

> What a nobility's in you that speaks now!

HIPPOLYTUS

> May your legitimate sons be as noble!

THESEUS

> What a magnificent person now leaves us!

HIPPOLYTUS

> Joy to you, joy to me also, my father!

THESEUS
   Do not desert me, my son; still struggle!

HIPPOLYTUS
   Struggling's over, my father. I leave you.
   Cover my face quick, quick, with my mantle.
(He dies.)

THESEUS
   Marvelous Athens, proud Pallas' city,   1490
   Oh what a wonder you had, and have lost him!
   Cypris, I'll always remember your doings.

CHORUS
   Down on the city
   strokes without warning:
   all's desolation.
   Rain down, O flowing
   tears of our mourning.
   Death of a great one
   wails among nations.
(Curtain.)

Suppliant Women

Translated by
John Frederick Nims

It seems to have been an incident of 424 B.C. that sparked the writing of the *Suppliant Women*. That fall an Athenian army left Attica for Delium, in hostile Boeotia. There they seized and fortified the shrine of Apollo. A Boeotian army, with substantial Theban forces and under a Theban commander, moved to oppose them. Having prevailed in the battle, the Boeotians turned down a herald's request to let the Athenians bury their dead. It was not until a couple of weeks had passed that the Boeotians, having recaptured Delium, allowed the Athenians to remove the neglected bodies from the battlefield.

Thucydides, in describing the many battles of that war, more often than not concludes with some mention of the recovery of the dead under an armistice. This was even more important to the Greeks than the recovery of our own MIAs is to us. Not only would the exposed bodies be savaged by animals and birds of prey, but the spirits of those not hallowed by burial would be excluded from their afterlife in the underworld. Antigone chooses death rather than leave her brother unburied.

The following spring the new play of Euripides expressed the anti-Theban anger in Athens. In his play, Euripides is adapting to the customs and politics of his own time a thousand-year-old story from the tragic Theban cycle, several times quarried for material by Aesychlus, and by Sophocles in *Antigone* and the two Oedipus plays. Euripides' drama deals with the aftermath of the disastrous campaign of the Seven against Thebes: with the withholding of their bodies after the defeat, the recovery of those bodies by Theseus, and the mourning, before and after the recovery, for the many dead.

Myth and history were no doubt mingled and enhanced as the centuries went by. Was there really a dramatic battle, as Herodotus says (ix.27.3), or was there a settlement "by persuading them to a truce," as Plutarch would have it in his life of Theseus (xxix.4)? Whatever the truth was, Euripides chose the more dramatic version. It was his imagination that contributed the Evadne-Iphis episode near the end of the play, a scene which in its pathos and horror is not only unique in Greek tragedy but, as a recent critic has said, "We would be hard pressed to find a more theatrically daring moment in the history of the stage." [1]

The ancient "hypothesis" or "argument" prefixed to the text says the play is "an encomium of the Athenians," praise, that is, of Athenian institutions and of their national hero, Theseus. Regarded as the contemporary and companion of Heracles, he was credited with setting up democratic government in Athens as against the "tyrannies" that prevailed elsewhere in Greece, a government the Athenians of Euripides' time had reason to be proud of, especially when it was compared to Sparta's more rigorous absolutist regime. It was also praise of the Athenians in showing how their ancestors were willing to go to war to preserve the venerable sanctities of the Hellenes against those who would desecrate them. But that praise took a more gratifying form. The Thebans at Delium had delayed the burial of Athenian bodies; now an Athenian audience could see the stage Thebans committing the same kind of impiety, but this time getting their humiliating comeuppance. Praise of the Athenians, however, is by no means the whole story for Euripides, who is even more concerned with the grief and suffering brought on humanity by the folly and futility of war.

Suppliant Women is set at Eleusis, not far from Athens, where the temple of Demeter and Persephone was the site of the celebration of those mysteries that attracted visitors from all of Greece. The obvious reason for its being set there is that history demanded it. As Plutarch wrote in his life of Theseus, "And the graves of the greater part of those who fell before Thebes are shown at Eleutherae, and those of the commanders near Eleusis" (xxix.5). But there were other reasons as well. The association between Athens and Eleusis had been close, especially after Athens, some time before 66 B.C., took charge of the mysteries, partly as a religious buttressing of the regime. We are told by Vitruvius that Eleusis benefited substantially from the great building program sponsored by Pericles in mid-century. And no doubt Euripides had in mind the symbolism of the earth goddesses, representing life and rebirth as against the holocaust of war. The play opens with a cere-

---

1. Rush Rehm, *Greek Tragic Theatre* (London and New York: Routledge, 1992), pp. 129–30.

mony in their honor. Near the conclusion, when Evadne leaps to her death on the pyre of Capaneus, she sees the reunion with her dead husband as taking place "in the wedding chamber of Persephone."

Nearly a thousand years after Euripides' time, the anthologist Stobaeus, culling from earlier collections, preserved a number of quotations from *Suppliant Women*, showing what an impression this eminently quotable play must have had in antiquity. But its popularity seems not to have endured through later centuries. Looking it up in histories of literature, we are likely to come upon summaries as dismissive as this one of 1904: "a play written for an occasion . . . its dramatic value is mediocre." The most disparaging judgment is that of Gilbert Norwood in his *Essays in Euripidean Drama* (1954); he feels that Euripides, "fine poet that he was, here totters on the brink of insanity."[2] In his analysis he has recourse to such language as "repellent," "rubbish," "intolerable flatness," "a heap of lumps thrown together by some meddling dullard." His opinion, shared by few if any, has been labeled "bizarre."

One reason for the underestimation of *Suppliant Women* is the ambiguity of the play itself. Critics were likely to miss the point of it: Wonder what it was up to, after all? H. D. F. Kitto in his *Greek Tragedy* says, "With the exception of the *Heracles* no play of Euripides is more baffling and 'unsatisfactory.'"[3] L. H. G. Greenwood, in his *Aspects of Euripidean Tragedy*, agrees. A point he stresses is that Euripides often writes tongue in cheek; he "says one thing and means another,"[4] writing on one level for the naive listener but hoping that a more sophisticated one will sense the intended irony.

Günther Zuntz deserves much of the credit for the far more favorable attention the play has received in recent decades. "A document of the immense skill and the passionate heart of its creator," he writes, "and the ideal image of his city.[5] Kitto, in spite of some reservations, would agree, "Few

2. Norwood, *Essays in Euripidean Drama* (Berkeley: University of California Press, 1954), p. 117.
3. Kitto, *Greek Tragedy: A Literary Study* (1939; 3d ed. London: Methuen, 1961), p. 232.
4. Greenwood, *Aspects of Euripidean Tragedy* (Cambridge: Cambridge University Press, 1953), p. 92.
5. Zuntz, *The Political Plays of Euripides* (Manchester: Manchester University Press, 1955), p. 25.

plays . . . surpass this one in tragic feeling and imagination" (p. 132). Greenwood, too, praises it as "a moving and beautiful picture of human misfortune and sorrow" (p. 93). A number of sympathetic critics besides those mentioned have walked us through the play almost line by line, among them Wesley D. Smith (1966), Christopher Collard (1975), and Peter Burian (1985), all eloquent in explaining away the twenty and more centuries of misunderstanding.[6]

Many readers will feel that *Suppliant Women*, falling into two parts, lacks the unity a well made play should have. Intending praise, it is even more powerfully swayed toward lamentation. The schizoid tendency, shown in its double structure, appears in details as well. War is seen as releasing humanity's worst impulses and as leading to endless agony, yet the war Theseus undertakes is seen as righteous. The goddess Athena seems to more than tolerate a war of vengeance, not just in predicting what is fated but in encouraging the young to look forward to its savagery. Schizoid too is the attitude toward Capaneus and his fellow commanders. Toward the end of the play they are praised as models the young Athenians should imitate— even Capaneus, who screamed his blasphemies at Zeus (and whom Dante, centuries later, put in hell for it). And what about Theseus? Does he go to war to preserve the pieties, or only to avoid being called a coward? For all his talk about democracy, is he a kind of big-city boss who gets his way? Thucydides had this kind of leader in mind when he wrote, "And so Athens, though in name a democracy, became in fact a government ruled by its foremost citizen" (II.lxv.9).

We might wonder whether the first two-thirds of the play are too talky. Theseus, though taunting the Theban herald for his garrulity, is at least as long-winded himself. In his speech on cultural evolution and the structure of society, is this young man showing off? Or is Euripides himself taking over and giving his own views, not those of his character, as he is often charged with doing? In defense of the talk we can say that it is lively and often eloquent. And the Greeks loved that kind of discourse. Theirs has been called a "performance culture." Talk, as well as action, was their per-

6. Smith, *Expressive Form in Euripides' Suppliants*, Harvard Studies in Classical Philology 71 (Cambridge, Mass.: Harvard University Press, 1966; Collard, ed., *Supplices/Euripides* (Groningen: Boumas, 1975); Burian, *Directions in Euripidean Criticism: A Collection of Essays* (Durham, N.C.: Duke University Press, 1985).

formance—on the Pnyx, in the Agora, in the law-courts with their constant suits and countersuits. They also were more polysemous in their talk than we can be today; some critics have found a continual political allegory in certain plays, even called them a kind of electioneering, with the characters seen as actual political figures of the time.

When we look at a text of Euripides, we are looking at lines that have been recopied and worked over by scholars, real or would-be, for nearly twenty-five centuries. How did a work so ancient make its way to us at all? In antiquity there would have been editions of his ninety-two plays on rolls of papyrus. Almost none survived the classical age. Some eight hundred years after they were written, a couple of rolls, containing nine plays, were transcribed into an uncial codex (a book first of papyrus, later of vellum). Somehow, probably at Constantinople, this codex endured until its rediscovery in the late twelfth century by a bibliophile who, it seems, made a copy in minuscule. In the early fourteenth century, the Byzantine scholar Triclinius came on this work and had it transcribed for his projected edition of Euripides. This manuscript he worked over: recopied, corrected, annotated, emended, sometimes made erasures on, added marginalia to. Much commented on in inks of different colors, it found a home in the Laurentian Library in Florence, where—a copy of a copy of a copy—it is the basis for the Euripides we read today. Three more copies of it survive from the late Renaissance. There were editions in 1571, 1684, 1763—and from then on too many to mention.

When I first read *Suppliant Women* in a Greek class, years and years ago, what we used was the third edition of Gilbert Murray's 1904 Oxford Classical Texts *Euripidis Fabulae*, reprinted in 1937.[7] Since then, scholarship has been industrious. When Christopher Collard published his *Supplices* in 1975 (two volumes, with extensive commentary), he noted over one hundred differences between his text and Murray's. James Diggle did further work in his O.C.T. edition (1981). In 1984, in his Teubner edition of the play,[8] Collard acknowledges his indebtedness to Diggle and others in his Praefatio, written in the elegant Latin scholars use even today. He thanks earlier editors, "Jacobo Diggle praeter omnes," for the twenty readings of

---

7. Murray, *Euripidis Fabulae* (Oxford: Clarendon Press, 1937).
8. Collard, *Supplices/Euripides* (Leipzig: Teubner, 1984).

theirs he had come to prefer to his own in the ten years since his earlier edition.

If we do a line-by-line comparison of Diggle's text and the newer Collard, we find few differences substantial enough to concern a translator. A rare exception: in line 371 the chorus are wishing that Theseus would arrive and end their grief by recovering the bloodstained bodies of their loved ones. The word I translate as "loved ones" is ἄγαλμα (*ágalma*), which means "glory, delight, honor, etc." It was often used of one's children, as we call them our "pride and joy." Diggle objects to it mostly because it is used in a different sense eleven lines later, a repetition he thinks "betrays clumsiness to a high degree." He suggests instead the word ἄμυγμα (*ámugma*), which means "a scratching, tearing."[9] With that reading, the chorus would be praying that Theseus would remove the reason for their bloody face-scratching, a sign of mourning. Collard's comment: "I cannot believe he is right" (p. 205). The Greek text I have translated is Collard's 1984 one. To the knowledge he has shown in his earlier (1975) commentary on every aspect of the text, I am gratefully indebted.

In his "Ars Poetica" (Epistle II.iii) Horace has some advice about translation. Among other things, he cautions us not to attempt translation word for word (ll. 133–34):

nec verbo verbum curabis reddere
fidus interpres . . .

Such translation is easily shown to be impossible: languages do not jibe word for word. An Italian may express boredom by saying, perhaps with an eloquent gesture, "Che barba!" The word-for-word translation is "What a beard!" which is no translation at all. Spaniards may greet each other with "¿Qué tal?" But its word-for-word translation, "How such?" means nothing.

"Literal" translation is even more impossible with poetry, in which the sense is often no more important than sound, rhythm, connotation. But a translator always *starts* with something like a word-for-word translation in mind, and then asks: How would we say that in English? Two examples.

9. Diggle, *Euripidea: Collected Essays* (Oxford: Oxford University Press, 1994), pp. 64–65.

The literal meaning of line 92 of the Greek is "What thing (is this)? I see strange comings-in of words." My translation departs from the word-for-word to give

"So what goes on here? Explain, if there's any way to!"

Line 112 of the Greek literally reads: "For terminus (there's) none, not going by way of tongue." I have Theseus say:

"Speak up. We're getting nowhere till you talk."

Neither of the lines I suggest is the one right way to render the Greek. There is no one right way; we have many ways of saying these things. But there is one wrong way: doing it word-for-word.

In translating, we ought to care not only about the meaning of words but about their level in the language. Are they learned words? Demotic words? Zuntz reminds us that Euripides often uses colloquial expressions, "popular, even vulgar" ones, when the tragedians would have "given (it) a nobler turn" (pp. 38–39n).[10] Colloquialism is especially frequent in the stichomythia (line-by-line exchanges), which, says Peter Levi, "properly read aloud, ought to sound like a quarrel between fishwives."[11] I once heard that admirable poet and translator Robert Fitzgerald declare that rhythm was the soul of poetry. Should a translator be indifferent to soul, or to the meter that expresses it?

The meter of the dialogue and of the nonchoral parts of Greek tragedy is the iambic trimeter, a line of six iambic feet; their iambic unit is the double iamb. The meter is appropriate; Aristotle considered the iambic rhythm the most conversational (μάλιστα λεκτικόν) of the meters. Gerard Manley Hopkins, reading this, added, "and the same holds for English."[12] No wonder our iambic pentameter became the vehicle for English drama during its

10. For thorough documentation, Zuntz refers us to Philip T. Stevens, *Colloquial Expressions in Euripides* (Wiesbaden: Steiner, 1976).
11. *The Oxford History of the Classical World*, ed. John Boardman, Jasper Griffin, and Oswyn Murray (Oxford: Oxford University Press, 1986), p. 170.
12. "Rhythm and the Other Structural Parts of Rhetoric—Verse," in *The Journal and Papers of Gerard Manley Hopkins*, ed. Humphry House and Graham Story (Oxford: Oxford University Press, 1959), p. 274.

great age, and for much of our later poetry. It is the meter used for dialogue and narrative in this translation.

But the choruses are in far more complex meters, often strange to modern ears. I happen to think it worth the considerable effort it takes to replicate them, using our unaccented and accented syllables for their shorter and longer ones. With one exception: coming on a run of several Greek syllables all of one kind (all short or all long), I have had recourse to syllabics for that run alone, since such runs are rare or impossible in a language like ours which likes to alternate its degrees of stress (e.g., "incomprehensibility").

Why bother? Because the words of the chorus were *choreographed*, set to music and the ballet-like dance we see depicted on many a Grecian urn. As Wesley Smith says, distinction between meters "would seem to be an indication of the staging" (p. 156). It seems worthwhile, then, to try to give at least some adumbration of what those movements were like—faster, slower; agitated, stately.

For example, the first chorus, beginning with line 42, is an appeal to Aethra for help. Its urgency is emphasized by the heaviness of the ionic meter ($\smile\smile--$), felt most clearly in the first lines of strophe and antistrophe, and varied in the lines that follow:

> At your feet now, O revered one,
> As we kneel here, who are old too . . .
> Since you also had a son born
> And it brought joy to the bride-bed . . .

But there is a change in the strophe and antistrophe of lines 71–86. As described by Collard, "When the appeal is over . . . the change to mixed iambo-trochaic for the last pair of stanzas marks freer emotion" (p. 116).

> No end to this exultancy in pain: a strange
> agonized release, still heavy; as mountain crags
> disgorge their wild torrents . . .

A different rhythm, a different mood—calling for a different music, a different kind of dance. We can't know exactly what this meant to a Greek audience, but at least the change of meter shows that something was indeed happening.

BACKGROUND

After the downfall of Oedipus, his two sons Eteocles and Polynices had quarreled over the succession. When Eteocles prevailed, Polynices fled and appealed for help to Adrastus, king of Argos, whose daughter he had married. Under the king's command, Polynices and six legendary warriors—the famous Seven against Thebes—led their forces against that city. When all seven were killed in the assault, the Thebans refused to release their bodies for the burial to which, in Greek belief, the dead were entitled. As the play opens, Adrastus and the mothers of the Seven (or their surrogates, since not all were alive and available) have come to Eleusis, near Athens, to implore Aethra, mother of Theseus, to persuade her son to use his power as ruler of Athens to secure the release of the dishonored bodies.

ANNOTATIONS

Line 31. Pausanius, in his section on "Attica," mentions that grain was first grown on a plain near Eleusis. The wandering Demeter, giving the first seed to Triptolemus, son of a family that had sheltered her, taught him the art of sowing and the use of the plow. Thanks to a dragon-drawn chariot she also provided him with, he was able to disseminate and propagandize his knowledge of agriculture and bread-making.

Line 160. Amphiaraus, thought to be an infallible interpreter of the gods, was the brother-in-law of Adrastus (see Glossary). Foreseeing the outcome, he at first refused to take part in the expedition against Thebes, but was compelled to do so by his wife, who had been bribed by Polynices. After he was driven off in the attack, Zeus' thunderbolt opened a chasm in the earth before him, swallowing him up, chariot, horses, and all.

Line 182. Because a line or lines are missing from the Greek text, the connection between the thought of lines 180–83 (on the sympathetic observation of others) and that of lines 184–87 (on the unhappy poet) is not apparent. Perhaps Euripides intended something like the two-and-a-half italicized lines in the translation, confected by the translator.

Line 253. The Greek text is corrupt here; as Collard says, "the whole verse lacks meaning or grammar." The proverb supplied, anachronistic as it is, is a possible equivalent of the lost words.

Line 256. Editors believe this line an intrusion in the text because of a copyist's dittography—the unintentional repetition of something from another line (here line 260).

Line 267. The line, missing in the Greek text, would have said something like this.

Line 282. The two lines in the Greek text that follow "sons that I lost . . . "are omitted here as "unmetrical and ungrammatical," probably interpolated by actors "to embellish the pathetic context."

Line 330. The "savage boar" was no ordinary wild boar, but the monstrous Crommyonian sow (some say boar), which the young Theseus confronted and killed, Plutarch says (*Theseus*, ix.7), "at the risk of his life."

Line 385. In his commentary Collard has μεγάλα ("of great importance"). In his 1984 edition of the play his reading is μεγάλᾳ (with the iota subscript below the final alpha), which would link the word with πελασγιᾳ (also with the iota subscript). But does that fit the Greek meter, which calls for a short syllable in that position? The translation goes well enough with either reading.

Lines 453–56. John Milton quotes in both Greek and English these four lines as the epigraph to his *Areopagitica*. His English version is

> This is true liberty, when free-born men,
> Having to advise the public, may speak free,
> Which he who can, and will, deserves high praise;
> Who neither can, nor will, may hold his peace:
> What can be juster in a state than this?

The first two lines echo the proclamation ("Who wishes to speak . . . ?") made formally in the *ecclesia*, the general assembly of Athenian citizens.

Lines 511–12. . . . . clapped . . . caped . . . captain Capaneus . . . This is a sad attempt to reproduce an effect translators generally have to ignore: sound effects that involve a pun. In the Greek, the lightning-blasted "Kapaneus" is linked with "kapnountai" ("is turned into smoke"). The alliteration on "k" is continued in two other words. See line 522 for another effort to carry over a play on words.

Line 515. The "bird-inspector" is Amphiaraus (line 160), who did make use of ornithomancy as well as other kinds of divination.

Line 593. When Thebes was founded by Cadmus, on the advice of Athena he sowed a field with the teeth of a dragon he had killed. From these grew a crop of warriors who started fighting among themselves. Five, presumably the feistiest, survived to become the ancestors of the Thebans.

Lines 669–73. Students of military history may be interested in Collard's Addenda to his remarks on these lines (pp. 443–44), in which he discusses and takes issue with Diggle's analysis of the battle formation.[13]

Line 728. The club had belonged to Periphetes, the lame son of the lame god Hephaestus, who waylaid travelers on the outskirts of Epidauros and murdered them with his bronze weapon. He was killed by Theseus, who appropriated the club. Plutarch (*Theseus*, viii.1) tells the story.

Lines 759–60. These lines, which Collard thinks interpolated, were rejected by Wilamowitz and others, the first line as incorrigibly unmetrical, the two together as duplicating and disrupting what Adrastus says in lines 752–57.

Line 778. This line is missing from the Greek text. We can guess its meaning from the response to it.

Line 820. The words are missing in the Greek. Again we can surmise the meaning they must have had.

---

13. First published in *Greek and Byzantine Studies* 14 (1973) and reprinted in *Euripidea: Collected Essays*.

Line 850. Because of corruption of the text, we cannot be certain what Theseus is saying in his first few words.

Line 911. This and the following line are thought to be an interpolation because, unlike the three preceding portraits, this one does not end with remarks about the man's civic virtue. Remarks about the extent of his love-life also seem inappropriate in a funeral encomium.

Line 916. The five lines beginning here also seem an interpolation, perhaps by actors. In a funeral encomium, one is not likely to remark that the dead man was not as smart as his brother (who himself had no reputation for intelligence). The lines are also repetitious. Collard suspects that these lines have replaced the original characterization, which should have concluded with a mention of Tydeus' attitude toward the city.

Line 937. The "noble son" was the Amphiaraus of line 160.

Lines 1004ff. The text of Evadne's monody is, says Collard, "as seriously corrupt as any passage in the extant plays." The "worst damage" is in lines 1004–8 and 1039–49, perhaps because these lines were back-to-back on a single sheet that was somehow damaged. The first passage is about happy memories of Evadne's wedding to Capaneus, but we can't be sure what precisely the "parade" or the "nymphs" or the "cavalcade" of the translation refer to. Collard calls lines 1007–8 a "*locus desperatus,*" saying that "Sense and grammar are uncertain; the meter is at fault and response lacking." ("Response" is a correspondence between the meter of strophe and antistrophe.) The "desperately corrupt" final lines, which Wilamowitz called "heillos entstellt" ("hopelessly garbled"), begin with nuptial cries and seem to hope that the marriage and its *Liebestod* will be an inspiration to other Argive wives.

Cast

AETHRA, mother of Theseus
THESEUS, ruler of Athens
ADRASTUS, king of Argos, leader of the Seven against Thebes
THEBAN HERALD
MESSENGER, an escapee from Thebes
EVADNE, widow of Capaneus, one of the Seven
IPHIS, her father
ATHENA, goddess of wisdom
CHORUS of elderly Argive women, speaking as mothers of
    the Seven
SECONDARY CHORUS of boys, sons of the Seven
NONSPEAKING
    priests of Demeter
    handmaidens
    Athenian herald
    soldiers

*(Stage painting represents the temple of Demeter and Kore at
Eleusis. Aethra is seated next to the altar, encircled by the chorus
of suppliant mothers from Argos. The secondary chorus of boys is
grouped around Adrastus, who is prostrate near the entrance to
the temple. Priests are in the background; handmaidens are
also present.)*

AETHRA
Our lady of hearth and home here in Eleusis,
Demeter, and you, her priests who tend the temples,
grant happiness to me and my son Theseus,
and to the city of Athens and lands where Pittheus,
my father, raised me in homes by fortune favored—
his Aethra—until, because of Apollo's oracle,

he contrived that I marry Pandion's son, Prince Aegeus.
   While making this invocation, I couldn't take
my eyes from these poor women, who left their Argos
to fall with suppliant fronds here at my knee,   10
having suffered the worst of sufferings: childless now,
their seven noble sons being cut down dead
before the gates of Thebes. The King of Argos,
Adrastus, had marshaled them, heart set on wresting
for his daughter's outcast husband, Polynices,
a fair share of what Oedipus possessed there.
Wishing to bury their dead, sons killed in battle,
these mothers were turned away by the Theban authorities.
Forbidden to care for their dead! Heaven's sanctions flouted!
Sharing, like these, the need to appeal to me,   20
Adrastus lies over there with tear-stained face,
bemoaning the bloodshed and the dire campaign
that routed them out of their homes to utter ruin.
He begs me now to prevail upon my son
to negotiate their release, or, resorting to arms,
to enforce it and be co-sponsor of the rituals.
He'd have this a joint endeavor for both my son
and the city of Athens. I'm here, as it happens,
on behalf of the land, to sacrifice in seedtime,
come from my home to this holy place, where first   30
the wheatfields bristled with new grain. Encircled
by chains that don't really chain, a festoon of leaves,
I wait by the hearthstone of the holy pair,
Demeter and Kore her girl, wait full of pity
for these, the gray-haired mothers without sons,
and in awe of their sacred garlands. I've sent a messenger
to summon Theseus here to cleanse the land
of a spectacle so distressing, or absolve us
from our bounden duty to these suppliants
by some act pleasing to heaven. Best to let   40
men do the maneuvering, as wise women know.

CHORUS

    Strophe

At your feet now, O revered one,
as we kneel here, who are old too,
supplicating you: secure
the release of our dead children's remains
that are left scattered in limb-slackening death
by the wicked, as obscene food for the wild beasts of the hills.

    Antistrophe

For you see us, see the heartbreak
as our tears well under eyelids,
as our nails furrow their grief   50
in our wrinkled and wan flesh. As they must.
Not allowed holy devotions for our dead
in their own homes? Hold no grave-rites? See no tumulus arise?

    ·   *Strophe*

Since you also had a son born
and it brought joy to the bride-bed
and a glad heart to your lord,
let us sympathize in sharing
what we feel now. Only share my desolation
for the lost ones that I bore!
So I beg you, have your son come to Ismenus,   60
Theban river, and entrust there to our own arms
all the bodies robust once, now with no homes in the earth.

    Antistrophe

Not as votaries we've come here to adore, but
out of dire need to invoke you
at the shrine torches bedeck.
We've a just cause, you've condign power,
being so blessed in a brave son who can help us
and can free us from despair.

You can see how we bemoan here; I entreat you,
let your son lay in my poor arms the remains of   70
such another beloved boy for a last heartsick embrace.

Strophe

Again, antiphony of wail on wail competes,
sob huddling on sob. Loud, the thud of maiden palms.
Go, souls in one key of grief,
go, souls that share others' pain,
to dance the dance Hades hails.
Over your cheek and its pallor rake your
nails until the skin's a lace of blood.
Whatever ways suit the dead become us.

Antistrophe

No end to this exultancy in pain: a strange   80
agonized release, still heavy; as mountain crags
disgorge their wild torrents, so
without surcease flow my tears.
A special grief women know
when their own children are the ones taken,
a grief unique in its anguish.
Oblivious death, end my sorrow, come soon.
(Theseus enters.)

THESEUS

Who's wailing here like this? Who's pounding her breast?
Some dirge for the dead? The very temple reverberates!
Fear has me all on edge. Has something happened   90
to my mother? I'm looking for her. It seems she left
home quite a while ago. Has something happened?
Good god!
So what goes on here? Explain, if there's any way to!
Here's poor old mother seated by the altar
and, with her, women I don't know, distraught

and showing it in different ways: old eyes
fairly a-stream with pitiable tears;
thin hair cropped short, dress hardly fit for rituals.
    Mother, what's this all about? You tell me;   100
I'm listening. Something very odd is going on.

AETHRA

    O son, these women you see here are the mothers
    whose sons have fallen before the gates of Thebes,
    leaders, all seven. Now with suppliant fronds
    we see them in a circle, eyes on me.

THESEUS

    Who lies moaning at the entrance there?

AETHRA

    Adrastus, lord of Argos, so they tell me.

THESEUS

    Those boys around him? Sons of these women, are they?

AETHRA

    Grandsons. The children of the men who died.

THESEUS

    But why come here as suppliants? Why to us?   110

AETHRA

    Reason enough, I know. But let them tell it.

THESEUS

    You there, all swathed in robes, I'm asking you.
    Uncover your head and spare us further moaning.
    Speak up. We're getting nowhere till you talk.

ADRASTUS

> Oh glorious in your victories, lord of Athens,
> I've come your suppliant, Theseus, and your city's.

THESEUS

> What is it you want? It's something, obviously.

ADRASTUS

> You heard of my ruinous military venture?

THESEUS

> Hardly hush-hush, your traipsing around Greece.

ADRASTUS

> Such men I lost! The very pride of Argos.   120

THESEUS

> That's what war's all about. You didn't know?

ADRASTUS

> Anyway, they died. I asked Thebes for the bodies.

THESEUS

> Through heralds, the agents of Hermes? You asked to bury them?

ADRASTUS

> I did indeed. But the killers turned me down.

THESEUS

> Turned down what the heavens ordain? Their reason being—?

ADRASTUS

> Winners don't deal in "reasons." They're above it.

THESEUS

> You've come to me for advice? Or else for—what?

ADRASTUS
 O Theseus, give Argos back her sons!

THESEUS
 Argos! Old big-mouth Argos! So who cares?

ADRASTUS
 We were wrong, we confess. We're done for. We came for help. 130

THESEUS
 You came on your own? Or is Argos in on this?

ADRASTUS
 No Argive but implores you: honor the dead.

THESEUS
 What possessed you to lead the seven hosts to Thebes?

ADRASTUS
 I was trying to lend a hand to my sons-in-law.

THESEUS
 What Argives did you give your daughters to?

ADRASTUS
 I didn't say they married within our people.

THESEUS
 You gave your true-born Argive girls to foreigners?

ADRASTUS
 To Tydeus, yes. And the Theban Polynices.

THESEUS
 What hankering led you to a deal like that?

ADRASTUS

Apollo is why. His riddling oracles got to me.   140

THESEUS

What did he say that influenced the weddings?

ADRASTUS

Wed them, he said, to a lion and a boar.

THESEUS

Now how make sense of an oracle like that?

ADRASTUS

One night there came to my door a couple of fugitives—

THESEUS

A couple? Let's be specific. Identify them.

ADRASTUS

Polynices, Tydeus. What a brawl they got into!

THESEUS

Aha! Like the beasts of the oracle. So you gave—

ADRASTUS

My daughters to them, of course. They fought like animals!

THESEUS

But why did they leave their country in the first place?

ADRASTUS

Because of bloodguilt Tydeus fled. He had to.   150

THESEUS

But the other, Oedipus' son. Why did he leave Thebes?

ADRASTUS
His father's curse. Afraid that he'd kill his brother.

THESEUS
Good thinking there. Smart move to get out of town.

ADRASTUS
But the ones that stayed proved false to the ones that left.

THESEUS
Don't tell me a brother made free with their possessions?

ADRASTUS
He did. So I came to see justice done. I lost.

THESEUS
You queried the prophets first? Watched offerings burn?

ADRASTUS
No, damn it! You've got me there. My worst mistake.

THESEUS
Seems the gods weren't exactly in favor of your project.

ADRASTUS
Worse. Amphiaraus said no. I overruled him.   160

THESEUS
Ignoring the will of the gods! Without a thought!

ADRASTUS
The young were raising such hell it left me reeling.

THESEUS
High spirits mean more to you than level head.

ADRASTUS
And that's the thing that ruined many a general.
     But you, O lord of Athens, most valiant soul
in the whole of Greece, I'm overcome with shame
as I fall to the ground, arm reaching for your knee,
an old man, once a king and blessed by fortune,
with now no choice but to yield to the way things are.
I beg you, restore our dead, have pity on   170
me and these mothers whose sons are slain, these mothers
to whom the snows of age bring only bereavement.
They had the courage to come here, to entrust
to foreign soil limbs they could scarcely stir,
and not to look in on the mysteries of Demeter,
but only to see that in decency were buried
those who should have buried them when the time came round.
     It only makes sense for the rich to consider the poor,
for the poor to keep a competitive eye on the rich
and learn to evaluate rightly the worth of possessions.   180
Those lucky in life should muse on the down-and-outers
or there's no understanding. You—you're on top of the world;
me, I've come crawling. Don't mock. Try to understand me.
Say a poet intends ecstatic songs of joy,
but isn't happy, at sixes and sevens within.
Distraught as he is, he won't delight his readers.
If wouldn't be right if he did. *Don't expect me to charm you.*
     So perhaps you'll ask: Why give a bye to Sparta
and lay this responsibility on the Athenians?
It's only right I explain the reason why.   190
Sparta's too harsh and has a checkered history;
our other towns are poor and puny. Yours
is the only one that can really handle this,
the one with a heart that can sympathize with others,
and a leader who cares—a true shepherd! Youthful too.
For lack of that, how many a town has toppled!

CHORUS
    I'm with him there. Indeed, he speaks for me,
    Theseus. Do look with pity on our plight.

THESEUS
    I've had lively debates with others in this regard.
    There are those, I know, who maintain that the worse occurs   200
    more often in life than the better does. Not so!
    I couldn't be more opposed to such ideas.
    I hold there's more good in this world of ours than evil.
    If it hadn't been so, we wouldn't be here at all.
    My homage goes to the god who out of chaos
    and brutishness plotted the orderly world we live in,
    first giving us thought, then a tongue that turned that thought
    into airy words that the ears could catch and fathom.
    Next, gave us fruit and grain; for its cultivation
    sent falling rain from heaven for thirsty earth   210
    and its thirsty people. Besides, gave means of warmth
    against the winter, protection from summer's heat.
    Then taught us to ply the sea with oar and sail
    in commerce, exchanging our surplus for our dearth.
    For what's mysterious, past our understanding,
    we've prophets to read the riddles: they study flames,
    pore over twisted entrails, watch the birds.
    Then aren't they finicky folk who cry "Too little!"
    given all that providence has supplied us with?
    But we, in our arrogant drive to be more than gods   220
    arrive at so heady a pitch of self-conceit
    that we tell ourselves we're wiser than heaven itself.
        You too, it appears, are one of that crew, naive
    in tying your girls to the oracles, giving them
    to outsiders in nuptials you thought were the gods' idea.
    That way, you've slubbered with mud your splendid home—
    infected it! No right-thinking man would invite
    the healthy and the diseased to intermingle.

The wise want friends in their home who are blessed by heaven.
God sees our human fates as intertwined   230
and in the deserved calamities of the criminal
brings down his associate too, though innocent.
As you led your Argives on to Thebes, the prophets
spoke. But contemptuous of both them and the gods
you stubbornly went your way—and brought down your city,
seduced by the young, who, enjoying their celebrity,
escalate wars without just cause for doing so,
no matter the casualties. One struts as general;
another's unblushing in his grab for power;
another's out just for the payoff, the public be damned.   240
None care how the people suffer by what they do.
Now look: We've three classes of citizens: first the rich,
dead weights on the state with their itching for more and more;
then the poor, who have nothing, just nothing to live on at all—
they're scary! With envy the ruling emotion in most,
they snipe with their venomous barbs at the flourishing rich,
and themselves are but dupes of the sleazy no-good politicians.
There's a third class, in between: they preserve our cities,
watchdogs of the constitution by each established.

All this being so, you expect me to join in your squabbles?   250
What sound excuse would I have to give my townsmen?
No. So be on your way. If you managed matters badly,
you made your bed—and you know how the saying goes.

CHORUS

No question he acted in error. As young men do.
It's in their nature. What's called for is forgiveness.
Just as a healer, lord, we came to you.

ADRASTUS

Far from choosing you as the judge of my misfortunes,
or, if it's clear that what I've done is wrong,
as the one who'd assign the punishment, my lord,
just as a helper I sought you. If you're against me,   260

no choice but give in to your will. What else can I do?
   Old women, so let's go home. But leave them here,
your gray-green olive branches twined with wool,
calling on heaven and earth, on the light of the sun,
on Demeter, our lady of torches, to bear us witness:
we made our prayer to the gods. To no avail.

CHORUS

   Theseus, son of Aethra, the daughter of Pittheus,
who was Pelops' own son, we too of the land of Pittheus
share in the same ancestral blood as you.
What is it you're doing? Betraying that bond? Expelling   270
old women unjustly done out of their sacred rights?
Don't do it! The very beasts have caves for refuge,
the slave finds safety at altars, city with city
clings closer in time of trouble. Nothing human
endures in unshaken prosperity forever.

HALF-CHORUS A

   Step now, unfortunate woman,
away from the ground of Persephone,
step now, go plead with him there
at his knees, and, arms reaching, implore him
to bring back the bodies of sons   280
who were slaughtered—oh, anguish to say it!—
sons that I lost in the strife
under ramparts of Cadmus—my young ones!

HALF-CHORUS B

   I entreat, by your beard, dear friend,
whom all Hellas holds highest in honor,
entreat as I kneel here and reach
for your knee with my feeble old fingers.
Pity me now for the young
who are lost to me, wayfaring beggar
wailing my pitiful song,   290
wailing my pitiful death-song.

HALF-CHORUS A

>Don't look away as they lie
>in the kingdom of Cadmus, unburied,
>feast for the scavenging beasts—limbs
>vigorous once as your own are.

HALF-CHORUS B

>Look at my eyes overflowing
>with tears as I grovel here, heartsick;
>all that I'm praying for now
>is a grave for the sons that have fallen.

THESEUS

>Now mother, why these tears? Why hide your eyes   300
>beneath your cloak? Because of the stricken sobbing
>of these women here? It touched me too, and keenly.
>Lift up your poor gray head. No shedding tears
>when you're curled so close to Demeter's holy hearth.

AETHRA
(sobs)

THESEUS

>But the troubles they have aren't yours to grieve for.

AETHRA

>Poor, poor old ladies!

THESEUS

>   They are. But you're not one of them.

AETHRA

>May I say something, son, for your good and Athens'?

THESEUS

>Of course. We often hear good sense from women.

AETHRA

    It doesn't come easy to say what I have in mind.

THESEUS

    Shame! Shame on you! Keep back what's meant to help us?   310

AETHRA

    I'd not be silent, knowing that some day
    I'd think that silence a reproach to me.
    Nor would I hush the god's truth as I see it,
    fearing fine words are out of place in women.
       But I urge you, as my son, to scrutinize
    the will of the gods in this, lest you dishonor them,
    and, blameless in the rest, be guilty here.
    Besides, it's a question of courage, this helping the victims
    of any injustice. If it weren't, I'd have nothing to say.
    But just imagine the honor you'll derive   320
    (the more since I've no misgivings in the matter)
    if you take decisive action by calling a halt
    to these lawless bravos who deprive the dead
    of the graves and grave-rites piety prescribes.
    You could curb these ravagers of the ancient ways
    all Greece reveres. He who preserves what time
    has sanctioned gives our cities a firm foundation.
       But someone is certain to say you're a coward at heart
    if you hang back when you could have crowned our Athens
    with glory. It's true you took on the savage boar,   330
    mere child's play for you—no fight for life. Now facing
    armed men with honest-to-god real spears, you'd seem
    to be just the thing they'd say you are—a coward.
       Don't do this, don't! As a son of mine, don't do this!
    You've seen how, when your country's mocked as reckless,
    with gorgon eye she'll petrify the mockers?
    She thrives on difficulties. Sluggish cities
    work under wraps, make shady deals, conceal
    their gaze beneath a bleary mask of caution.

And you'd not help the dead, their weeping women,   340
not lend a hand—son! son!—to those who need you?
Not even seeing the Thebans riding high
do I fear that you'd come to harm, god's justice with you.
The dice the Thebans cast will come up balky,
I'm sure. For god plays turnabout with all.

CHORUS

Well said there, dearest lady. Double joy
in this, for his own ear, and mine alike.

THESEUS

In mine, the words rang true that I spoke before,
mother, in his regard. I spoke my mind
about the way he blundered in his policy.   350
However, I see the point of your admonishings.
It doesn't suit my character at all
to shrink when danger threatens. I've made it clear
to all of Greece the kind of man I am:
one who comes down hard on evildoers.
What would they say of me, my opposition,
when even my mother, who trembles for my safety,
is herself the first to urge me to undertake this?
    Here's what I'll do. I'll go and reason with them
about those bodies. If that fails, it's war!   360
That's it. And I'll do it without transgressing heaven.
It's a course I'll have to justify to the city,
but they'll go along if I say so. By talking with them
I can win their support, I'm certain. I established
rule by the people as their government,
full freedom, with an equal vote for all.
I'm taking Adrastus with me before the people
as living proof of my words. Having made my point
I'll muster a chosen corps of young Athenians,
and it's "Forward, march!" Encamped, in arms, I'll send   370
an ultimatum to Creon demanding the bodies.
    But now, good grannies, release from the suppliant boughs

my mother, whom I'll take home to old Aegeus,
holding her by the hand I love. The son
who won't return a parent's care is a sorry one!
It's a beautiful duty—to observe it means rich return
from one's own children, in time, for affection shown.
(Exeunt Theseus, Aethra, Adrastus. The following chorus spans a time
interval of some length, while Theseus returns to
Athens (about fourteen miles), assembles and
addresses the populace, musters his army, and
returns to Eleusis.)

CHORUS

Strophe

Argos where the horses range, O land of my ancestors,
did you listen, did you listen to these
devout words respecting the gods, these words   380
boding well for all southern Greece and Argos?

Antistrophe

Would that he could devise an end to assuage the grief we feel
by restoring to their mothers' arms
those forms, ensanguined now, they idolized,
making a peace with Argos too by helping.

Strophe

Exertions born of piety make the cities shine
with gratitude that endures. But
whatever will the city do? Make a friendly pact
with our Argos? Help to bed our sons in earth?

Antistrophe

A mother's prayer to Athena's town: Repel the ones   390
depraving our ancient ways; you
hold justice high; injustice you trample underfoot,
and toward the helpless still reach helpful hands.
(Theseus and Adrastus enter, Theseus talking to an Athenian herald.)

THESEUS

    You know your office and you serve us well,
    myself and the state, going back and forth as herald.
    A message now for Thebes, beyond the rivers:
    To his Cadmean majesty from Theseus:
    would he kindly be so kind as to honor the dead?
    I deserve that favor as a neighboring ruler.
    He might like to have our people a not unfriendly one.   400
    If he agrees, bow, smile, come straightway home.
    If he refuse, though, then there's this to say:
    How'd he feel about having a romp with my merry crew
    all a-bristle with spears and shields? They're encamped right now
    by the Spring of the Beautiful Dances in Eleusis.
        Our city is willing—no, more than that—is chafing
    to take on a project so close to my heart—
                          Who's this, though,
    this fellow interrupting what I say?
    From his dress a Theban, far as I can tell;
    a herald too. So wait a bit. He may   410
    save you some trouble, meeting us halfway.
(Theban herald enters.)

THEBAN HERALD

    Who's monarch here? To whom am I bound to deliver
    the words of Creon, king in the lands of Cadmus
    now that Eteocles died at the seven gates,
    cut down by the hand of his brother, Polynices?

THESEUS

    You're off to a bad start, stranger. A slur, I take it,
    when you talk of "monarch" here. Our city's free.
    There's no one person rules it. The city itself
    is its own ruler, with all taking part in annual
    rotation, so that no rich man gets to hog   420
    more than his share. The poor have a say as well.

THEBAN HERALD
Aha! That gives me a leg up in the game.
Now take the city that I come from: one man,
and I mean *one man*, is in charge, not just some mob.
No rabble-rouser full of hot air can twist,
for private gain, our policy every which way,
charming, no doubt, at the moment, making friends,
though there's hell to pay as a consequence. Smear tactics
conceal the scandals and your crook goes free.
Besides, unless the speakers level with them,   430
how can your people know enough to manage?
Weighing things soberly gives a better perspective
than snap decisions. For example, your poor farmer—
just assuming he's not a lunkhead—has no time,
with all of that heavy lifting, to think politics.
It's nauseating for the abler citizens
when some no-goodnik scrabbles his way to the top
by his gift of the gab—to the top! a former nobody!

THESEUS
Some herald we've got! With a hankering to speechify.
So it seems I'm challenged to a duel of words.   440
It's your idea, a debate. Your turn to listen.
    There's nothing corrupts a city like one-man rule!
For, first of all, there are no laws in common.
He's cornered all the laws; they're his monopoly.
That means no equal justice for the citizens.
With our laws written out for all to see,
the poor are on a par with the super-rich.
When libeled, the poor are free to take legal measures
against the high and mighty; if proven right,
impoverished as they are, they win in court.   450
That's liberty. Say we hear: "Who wishes to bring
to public attention some matter affecting the state?"
One can speak right up, win applause for his stand. Or not speak.
No harm either way. Both free. Can a city be fairer?
    Now when a city is master of itself

it's happy to have a store of husky youngsters.
But how a monarch detests potential rivals!
Just out of nervousness about his sovereignty
he kills off all the likeliest and best.
How in the world, then, keep a city strong   460
when, as if topping shoots of grain in springtime,
one culls and kills the bravest of the young?
Again, why strive to save up for one's children
when it's labor lost?—a monarch confiscates it.
Why bring up daughters decently in our homes
as tempting bits for the monarch when he's horny?
For the sad providers, though, despair. I'd die
before I'd see my daughters brides of violence.
    I've just about emptied my quiver in reply.
What was it you expected to get from Athens?   470
We'd have made you pay, if you weren't a privileged herald,
for frothing off. A messenger should only
say what he's told to say, then scuttle home.
In the future, if Creon has dealings with my city,
he'd better not send a blabbermouth like you.

CHORUS

Disgusting! When heaven lets bad people prosper,
they swagger as if they'd be on top forever.

THEBAN HERALD

A further word or two, please. What you've argued,
believe in if you will. I hold the opposite.
    My orders, with all Thebes behind me, are   480
"Don't let Adrastus cross into your land,
or, if he has, then drive him out by sunset."
Never mind the mystic influence of those garlands.
And don't even think of hijacking the bodies;
none of your business, our affair with Argos.
Do what I say, and then it means smooth sailing
for your ship of state. Refuse, and—well, I tell you!

War's turbulent surf will engulf you, us, our allies.
    Think it over, and don't go flying off the handle
at my remarks—free cities allow free speech, no?   490
Don't try to make a mountain of this molehill,
and don't make hope your hope, which locked so many
cities in hopeless strife by gaudy forecasts.
For, when declaring war comes to a vote,
none reckons death is in the cards for him.
Bad luck for others? Maybe so. Not him.
Were death before his eyes while casting votes,
this warlust wouldn't devastate our Greece.
We all know, everyone, between two words,
which means the better. We know "good" from "bad,"   500
and we know how much better "peace" than "war."
Peace, first of all, is what the Muses love
and the Furies hate. Peace wants us blessed with children,
rejoices in prosperity—scrapping which,
ruffians among us take up war, so men
enslave the men that lose; so cities, cities.
    You, though, you'd help our enemies, even dead ones,
honoring with burial those their pride destroyed.
Wasn't it right that a clap of thunder caped
in smoke that captain Capaneus, charred him to cinders,   510
who had flung up scaling ladders against our gates,
swearing he'd sack the city, god willing or not?
Didn't a sinkhole seize the bird-inspector
and suck him, with his four-horse chariot, down?
Aren't the other captains strewn before the gates,
their craniums gaping from the crunch of boulders?
Now either commend the gods for blasting the wicked,
or flatter yourself you know better than Zeus himself.
Wise men should love their children first, then parents,
then their native land—should foster and not fluster it.   520
Fire-breathing generals are a hazard, like
your stumbling sailors. The wise know, in a crisis,
easy does it. And real men think ahead.

CHORUS

>Enough that Zeus doles out the castigation.
>Bluster from you, however, we don't need.

ADRASTUS

>Son of a b____!

THESEUS

>   Just button your lip, Adrastus.
>Don't butt in with your thoughts ahead of mine.
>He didn't come to you with his pronouncements.
>No, I'm his target. Rebuttal's up to me.
>   First, the first point you make. I'll answer that.   530
>I never thought of Creon as lord and master,
>or outranking me in power, so as to tell
>Athens just what to do. He's got things backward
>if he thinks we'll stand to be ordered around like that.
>I didn't start this war, didn't join the invaders.
>I'm merely convinced it's our duty to bury the dead,
>not prejudicing the city, not getting men killed,
>but only preserving a custom that all of Greece
>has cherished. What's wrong with that, I'd like to know?
>Even if you suffered indignity from Argos,   540
>the offenders are dead. You won. Your defense was exemplary.
>They lost, and looked bad in doing so. End of that.
>So let the dead have their blanketing of sod.
>Soul, body derive differently; let each
>return in death to its source: spirit to air,
>the body back to earth. It's only ours,
>this body, while we've a life to live, and then
>what brought it forth should have it back. You think
>that exposing the dead to shame is revenge on Argos?
>It's anything but! Depriving the dead of their   550
>one right, due honor in death, is an injury shared
>by all of Greece. It's why the brave are brave;
>undo that use and cowardice comes in vogue.

You came here making direful threats against me,
yet shake in your boots in fear of a body buried?
Expecting what? That they'll undermine your country,
being underground there? Or, in the lap of earth,
beget a generation of avengers?
A stupid waste of words, not worth discussing,
this terror you have of bugaboos and bogies.   560
    O thoughtless people, think! Our life's uneasy.
Always a struggle. Some may strike it rich
today, tomorrow, yesterday. Meanwhile,
gods loll and have the best of it. Our offerings
pour in from the down-at-heels, who hope to make it;
pour in from the ones on easy street, who, fearing
to lose the wind in their sails, exalt the deity.
Knowing this, don't rage at life's routine comeuppance,
or overreact in ways that hurt the city.
    So what's it to be? Those bodies of the dead,   570
restore them, and we'll see to the funeral honors.
Or the consequence is clear: I'll make you do it.
I'd never let any word get round in Greece
that when god's ancient venerable usage
came pleading to me and mine, I let it languish.

CHORUS

    Courage! Your holding high the torch of justice
    will spare you censure from the world of men.

HERALD

    Just a word or two, if you please? I'll make it short.

THESEUS

    Speak on, if you must. You don't mind talking, seems like.

HERALD

    You'll never get out of the country with those bodies.   580

THESEUS

Now listen in turn to me. If you don't mind?

HERALD

I'd listen, of course. How else? My turn, your turn.

THESEUS

I mean to remove those dead from Thebes. For burial.

HERALD

Assuming you run the gauntlet of our spearmen.

THESEUS

I've done as much in many another scuffle.

HERALD

You were just plain born, it seems, to stand up to anyone.

THESEUS

Anyone bumptious. I've no quarrel with others.

HERALD

You and that city of yours! The big buttinsky!

THESEUS

No. Much attempted, much achieved, I'd say.

HERALD

Go ahead then. Bite the dust our spearmen rose from.   590

THESEUS

Dragon's teeth! A squiggly snake begot your he-men?

HERALD

So young, so uppity! But you'll learn. The hard way.

THESEUS

    You won't get a rise out of me, for all your needling.
    I'm telling you, cool as a cucumber, leave our land,
    packing up that sack of fatuities you came with.
    Talk got us nowhere.

                All our armored men,
    let them get a move on now, every charioteer,
    every warhorse, cheekpiece chiming as they hurtle,
    foam flying from bridle and bit all the way to Thebes.
    I'm off on a march to the seven famous gates,   600
    me my own herald, with sharp sword in hand.
    Adrastus—I'm giving the orders now—stay here.
    I won't have your fortunes messing in with mine.
    With the spirit that guides my destiny, I go
    as fresh commander-in-chief in a fresh affray,
    needing just one thing, the favor of the gods
    who revere justice. This assurance with us,
    victory lies straight ahead. But mortal valor's
    of no avail without the consent of heaven.

(All exit except Adrastus and the Chorus. The choral song that follows
                 spans a time interval in which Theseus and his
                 men march the twenty-five or so rugged miles to
                 Thebes, the army is deployed, the battle begun, and
                 the Athenians, after some reverses, are triumphant.
                 A messenger then returns from Thebes to Eleusis
                 with the news.)

HALF-CHORUS A

    Strophe

Pitiful, pitiful, all! mothers, sons who lie slain!   610
How from its well in our hearts sallow terror spreads wide!

HALF-CHORUS B

    Antistrophe

What news then have you heard? What dire report?

HALF-CHORUS A

The force we sent, Athens' pride, do they prevail?

HALF-CHORUS B

In battle you mean? Or was a parley to be held?

HALF-CHORUS A

I wish words won the day. If not, the dead
in fields of blood! Beating of breasts! And city-wide
the sounds of grief! I'll be to blame! What bitter words
will shrill their guilt and rage in my ear?

HALF-CHORUS B

Antistrophe

But if there's glory in Thebes' recent triumph, some fate
still could reverse it and change all, and there's my one hope.   620

HALF-CHORUS A

You say so. Thinking then the gods are just?

HALF-CHORUS B

Who else is there could direct the course of things?

HALF-CHORUS A

If often appears the gods and mortals are at odds.

HALF-CHORUS B

You felt some stir of apprehension, no,
back there? But justice cries out for justice, blood for blood.
The gods afford tormented man relief at times.
In their hands lies the fate of all things.

HALF-CHORUS A

Strophe

Departing from waters of the Spring the goddess loves,
how could we reach Thebes, her fields and high towers?

HALF-CHORUS B

    If but some god would grant you buoyant wings   630
    to loft you to the doubly-rivered town,
    then you'd know how our friends
    had fared, know the drift of things.

HALF-CHORUS A

    Oh what destiny, oh what future
    this time awaits the valorous
    chosen lord of our land?

HALF-CHORUS B

    Antistrophe

    So once again we invoke the gods invoked before,
    trusting they'll give confidence against fear.

HALF-CHORUS A

    O Zeus, who fathered her, our Io, famed
    as ancient mother of the Argive race,   640
    we pray, help Athens now
    and keep yet a friendly heart.

HALF-CHORUS B

    Our young, the city's support and glory,
    oh, bring them back to righteous pyres,
    after such dishonor.
(Messenger from Thebes enters.)

MESSENGER

    Women, I've much to report to you, all of it good.
    I was captured in the battle which the seven
    generals, now dead, engaged in by the river.
    But I've just escaped, and I'll tell you how things went.
    Theseus won the day! He won! I'll spare you   650
    more words for now. I was slave to that Capaneus
    Zeus burned to cinders with his thunderbolt.

CHORUS

> A friend indeed! How good to see you safe
> and get the news of Theseus! Doubly welcome
> what you come to say if the army's safe as well.

MESSENGER

> As it is! And it did what Adrastus should have done,
> he and his men from Argos, which he assembled
> and paraded up from there to the city of Cadmus.

CHORUS

> So how did it happen Aegeus' son and his soldiers
> achieved this honor—a victory trophy! Tell us!   660
> You were there; we weren't. So tell!
> Let us share in the joy of it!

MESSENGER

> Bright sunlight fell on the earth, every inch of it
> distinct as the marks on a ruler. The Electra Gate
> is where I was, on a tower with a view of it all.
> From there I made out the three corps of Athenians.
> The armored infantry was deployed up toward
> the Ismenian Hill—for that's the name I heard.
> The commander-in-chief, Aegeus' famous son,
> and the men with him, of the ancient stock of Cecrops,   670
> made up the right wing, as the place of honor;
> to their left, by the spring of Ares, the other wing,
> Paralus and his soldiers. Farther off, to their right,
> the cavalry. Between them and Theseus' men
> was about an equal detachment of war chariots,
> ready for action just under the tomb of Amphion.
> The Theban army was drawn up in front of their walls,
> on view behind them the bodies the fight was for.
> It was cavalry ranged against cavalry; next to them
> the four-horse chariots lined up facing each other.   680
> First, Theseus' herald had an announcement to make:

"Your attention, soldiers. And yours too, Theban lines.
Quiet, and listen. We've come to retrieve those bodies
deserving of burial, as all Greece believes.
A belief we reverence. Bloodshed's not our aim."
To this there was no response at all from Creon,
tight-lipped where he leaned on his spear. Whereon the captains
signaled the charioteers, "Go to it, men!"
So each drove into the other's ranks, discharging
the fighting men they carried, weapons ready.   690
Iron clanged on iron as they fought on foot,
while the charioteers returned for back-up fighters.
Surveying the clutter of chariots and their tumult,
Phorbas, the cavalry general of the Athenians,
and whoever it was commanded the enemy horsemen,
sent in their forces headlong. The battle see-sawed.
Seeing this, not just being told of it—I was there!—
right there by the melee of chariots and their fighters,
With so much happening, much so awful, much so—
What can I say? What first? About the clouds   700
of dust sent up skyhigh, so dense—or bodies
tangled and dragged in the reins, jounced up and down,
or the crimson blood in rivulets from those fallen
or flung headfirst against earth from shattered chariots,
or those who in jagged wreckage met their end?
      When Creon took note that among the mounted troops
our side appeared to prevail, he seized a shield
and plunged into the thick of it to encourage his men.
That meant an end to the hopes of Theseus,
if he hadn't snatched, on the instant, his glittering arms.   710
Then the whole mid-part of the armies clashed in clamor,
intent on the business of killing and being killed,
spurring on each other with orders or roars of encouragement,
"Let 'em have it!" or "Steady your spears there against the
                    Athenians!"
That army of brawlers bred up from the dragon's teeth
was a mighty grim antagonist! Our left flank

gave way before them. On the right, though, worsted,
the enemy turned tail. It was even-steven.
That was the time our general deserved commendation.
He didn't seek glory by pushing on with the victors,   720
but hurried toward those exhausted and outfought,
with a shout so clear the very earth reechoed,
"Now, men, if you can't hold back these scaly spearmen
of the dragon's brood, we're done for, we and Athens!"
That stung them to greater courage, one and all.
He, wielding the club he won at Epidaurus,
waded into the midst of the enemy, lunging away
with blows that broke many a neck, sent helmets flying
like hulls at shucking, from the skulls he crumpled.
And how they squirmed to escape, the few that could!   730
Oh, then, how I shouted in triumph, cavorted for joy!
How I clapped my hands! As those routed rushed the gates,
within the city what wails of fear and anguish
from young and old. Crowds, panic-stricken, jammed
the temples. And though he could have entered the city,
Theseus held back. He hadn't come, he said,
to ravage the town, but just to recover the dead.
Now that's the kind of commander a city should choose!
One who has grit aplenty in facing danger,
who despises the overbearing when, doing well,   740
they'd swarm to the tiptop rung of fortune's ladder,
thus losing their chance for the happiness at hand.

CHORUS

I never thought I'd see so glad a day!
It restores my faith in heaven, shows all my troubles
a shadow of what I thought, since Justice won.

ADRASTUS

O Zeus, why is it said we wretched men
are capable of thought? We're like your puppets,
doing this or that according to your whim.
It seemed to us our Argos was unstoppable,

our men so many, so youthful, full of fight,   750
that when Eteocles proposed his settlement,
which was fair enough, we'd have none of it, and—aha!—
that was our undoing. Next, the swellhead Thebans,
like ragpickers striking it rich, began to swagger.
High and mighty they were, high and mighty they cut a swathe,
and—aha!—what a fall they took! O foolish men,
who all too often overshoot the mark,
till justice intervenes and makes you pay!
Friends talk and you won't listen; the main chance
your sole concern. Just having talks could mean   760
détente. But no, it's bloodshed every time.
      Oh, never mind. Right now I'd like to know
how you escaped. The rest I can get back to.

MESSENGER
    There was such a tumult in town because of the fighting,
    I slipped out the gates while the soldiers were slinking in.

ADRASTUS
    But those bodies the fight was for, you conveyed them away?

MESSENGER
    Those in charge of the seven companies they did.

ADRASTUS
    How's that? What about those others, the many dead?

MESSENGER
    All laid to rest in the glens of Mount Cithaeron.

ADRASTUS
    This side? Or the far side? Who did all the burying?   770

MESSENGER
    On the shady hill of Eleutherae. Theseus did it.

ADRASTUS
   And the ones that he didn't bury, where are they?

MESSENGER
   Nearby. The goal you worked for is right at hand.

ADRASTUS
   Grim work for the ones who removed the mangled bodies?

MESSENGER
   Even so, no slave laid a hand on the remains.

ADRASTUS
   Then Theseus did it all? He showed he cared?

MESSENGER
   You'd say so, if you'd been there. So very caring!

ADRASTUS
   He washed with his own hands the mangled flesh?

MESSENGER
   And arranged the place they lay. And arrayed the bodies.

ADRASTUS
   How awful to have to do that! How demeaning!   780

MESSENGER
   How is one demeaned by another's human woe?

ADRASTUS
   Oh, how I wish I could have died there with them!

MESSENGER
   Tears do no good. You'll have these women weeping.

ADRASTUS

I'll have *them* weeping? Have *them*! They taught me tears!
However, now I'm going to salute the dead
and sing death's own sad songs, his weeping ones.
Then address the souls I loved—I, left behind
to bewail my desolation. Breath of life
is the one thing lost there's no retrieving. Property,
Things, money—all replaceable. Never this.   790

(Adrastus and Messenger leave.)

CHORUS

Strophe

Now the best, now the worst, at once.
For honor comes, glory too
doubly dealt to Athens town
and the ones who led our troops.
For me to see lifeless limbs of sons I bore,
a bitter sight—but blessed too, if see I may.
Day I never dreamed could be,
to look on the greatest grief of all griefs.

Antistrophe

If the father of days, old Time,
had only let me remain   800
here unwedded all my life!
For why, oh why have sons?
And just to think I'd have feared a single life
as worst of fates that any woman could endure!
Now I know, and all too well,
to lose our sons, be bereaved, is far worse.

(Adrastus enters with soldiers bearing the bodies.)

CHORUS

Now that I see them, bodies of loved ones,
the limbs that I cherished—miserable me!

Couldn't I die now, here with my children,
join in their journey down to the dead?   810

ADRASTUS

Strophe

Let your lamentations here,
wretched mothers, echo mine
to mourn the dead, soon to lie beneath the earth.
Now let resound the deep grief.

CHORUS

Sons—bitter word in such an hour
when falling so from mothers' lips.
In death's darkness I invoke you.

ADRASTUS

Oh wail, oh wail—

CHORUS

for the woes that weigh on me!

ADRASTUS

Ay! Ay!—

CHORUS

for the anguish mothers feel!

ADRASTUS

Now we've suffered such—

CHORUS

accursed pain, nothing worse!   820

ADRASTUS

Argos, my home town, you also witness the doom I endure here?

CHORUS

> They see as well my wretched self
> left without a manchild.

ADRASTUS

> *Antistrophe*

> Now bring in the luckless men's
> blood-bespattered bodies, so
> unworthily slain, by foes unworthy—these
> between them fought the fight out.
> *(Bearers set the bodies down in the orchestra.)*

CHORUS

> Give them to me so I may fling
> my arms about them, tight oh tight,
> within my embrace enfold them.   830

ADRASTUS

> You have, you have—

CHORUS

> much too much the weight of pain!

ADRASTUS

(moans)

CHORUS

> For us mothers no lament?

ADRASTUS

> Oh, you hear it now.

CHORUS

> And so you mourn both our woes.

ADRASTUS
> Would that the close-ranked Thebans had buried me deep in the
>> dust there!

CHORUS
> And would that I had never laid
> flesh of mine in bride-bed!
>> *Epode*

ADRASTUS
> Behold it, the sea of evil, you mothers who
> possessed children once.

CHORUS
> Our nails have dug furrows down our cheeks, we've poured
>> the dust
> upon our poor gray heads in grief.   840

ADRASTUS *(moans)*
> May the deep earth close over me,
> may the whirlwind strew my torn limbs,
> may fire of god's own thunderbolt fall upon my head.

CHORUS
> The bitter bride-fests you knew,
> the bitter words Phoebus spoke.
> She's come now, come to us from Oedipus'
> household, the same wailful Fury, tear-drenched.
(Theseus re-enters.)

THESEUS
> I was about to ask, when you were mourning
> the soldiers—a dismal task—but didn't want
> to interrupt. Now, however, I'd ask Adrastus: 850
> How in the world did these men get to be
> outstanding exemplars of courage? As one who knows,

tell the young people here. You understand it;
they only know that words can't begin to describe
the derring-do these had hoped to take the city with.
Only spare us, please, the details. It gets to be ludicrous,
naming names, telling who fought whom as the battle heated,
or exactly where every spear-thrust left its mark.
That kind of report's not worth a hill of beans.
To think that anyone actually in battle,   860
with the spearpoints right in his face or whizzing by him
could be fussy about detail, pinpointing heroes!
I'd not have the nerve to ask, or trust for a minute
anyone with gall enough to attempt an answer.
It's all you can do to try to save your skin
when you're hand to hand with the hotheads out to kill you.

ADRASTUS

Well, hear me then. I welcome your request—
which is my wish too—that I speak some honest words,
honest and true, in tribute to my friends.

    You see this one the violent lightning riddled?   870
Capaneus, that's the one. A wealthy man,
yet far from reveling in his wealth, his thoughts
as little presumptuous as any poor man's.
He'd have nothing to do with your elegant gourmet
who disdained plain fare. He'd say, in temperance
there's virtue, but in stuffing your stomach, none.
Friends found him a true friend, those near and far,
although—so rare his like—close friends were few.
He never lied, was affable with all,
kept every promise he ever made, to those   880
in his own home, and to those only fellow citizens.

    Next, Eteocles, with his different kind of virtue.
Though rich in honors in the land of Argos,
that young man was in need of the means to live.
True, many a time friends offered help, in gold,
but he'd turn them down as if possessions were

the kind of shackle only slaves should wear.
Wrongdoers he held in aversion; never though
the city they had wronged, as being innocent
itself, however defiled by a crooked leader.   890
    The third man here, Hippomedon, was like this:
from boyhood he was sturdy and tough, by-passing
art, music, and such. They were soft, he thought—effete.
He preferred the outdoor life, hard exercise
he chose as the way to manliness; liked hunting,
was happy on horseback or plying the bow; believed
that's how to develop the toughness a city needs.
    On now to the son of Atalanta the huntress,
the boy Parthenopaeus—remarkably handsome!
By birth an Arcadian, he came to our town by the river   900
and there he was raised, in Argos. When grown up,
he behaved as immigrants ought to—but often don't, though.
He was never intrusive, never a thorn in our side;
he didn't mouth off disputatiously—foreigners do,
but so do some citizens also—both are a pain!
He served in the army, defending our city, as if
native-born. He rejoiced when the city did well. When it seemed
faring badly, he took it to heart, was seen to despond.
[Men aplenty were rumored his lovers, and women as well;
he was careful, in all his relations, to never offend.]   910
    For Tydeus, next, I've great praise in few words.
He wasn't a man for the words; no, weapons of war
were the source of his fame. He was death on your careless
               campaigners!
[But he wasn't as smart as his brother Meleager,
although, for his aptness in battle, equally famous.]
His music was making metal ring on metal;
a spirit richly aspiring, with a mind
attuned, if not to words, to vigorous action.
    From what I've told you, Theseus, no wonder
these had the courage to die beneath the towers.   920
Being rightly raised is what nurtures our integrity:

any man trained to do the right thing sickens
with shame if he stoops to shabby dealing. Manliness
can be taught, as surely as we teach a child
to talk, to listen, to absorb what's new to him.
What is early learned, one tends to keep in mind
right to old age. Take care! Teach children well!

CHORUS

Alas, my son, you I raised
for a wretched life. I endured the pain
of pregnancy, pain of childbirth too.   930
Now, though, dark Hades has you,
the offspring of grievous days,
and I without a child to care for me in age,
who once had my own son.

THESEUS

And certainly the noble son of Oecles
was honored by the gods, who snatched him down,
chariot and all, into the depths of earth.
And also the son of Oedipus, Polynices,
in all honesty deserves a tribute here.
He was a guest of mine before leaving Thebes   940
as a fugitive, on his own, and bound for Argos.
    Do you know, though, what my plans are for these men?

ADRASTUS

I only know that whatever you do, I'm with you.

THESEUS

Capaneus first, who was struck by Zeus' own fire—

ADRASTUS

Heaven had its eye on him. He's separate? Special?

THESEUS

Absolutely. For the rest of them, one pyre.

ADRASTUS
    And the separate memorial? You'd locate it where?

THESEUS
    We'll build the tomb right here. In the temple precincts.

ADRASTUS
    I assume the construction is something slaves can see to?

THESEUS
    Yes. As we'll see to these. Now, remove the bodies.   950

ADRASTUS
    Come closer, O mourning mothers, to your sons.

THESEUS
    No. That's not a good idea at all, Adrastus.

ADRASTUS
    It's not? Not right for mothers to touch their sons?

THESEUS
    Not the way they look right now. They'd die to see them.

ADRASTUS
    A bitter sight—blood, mutilated bodies.

THESEUS
    So why inflict more torture on these women?

ADRASTUS
    You're right.
                Women, wait quietly. Good sense
    in what Theseus says. We'll place them on the pyre;
    the ashes are yours to cherish.
    (The bodies are carried out.)

Doomed race of men!   960
Why clutch your spears and spill each other's blood?
Enough of that! Give up your endless wrangling!
Keep your towns peaceful in a peaceful world.
What a little thing life is! So we should live it
as easily and as trouble-free as we can.

(Theseus, Adrastus, and the secondary chorus of sons of the Seven exit.
The choral song that follows allows for another
time interval: long enough for the process of
cremation and the preparation of the
sepulchral urns.)

CHORUS

Strophe

Nevermore to be blessed with sons!
Nevermore to enjoy with those
Argive women the pride of motherhood.
No more will Artemis come,
goddess of childbirth, to those left.   970
My life's no more a life;
like a drifting cloud I am tossed
this way, that, as by winds of winter.

Antistrophe

Seven mothers; and seven sons—
how distinguished all Argos knows—
we gave birth to, we mothers bound for grief.
No son remains to us now.
I grow old in misery here,
no more reckoned among
those alive or the dreary dead,   980
as I hover betwixt, between them.

Epode

What is there left to me? Nothing but tears.
Mournful reminders at home of

sons lost to us: the pitiful
locks of hair with their garlands gone,
cups offered in rites for the dead,
and death's song, a desolate dirge
as gold-maned Apollo plays deaf.
And half-awake, grieving at dawn,
I press tight to my breast the rumpled robe   990
night-long tears have left sodden.

But there! There I see the darkening grot
of Capaneus' tomb a holiness haunts,
and outside the walls, for the other dead,
ceremonials Theseus granted.
*(Evadne, in her wedding dress, enters on what represents the cliff behind
the painted temple of the skene.)*

CHORUS

And look! There's Evadne, illustrious wife
of the leader the lightning destroyed,
Evadne, the daughter of Iphis.
But why is she standing so still on that rock
that looms over these buildings, high in the air?   1000
She followed the path to its summit?

EVADNE

What sunlight! What moonlight!
What rare glory in their parade
across heaven that wondrous time!
Lightfoot nymphs and the torchlight too!
Cavalcades in the dark night!
Ah, that time of my wedding feast,
when the city of Argos
with an exuberance of song
sent skyhigh our happiness: mine   1010
and his, my bronze-clad Capaneus.

In such rapture as Bacchants feel
I've come rushing headlong from home
toward torchlight and tomb I'm
to share soon with my husband,
in death ridding myself of life's burden,
day after day of struggle and stress.
There's no death—no!—ever so sweet
as one shared with those we love,
at the pleasure of heaven.   1020

CHORUS

No doubt you can see the pyre there, just below you.
We could call it Zeus' own treasury, now that it holds
your husband, done to death by fire from heaven.

EVADNE

From this rock where I've come
I see now how it ends. My fate
and my feet were in tune. From here
impends glory: to hurtle down
dizzily from this sheer crag,
nestle deep in the glowing pyre,
blend this flesh that he treasured   1030
with his, in a halo of flame,
lying body to body, we two,
nuptial in Persephone's bower.
My lover I'll never desert
for life here, him bedded in earth.
Light the torch! Start the hymn!
Now let other devout souls
of those honorably wed back in Argos
show, through their children, such a love
as we two, affectionate pair: 1040
his ash mingling with mine, that knew
every tremor of true love.

CHORUS

> And look! He's come, the very one, your father,
> the old man Iphis. How your shocking words,
> so unforeseen, will agonize him now.

(Iphis enters.)

IPHIS

> Unhappy women! I've come, unhappy too
> and old, weighed down with double grief and worry
> for two close to me, Eteoclus my son
> the Thebans killed—his body I'll take home
> aboard ship. And where's my daughter, the dear wife   1050
> of Capaneus? She darted away from home,
> in love with death since her husband died. Before,
> she'd been carefully watched in the house, until the recent
> troubles distracted me. Surveillance failed;
> she eluded us. This is far the likeliest place
> where she might be. So you've seen her, maybe? Tell me!

EVADNE

> But why ask them? I'm here myself on this rock,
> like some mournful bird, a-hover above the pyre
> of my Capaneus—just barely poised, on tiptoe.

IPHIS

> What notion took you? What errand's this? What reason   1060
> whisked you from home, dear child? What brought you here?

EVADNE

> You'd only be angry if you knew my reason.
> I'd rather you didn't hear about it, father.

IPHIS

> How's that? It's wrong for a father to know your mind?

EVADNE

> You're not the one who could judge. Or sympathize.

IPHIS

But why such festive regalia? Some ceremony?

EVADNE

Why the bridal dress? For a great occasion, father.

IPHIS

It doesn't look right at all for mourning a husband.

EVADNE

I'm dressed this way for a very special reason.

IPHIS

But to wear by a tomb? By a pyre? You think it suitable?   1070

EVADNE

It's suitable. For my glorious victory, yes.

IPHIS

Your glorious victory? Over what? Or whom?

EVADNE

Over all of them. All women under the sun.

IPHIS

For some woman's work—embroidery? Good counsel?

EVADNE

For doing what my honor asks of me. Dying with him.

IPHIS

What? What! This is really sick, your riddling way!

EVADNE

What I rush to is—look!—below. The pyre of Capaneus.

IPHIS

O daughter, to say things like this when people are listening?

EVADNE

I want them to. I want every wife in Argos to.

IPHIS

But I won't go along with this! I just won't stand for it!   1080

EVADNE

Doesn't matter. I'm out of reach. No way to stop me.
Look, I'm leaning . . . I'm letting me fall. Not what you want,
but what I want. And the man I'll share the flame with.
(She leaps into the pyre.)

CHORUS

Ooooh!
O girl, what you've done!
What a horrible thing!

IPHIS

Miserable me! This is killing me, women of Argos!

CHORUS *(wailing)*

Awful for you to endure! So desperate an act!
                                        Can you look on this?

IPHIS

There's not a man more damned on all this earth!

CHORUS

Poor, poor man!   1090
Now you share the fate
                        Oedipus brought on all.
You inherit a part,
                        you and Argos alike.

IPHIS

Why aren't poor mortals ever allowed this,
to run life's course again, its youth and age?
As in our home, if something goes awry
we have a second chance, can rectify it.
But not so in our lives. Now just suppose
we could relive it all—twice young, twice old—
if we made some hideous blunder, we could fix it.
When I saw others having children, oh   1100
I was wild to have them also! Dying to!
But if I'd had the experience of fatherhood,
knew what it was, as father, to lose children,
I'd never have found myself so desolated.
I who have had a son, and a fine one too—
the very best!—and had him taken from me!
   Well, done is done. What next, for one so crushed
by fate? Just go back home? To see the emptiness
of all those rooms once so alive with family?
Or should I go to Capaneus' old house,   1110
the sweetest place of all, with my daughter there?
But she's not there any more! The little girl
who'd always kiss me, draw my head to hers
and hug me tight. Nothing old fathers love
as dearly as a daughter. Manly spirits
are grander, but not so good at hugs and kisses.
Take me back—won't you?—quickly to my home,
there shut me up in darkness, let me starve
this ancient body till it wastes away.
Why wait to fondle my children's bones? What use?   1120
   Old age, so difficult to grapple with!
I hate it. And hate those who'd live forever.
Their "Mustn't eat this!" and "Do drink that!" their magic
supplements to divert life's onward current!
What they ought to do, when they're no use on earth,
is die, for god's sake! and stop bugging the young!
(Iphis leaves. The chorus of sons of the Seven return, some carrying the
sepulchral urns.)

CHORUS (*wailing*)
> Now they bring the bones of our sons who are dead.
> Maids who help us here, take my arm, I pray,
> for I'm old and weak. I've no strength at all
> with this weight of grief for the dead ones.   1130
> I've lived too long, and I'm worn away
> as by falling tears, by my grief on grief.
> And what greater pain can we ever find
> for a soul to endure
> than to look on one's own dead dear ones?

CHORUS OF BOYS

Strophe

> I bring, I bring
> my father's ashes, mournful mother, from the pyre,
> a weight no weight, but heavy now with mortal woe.
> Yesterday my all in all, but now dust.

CHORUS (*wailing*)
> Child, a burden of tears for your   1140
> mother mourning those who died,
> a dismal trickle of dust for noble forms we once
> gloried in—your idols then, Mycenae.

CHORUS OF BOYS

Antistrophe

> No son! No son
> for you! No father left for me—a father lost!
> To live as orphans must—in a forsaken house;
> never again, loving arms to guide me.

CHORUS (*wailing*)
> What's it come to, a mother's care?
> Painful joy of giving birth,

the nursing, coddling, the sleepless nights by cradleside,   1150
nuzzling our warm cheek against our infant's?

CHORUS OF BOYS

> *Strophe*

Gone, all are gone! With us no more! Father gone!
Gone, all are gone!

CHORUS

> Souls adrift in thin air,
> their bodies burnt away to ash;
> themselves flown far away as Hades.

CHORUS OF BOYS

> You hear now, father dear, your son's lament?
> There comes a day we'll take up arms, yes! and we'll avenge—

CHORUS

> Fully your death! Come that day, my children!

CHORUS OF BOYS

> *Antistrophe*

If god is willing may it come, vengeance for
our fathers.   1160

CHORUS

> It smoulders on, this evil?
> Unfriendly fate! Enough of grief!
> On all sides anguish, much too much now.

CHORUS OF BOYS

> But one day Theban streams will mirror there
> a bronze-cuirassed tall general, Argos' own, who's come—

CHORUS
Ah! to avenge him, the father killed there!

CHORUS OF BOYS
Strophe
O father, your form hovers before my longing eyes—

CHORUS
As leaning for a father's kiss, warmly, cheek to cheek.

CHORUS OF BOYS
Your words, their encouragement, their cheer,
dwindle in empty air, are heard no more.   1170

CHORUS
He left us grief, mother's grief for me,
for you, son's heartache of loss forever.

CHORUS OF BOYS

Antistrophe

A burden so crushing for me I could die of it!

CHORUS
Give me! I'll press these ashes against my anguished heart.

CHORUS OF BOYS
These ashes! Most hateful words of all!
Just hearing, I'm all tears. They pierce the heart.

CHORUS
Gone from me, O son! Never to behold
my fondest hope, pride and joy of my life.
(Theseus and Adrastus enter.)

THESEUS

    Adrastus and you ladies, natives of Argos,

    you see these boys who carry in their hands   1180

    the remains of their noble fathers, which I've retrieved,

    and which my city and I entrust to them.

    Knowing now, as you do, what I've managed in your behalf,

    it's only right that you keep this day in memory,

    and suggest to your children that they do the same.

    They should always think well of our city, father to son

    passing on the remembrance of kindnesses we've done you.

    Zeus himself is aware, and all the gods in heaven,

    of the honor we paid you in doing these many favors.

ADRASTUS

    Indeed we are conscious, Theseus, of the benevolence   1190

    you've shown the land of Argos in its need.

    The memory's ineffaceable. Nobly treated,

    we're under obligation to make return.

THESEUS

    And now is there anything further I can do?

ADRASTUS

    Fare well. For you deserve to. You and your city.

THESEUS

    We shall, I trust. With the hope you do the same.

    (As they are about to leave, Athena enters on the platform which is the

                roof of the skene, recognizable by her aegis, spear,

                and owl-crowned helmet.)

ATHENA

    Attention, Theseus. Hear Athena's words,

    and what you must do to put them into effect.

    You are not to surrender these bones so casually

to the boys so they can take them back to Argos.   1200
But in fair return for your efforts and those of the city,
seal matters with a oath. Adrastus here,
as ruler, has full authority to swear
a binding oath in the name of the Argive nation.
Its provisions: the land of Argos will never—never!—
involve itself in armed conflict with our city;
and if another attacks us, will intervene
against them. If Argos breaks that oath and attacks,
be it cursed: may their city be wiped from the face of the earth.
As for the bowl you'll sacrifice with, listen: 1210
You've a tripod in your house, bronze-footed, which
Heracles, having devastated Troy
and about to dash off on another of those feats of his,
told you to store at Delphi's holy hearth.
So take three sheep, cut their throats right over the bowl
of this tripod, have the words of the oath inscribed there,
then leave it in custody of the Delphic god
to vouch for the terms of that oath to all of Greece.
The keen-edged knife that gashed the sheep and set
the blood a-flowing, bury in earth beside   1220
the seven pyres on which the bodies burned.
Then, if they march against us and that's exposed,
like an apparition it warns them: *no returning.*
That done, you can let the bodies leave your land.
Consecrate a spot where the dead were purged in fire
right there where the road to the Isthmus branches off.

   These words are meant for you. To the boys from Argos
I'd say: When you grow up you'll ravage Thebes
in righteous vengeance for your fathers' death.
You, Aegialeus, will fill your father's shoes,   1230
though young, as leader, jointly with Tydeus' son
from Aetolia, called Diomede by his father.
Just when your first beard darkens, time to march
your Argive army, formidable in bronze,
against the towers and seven gates of Thebes.

Bitter for them your coming! Like lion cubs
grown to full strength, you'll prove to be that city's
devastators—no maybe about it!—the famous "Descendants,"
as all of Greece will call you: a theme for epic,
so mighty your campaigning, with god's help.   1240

THESEUS
Athena, queen, I'll do as you direct me.
You steady me, keep me from going awry.
This man I'll bind with an oath. I only ask now:
Keep me on course. Look favorably on our city.
And then we'll manage safely for all time.

CHORUS
So, Adrastus, let's leave, having made our vow
to this man and his town. Those who've done so much
deserve our respect and compliance.

Helen

Translated by
Rachel Hadas

My decision to translate Euripides' *Helen* began with what seemed like a choice. Not that the range of possibilities was vast; even so, as often happens, more than one path presented itself. More than two, as a matter of fact; *three* roads diverged when David Slavitt, the series editor for the University of Pennsylvania Press complete presentation of newly translated Greek drama, told me that there were three plays of Euripides still unaccounted for. Which would I prefer to translate: *Hecuba, Iphigenia Among the Taurians,* or *Helen*?

Having taken a look at all three of the plays and pondered their respective heroines, I wrote, as a kind of study aid or decision-making device, the following poem:

Three Heroines

Features worn harsh and flat,
whole body a clenched fist,
she offered her own breast
to the marauders: *Kill me, spare my son*
(or daughter—there were many, then were none).
Doomed bargain—who would savor such stale flesh?
The triumph in surviving everyone
was bitter, and her eyes as dry as salt,
her wrung-out belly hard as adamant.
One version calls her bitch, the barking one.

Given the choice, which one do I become?

The sister and the daughter,
the virgin sacrifice,
duped and lured from her place

and dragged bound to the altar,
then, in one version, snatched away from danger
into a wilderness,
ambiguous haven from the land of lies,
into reunion with a brother,
rescue, revenge—but for the deadly snare
there had to be a late-exacted price.

Given the choice, which one do I become?

My bonny lies over the ocean . . .
Lightly she up and left.
The harbor boiled with ships
but she was far away,
shrouded in mist, a ghost,
at once condemned, unrecognized, and lost
(waiting, according to one version, in
the patient amber of Egyptian sun)
and found. What if she was no longer young?
They had a place to sail to; they went home.

Given the choice, which one do I become?

Really, it was no contest. Given the eponymous heroines of these three dramas drawn from the wealth of material of the postwar portion of the Epic Cycle, what translator, especially if she happened to be a middle-aged woman, wouldn't choose to immerse herself in a play about the radiant if ambiguous figure of the survivor—and more especially in a play built on the version of the tale that exempts this heroine from the opprobrium of having caused the Trojan War?

When I came to read and reread *Helen* with close attention, the unique charm of the play turned out to transcend plot. Nevertheless, the story this play tells is one that bears, if it doesn't actually demand, a good deal of retelling. (Indeed, given the amount of plot recapitulation Euripides fits into the play, it's amazing that *Helen* avoids tedium. The reason is that many people in the play are at least as bewildered as the audience or reader, and these characters' successive enlightenments become part of the action.) Let me quote the helpful prose passage with which the poet H.D. prefaces her long poem *Helen in Egypt*. For no less than H.D.'s poem about Helen, Euripides' play about her is in need of an explanatory proem. H.D. writes:

We all know the story of Helen of Troy, but few of us have followed her to Egypt. How did she get there? Stesichorus of Sicily in his *Pallinode* [sic] was the first to tell us. Some centuries later, Euripides repeats the story. Stesichorus was said to have been struck blind because of his invective against Helen, but later was restored to sight, when he reinstated her in his *Pallinode*. Euripides, notably in *The Trojan Women*, reviles her, but he also is "restored to sight." The later, little understood *Helen in Egypt* [Euripides' play is usually known as simply *Helen*], is again a *Pallinode*, a defense, explanation or apology. According to the *Pallinode*, Helen was never in Troy. She had been transposed or translated from Greece into Egypt. Helen of Troy was a phantom, substituted for the real Helen, by jealous deities. The Greeks and the Trojans alike fought for an illusion.[1]

Euripides' play and H.D.'s poem both go well beyond Stesichorus' claim that Helen never went to Troy. But the Helen-absolving version that H.D. turns into a mystical palimpsest, complete with Amon-temple, traumatic and half-repressed memories of the war and of an affair with Achilles, and a benignly Freudian figure of Theseus, is in the hands of Euripides not at all hermetic but something clear, sparkling with wit, and frequently cheerful.

Indeed, it is tempting, and not totally wrong, to call this *Helen* a romantic comedy. There are certainly elements of comedy and farce here, in addition to the thick texture of family relationships (interwoven with heroic genealogies and war stories) so crucial to the epic cycle. And yet this play is frequently sad; as was said in antiquity of the *Odyssey*, *Helen* is splendid like the setting sun, not—as is the case with the *Iliad*—like the rising sun. Or, to cite a more recent critic's comment on a very different literary work, I am reminded of Edmund Wilson's evocation of the tone of Dickens's final, unfinished novel, *The Mystery of Edwin Drood*. Wilson writes: "There is

1. H. D. (Hilda Doolittle), *Helen in Egypt* (New York: New Directions, 1961), p. 1.

plenty of brightness in *Edwin Drood* . . . but this brightness has a quality new and queer. . . . We have got back to the fairy tale again. Yet this fairy tale contains no Pickwick."[2]

Like the *Odyssey* and, even more, like the late Shakespearean romances, *Helen* has in some ways "got back to the fairy tale again," with its sunlit clarifications, reunions, and happy ending. But its brightness is porous; plenty of suffering makes its way through. The enormous and tragic waste of the war, the pain of exile, isolation, and blame—the beauty of *Helen* shines through these elements without ever avoiding or denying them. On the one hand, the happily-ever-after fairy tale feeling prevails, with the help, if not of Pickwick, then of a pair of gods out of the machine. On the other hand, happiness in this play has been paid for dearly.

Since the pain attendant on the Trojan War is obvious, let me try to give some sense of how and when this play is still sprightly. First, the whole idea of an alternative scenario brings with it the intoxication of an awakening from the nightmare of history. But along with vindication comes confusion, and Euripides delights in showing us one jaw after another dropping as various characters take in that this is the real Helen, that the true story went like *this*. Each person knows, or thinks he or she knows, what has been experienced and also what has been told; and almost everyone in the course of the play must radically revise this authorized version. Since Teucer leaves before the revelation comes, his final words show that he's grasped only part of the truth—not who Helen really is, but what sort of person she is: "You resemble Helen, but / how different from hers is your good heart!" And puzzling over the problem of apparent twin Helens, Menelaus ponders (lines 485–500):

> I brought my wife here, taking her from Troy,
> stowed her for safety in a cave nearby.
> But there's another one, with the same name,
> living in this house at the same time,
> and Zeus' daughter was the porter's claim.
> Can it be Zeus is a common name

2. Wilson, "Dickens: The Two Scrooges," in *The Wound and the Bow* (New York: Oxford University Press, 1965), p. 83.

in Egypt? No, there's one Zeus—in the sky.
And where else in the world could Sparta be
except along Eurotas' reedy stream?
Could two men bear Tyndareus' name?
Can any place exist synonymous
with Sparta or with Troy? I'm at a loss.
Yet is it so astounding, after all?
The world is big; therefore, identical
names for women, cities, men should be
common.

Such delicious moments are absent from Stesichorus and H.D., who are after all not dramatists. But how could any one teller capture all the joy, despair, and absurdity of this story? One poet who does notably convey the beauty and bewilderment, the paradoxical linking of pleasure and horror inherent in the tale, is the Greek George Seferis. Seferis in *his* "Helen" takes Teucer to Cyprus, where (as we are told in Euripides' play) he is destined to found a city. Teucer is speaking:

Lyric nightingale
on a night like this, by the shore of Proteus,
the Spartan slave girls heard you and began their lament,
and among them—who would have believed it—Helen!
She whom we hunted so many years by the banks of the
        Scamander.
She was there, at the desert's lip; I touched her; she spoke to me:
"It isn't true, it isn't true," she cried.
"I didn't board the blue-bowed ship.
I never went to valiant Troy."

Breasts girded high, the sun in her hair, and that stature
shadows and smiles everywhere,
on shoulders, thighs, and knees;
the skin alive, and her eyes
with the large eyelids,
she was there, on the banks of a Delta
                                And at Troy?

142   *Helen*

At Troy, nothing: just a phantom image.
The gods wanted it so.
And Paris, Paris lay with a shadow as though it were a solid being;
and for ten whole years we slaughtered ourselves for Helen.[3]

The checkered nature of the situation is reflected in the checkered imagery. Similar contradictions of feeling make themselves felt in the suggestive contrarieties of Shakespearean lines like the following, both from plays set by the ocean and both spoken by lovers:

Though the seas threaten, they are merciful. (*The Tempest*,
     V.i.178)

and

O my soul's joy!
If after every tempest come such calms,
May the winds blow till they have wakened death;
And let the labouring bark climb hills of seas
Olympus-high, and duck again as low
As hell's from heaven. (*Othello*, II.i.182–87)

Something like such swelling danger coupled with swelling joy marks the reunion of Helen and Menelaus in this play. But to the operatic duet of his reunited married lovers Euripides adds both a spice of comical incomprehension (Helen flees from Menelaus at first; when she does recognize him, he initially rejects her embraces) and then the suspense of a chase scene—will they escape the powerful and jealous king who wants to marry Helen himself?

One more reason for the play's beautifully high spirits springs from the way Helen's beleaguered though steadfast sense of identity colors her exchanges with the Chorus. To these women, her fellow Greeks and exiles, she can let down her hair, weep over the loss of her mother, openly express her moments of weakness, despair, and terror. Thus the choral songs, far from seeming stilted or static, provide intimate interludes, as natural as

3. Seferis, "Helen," in *Collected Poems*, rev. ed., trans. Edmund Keeley and Philip Sherrard (Princeton, NJ: Princeton University Press, 1995), p. 178.

weeping, and furnish something like the kind of relief we feel at Hamlet's soliloquies. But Helen lacks Hamlet's bitter introspectiveness; like everyone else in this play, she is more concerned with actual events than with their inner meaning. Only a couple of understated choral passages (lines 1151–61, 1713–20), one at the end of the play, to be sure, address the larger—and largely inscrutable—implications of these strange events:

> Divine or not divine
> or something in between:
> what mortal man
> after long scrutiny
> of the mind of god
> could undertake to see
> and then come back
> and somehow make it plain,
> all he had understood—
> with what impossible luck
> leaping the mortal gap?

And at the close:

> What is divine
> is multiform.
> What we await
> may remain incomplete.
> What seemed implausible
> God may make possible.
> And so it was
> in this case.

This element of sheer inscrutability adds a further dimension to the laughter and tears of *Helen*. Even in the *Iliad* she is a figure of almost Proustian mystery: she attracts everyone, but it is hard to be sure of her motivation, her thoughts and feelings. What is opaque in Homer is here more dramatically contradictory, for both Helen and Menelaus inhabit a world of disguise, a narrow ledge of life where the only choice is to wait or escape. Helen lives in a palace yet is homeless; she prefers to crouch, a suppliant, at the altar in the yard. Her beauty, which makes her Egyptian host want to marry her (and I'm reminded of Miranda's magnetism in *The Tempest*), makes the war veteran Teucer detest her and even threaten to shoot her if only he had his bow. Menelaus, equally marginal, is at once war hero and wandering beggar, boasting in one breath and begging in the next. He's a figure of mild fun; the humor inherent in the situation escapes Seferis and H.D. but most certainly not Euripides. But even if we laugh at Menelaus, we can be moved by his reunion with Helen.

Fairly early in the action of *Helen*, a messenger describes how the Helen-shaped cloud has been called back into the sky. Yet until the play's final moment, when we are told how Helen and Menelaus vanish over the waves under the protection of the Dioscuri, the effects of this cloud linger. The suffering and confusion that are the legacy of war cannot dissolve into air like phantoms; they are all too real. The question of blame remains, even if its focus shifts. Private happiness prevails; public suffering leaves scars. The play is romantic, comic, and tragic. It could have been either a farcical froth or a diatribe against the capricious and arbitrary Olympian gods, but it stays in the memory as something richer and stranger, funnier and more beautiful than either.

A word on the translation. I have used loosely rhymed pentameter couplets to render the dialogue. Choral portions are unrhymed or rhyme irregularly, and use shorter lines. In translating the choruses, I've tried, probably with incomplete success, to avoid the Swinburne-flavored elaborations of diction which, following Gilbert Murray, were once so prevalent in translations into English of Greek lyric, and which are still alive and well in many Loeb translations. T. S. Eliot long ago observed: "As a poet, Mr. Murray is merely a very insignificant follower of the pre-Raphaelite movement. As a Hellenist, he is very much of the present day," and complains elsewhere in the same essay:

> that he should stretch the Greek brevity to fit the loose frame of William Morris, and blur the Greek lyric to the fluid haze of Swinburne; these are not faults of infinitesimal insignificance.[4]

4. Eliot, "Euripides and Professor Murray," in *The Sacred Wood* (London: Methuen, 1920; rpt. 1960), p. 74.

But while I've tried to prune excess verbiage from my renderings of the choral portions of *Helen*, these parts of the play should retain, if not a fluid haze, some kind of difference of affect from the rest of the action. The choral parts are by and large, as I've said above, where the mask drops and emotions are revealed. They also have a sweep and pace that contrasts with the earthbound limitation of mere mortals. Helen seems to have crouched at the altar for years—years during which Menelaus has fruitlessly circled the seas. Only Zeus, or the swan he turns into, can swoop and dive and soar effortlessly between heaven and earth—a memory the chorus returns to again and again. Only the gods can negotiate such disparate realms with ease and grace, creating a cloud, conjuring a bloody river and a fallen city, or even, initially, assuming the form of a bird to seduce a woman. Only the gods can maneuver vertically, like the bark Othello envisions climbing "hills of seas / Olympus-high"—only the gods and human memory expressed in language, which is to say only the gods and poetry.

Cast

HELEN
TEUCER, son of Telamon, half-brother of Ajax
MENELAUS, king of Sparta, husband of Helen
DOORKEEPER
MESSENGER
THEONOE, prophetess, daughter of Proteus
THEOCLYMENUS, brother of Theonoe
DIOSCURI, Castor and Pollux, Helen's divine brothers
SECOND MESSENGER
CHORUS of Greek women

(Helen is standing alone in front of an imposing palace in the Egyptian style.)

HELEN
This is the river Nile, whose waters flow—
fed not by rain but gleaming melted snow—
through Egypt, where King Proteus held sway,
living on Pharos island. Psamathe,
one of the daughters of the Sea, he wed
after she left Aeacus' marriage bed.

To Proteus Psamathe bore both a son—
Theoclymenus, a pious name—
and daughter, apple of her mother's eye.
Eido they called her when she was a baby,   10
but when she grew to womanhood she was known
as Theonoe, for god's mind seems her own.
She understands things sacred—those that are
and also those that have yet to appear,
a gift inherited from her ancestor
Nereus.

As for me—well, not unknown
is the part of earth that I call mine,
Sparta. Tyndareus was my father. Some
say, though, that Zeus, assuming a swan's shape,
flew to my mother Leda to escape   20
an eagle in pursuit of him, and, so
disguised, entered her bed. It may be true.
At any rate, I'm Helen. Let me tell
all the misfortunes that then befell.
Hera and Aphrodite and the Maid,
three goddesses, converged on Ida's wood.
Beauty was the crux of their dispute,
and Paris was the person whom they sought
to ponder each one's beauty and decide.
Promising me to Paris as his bride,   30
Cypris won out. My beauty was the bait—
a pretty word for what gave rise to hate.
Leaving his mountain mangers, Paris came
to Sparta, where he thought that he could claim
his prize—my bed. But Hera, whose defeat
enraged her, had contrived a trick to cheat
the prince, bestowing on him in my place
a breathing phantom shaped from nothingness.
Paris was sure he was embracing me;
it was an empty image, sheerest vanity.   40

On top of this, Zeus had another plot.
To Greeks and to doomed Trojans he now brought
war with dual purpose: prune the population
while making known the hero of my nation,
the greatest of the Greeks.

                   So there I was
(or wasn't—it was just my name)—the prize
both armies fought for. Thanks to Zeus' care
Hermes came and folded me in air,

tucked me in cloudcover, set me down here.
Zeus judged that Proteus, most controlled of men,   50
would keep me pure until I could return
to Menelaus. So here I am.
My wretched husband tried to track me down.
Hot on my trail, the army that he led
to Troy killed many men who now lie dead
beside Scamander. For these reasons I,
I who have suffered so, am cursed. They say
that I betrayed my husband, caused the war.
You may well wonder what I'm living for.
This only: I've heard Hermes prophesy   60
that one day with my husband I shall lie
in our own bed in Sparta, and that he
will know no other man has lain with me
and know as well I never went to Troy.

While Proteus still saw the light of day,
this palace gave asylum to me.
But now that death has hidden him, his son,
aiming at marriage, tries to hunt me down.
A suppliant, I kneel at Proteus' tomb,
honoring the husband who was mine,   70
praying my bed will be reserved for him.
Throughout all Greece I bear an evil name,
but may my body here stay free of shame.
(Enter Teucer, moving cautiously. Awed, he stares at the palace.)

TEUCER
Who has command over the stronghold here?
This is how Plutus' palace must appear,
this royal courtyard and these massive walls.

Oh my god! What horrid sight appalls
my vision? For surely what I see
is that vile woman, vicious enemy,

my ruin and the bane of all of us.   80
May the gods spurn you—you with Helen's face!
If I were not on foreign soil, I vow,
this arrow would have shot you dead by now
for daring to be Helen's facsimile.

HELEN

Wretched man, whoever you may be,
why turn your anger at her faults on me?

TEUCER

Pardon me. But passion drove me wild.
All Greece, you know, abominates Zeus' child.

HELEN

Who are you, and what brings you to this place?

TEUCER

I am a Greek—of that unhappy race.   90

HELEN

It's not surprising you hate Helen, then.
But who are you? From what place and whose son?

TEUCER

Teucer is my name. My father was
Telamon. I come from Salamis.

HELEN

What brings you to the fields around the Nile?

TEUCER

I'm driven from my homeland in exile.

HELEN

Poor man, what made you leave your native hall?

TEUCER

My father, who should love me above all.

HELEN

Some great misfortune has befallen you.

TEUCER

My brother's death in Troy destroyed me too.   100

HELEN

Your sword killed Ajax, do you mean to say?

TEUCER

He fell on his own sword and died that way.

HELEN

Anyone who does that is insane.

TEUCER

Have you heard of Achilles, Peleus' son?

HELEN

He wished to marry Helen, did he not?

TEUCER

After Achilles died, his comrades fought
each other for his armor.

HELEN

                            How was that
dangerous for Ajax?

TEUCER

                        Ajax lost
that contest, and his own life was the cost.

HELEN

These were his troubles; they were not your own.   110

TEUCER

No, I should have died along with him.

HELEN

You too then went to fight the Trojan war?

TEUCER

I helped sack Troy, but hurt myself far more.

HELEN

Is all the city now burned to the ground?

TEUCER

Traces of walls are barely to be found.

HELEN

Helen, you wretch, the Trojans died for you!

TEUCER

Do not forget the Greek deaths she's caused too.

HELEN

How long since the destruction of the town?

TEUCER

Seven fruitful years have rolled around.

HELEN

How many years in all did you spend there?   120

TEUCER

Month after month piled up to ten long years.

HELEN

The Spartan woman—did you capture her?

TEUCER

Yes, Menelaus dragged her by the hair.

HELEN

Is this hearsay or something that you saw?

TEUCER

No less than with these eyes I now see you.

HELEN

And yet gods have been known to hoodwink men.

TEUCER

Please, let's change the subject if we can.

HELEN

You're absolutely sure of what you saw?

TEUCER

I saw with my own eyes, as I see you.

HELEN

Did Menelaus and his wife get home?   130

TEUCER

No, not to Argos, nor Eurotas' stream.

HELEN

Oh, this is dreadful news you're telling me.

TEUCER

The rumor is they've vanished, he and she.

HELEN
>The Greeks sailed in a convoy, didn't they?

TEUCER
>Until a storm arose that blew away
>some far from others . . .

HELEN
>>Just where would this be?

TEUCER
>About halfway across the Aegean Sea.

HELEN
>Since then, no one's seen Menelaus—yes?

TEUCER
>No one. Word of his death has spread through Greece.

HELEN *(aside)*
>Oh god.
(controlling herself, to Teucer again)
>>And Thestia's daughter—can you tell   140
>me, is she living?

TEUCER
>>Leda? Dead as well.

HELEN
>Could this death too have sprung from Helen's disgrace?

TEUCER
>They say it did. She fashioned her own noose.

HELEN
>Tyndareus' sons—are they alive and well?

TEUCER

Yes and no. Two versions of that tale
exist.

HELEN

Tell me the main one,

(aside)

God help me.

TEUCER

That both are gods now, shining in the sky
as stars.

HELEN

Good. But the other version says . . .

TEUCER

Shame for their sister made them end their days.   150
Enough of stories now! I'd not weep twice.
The reason I have come to this great house
is to see Theonoe the prophetess.
With you as my envoy, I'd find out
exactly how to steer my winged boat
to sea-surrounded Cyprus, where I know
I'll end my days—Apollo told me so,
and ordered me to give the place the name
of Salamis, to honor my old home.

HELEN

The sea will point the way for you. But go   160
now, quickly—our new king may hear of you,
the son of Proteus. He's off hunting now.
Whatever Greek he finds he's sure to slay.
I cannot tell, and please don't ask me, why—
nothing I say could help.

TEUCER

      But for your words
 and deeds of kindness, may you reap rewards
 from heaven. You resemble Helen, but
 how different from hers is your good heart!
 I hope she's dead, and someplace far away.
 But you—the best of luck to you. Goodbye.   170
(Exit.)

HELEN *(alone, giving way to grief)*
 No Muse has charge of agony.
 But, oh god, the relief
 of screaming, a shrill cry
 wrung out of grief.
 O winged Sirens, weeping virgins, come
 and add your tears to mine,
 a counterpoint of melody and pain,
 and let Persephone
 send a pale choir to keep me company.
 My tears will thank her even as they fall   180
 for those imprisoned in her deathly hall.
(Enter a Chorus of Greek women.)

CHORUS
 Down by the stream where the rushes grow
 we women wash our clothes.
 I'd rinsed mine, and was spreading them
 to dry in the golden sun
 when I heard a scream of grief and pain,
 hoarse and harsh, a shout
 such as a girl pursued by Pan
 in some rocky hollow would let out.

HELEN
 Women of Greece, O friends,   190
 dragged overseas with me,
 listen. A man has come

to this place of slavery—
has come from Greece, our home,
and brought me agony,
a crowd of griefs, not one!
Listen. Because of me,
or rather not through me,
only my wretched name,
Troy has been wrapped in flame,   200
the city of Troy is gone,
and I am to blame.
My mother Leda has hanged herself—
whose is the fault but mine?
My husband wanders, vagabond and lost—
it's all my fault. Castor and Pollux, twin
jewels of our father's house—
my brothers are lost too,
gone from the plain where their horses used to run,
gone from the meadow   210
where they played by the stream in the sun.
I am alone to blame.
The fault is all my fault; the shame, my shame.

CHORUS
Lady, we know your pain
overflows the brim.
Ever since the time
Zeus zoomed down on your mother in the white
shape of a snowy swan,
there is no evil that you have not seen.
Your mother's gone;   220
the twins' fair day is done;
your husband—God knows—lost
somewhere on the cold sea,
in salty billows tossed;
rumor assigns you to barbarian lechery;
and you are distant from
the town where you were born,

the temple of Athena where
you prayed when you were young
and free of any care.   230
Yes, you are far from home.

HELEN
God damn that man
who cut the pine
that made the ship
that Paris, Priam's son,
sailed in over the sea
to my house, my bed, my god-damned beauty,
goaded by the goddess of desire
whose savage cruelty
brought Greeks and Trojans sheer   240
disaster—death with impartiality.

Curled up in Zeus' clasp,
Hera from their gold throne
sent down the Messenger
to pluck me up, transplant me.
I happened to be
picking flowers—but he,
Hermes, seized me, flew me through the air
to this place of distress,
contention, ruin, every bitterness.   250
Troy went to war with Greece.
But more than this,
my evil reputation there
in the city where the rivers run with blood
is false—a void,
a rumor fashioned out of empty air.

CHORUS
I know all this is painful. Best to bear
lightly as you can your life's despair.

HELEN

> I'm trapped inside an evil destiny.
> My life and everything involved with me   260
> is monstrous. For some beauty, what a cost!
> If only I could somehow be erased
> as pictures are, and part of me replaced
> with something plainer, would the Greeks let go
> of that ill fame which long has dragged me so
> and keep instead some happy memory?
>
> If people suffer one great stroke of ill
> luck, it's hard, but it is bearable.
> My web of woes is more complex by far.
> First, though I have done nothing wrong, I bear   270
> this evil reputation—so unfair,
> far worse than if the charge were true. I'm banned
> from my own country to this foreign land,
> these alien customs—all without one friend.
> I'm treated like a slave here. Never mind
> parentage; places like this are bound
> by slavery. All but one of us are slaves.
> My only anchor in these tossing waves
> of trouble was the hope that one fine day
> my husband would come carry me away   280
> from here to safety. He cannot; he's gone,
> he's dead, my mother's dead. The fault is mine—
> all unintentional, but still a crime.
> My daughter, once so beautiful, begins
> to wither into spinsterhood. The twins,
> Castor and Pollux, are no more. And I—
> my heart is shriveled from this misery,
> and yet I go on living. If I should
> return to Sparta, what would be the good?
> At home they'd hate me, they would slam the door: 290
> "Helen for whom a war was fought—you whore!"
> Living, my husband might identify

me by signs known only to his eye,
but he is dead now; this can never be.
And I—what course of action's left to me?
Marriage might be a bulwark against pain,
but could I live with a barbarian,
no matter what his wealth? What bitterness—
hating my husband, loathing each caress.
Some women wear their beauty gratefully;   300
my beauty has destroyed me utterly.

CHORUS

Whoever that man was who spoke to you,
don't be too sure that all he said was true.

HELEN

But he said clearly that my husband died.

CHORUS

He said a lot of things. He may have lied.

HELEN

Yet often words mean just what we expect.

CHORUS

Why be so certain he has been shipwrecked?
Good things can happen.

HELEN

                                  But I am afraid,
and my fear pushes me to greater dread.

CHORUS

Can you depend on good will in this house?   310

HELEN

Except for him who'd marry me by force,
they're all on my side.

CHORUS

                    Here's what I'd advise:
stop sitting on the tomb here. Leave this place.

HELEN

What are you hinting? Please don't make me guess.

CHORUS

Go in the house and ask the prophetess,
Nereus' descendant Theonoe,
whether your husband sees the light of day
or not. When you have learned the truth from her,
then is the time for joy or else despair.
Before you're sure, what is the point of grieving?   320
Do as I say. Your first step should be leaving
this tomb. Then go and ask her, for she knows.
This way the answer to your problem lies,
and nowhere else. Let me accompany
you; I too want to hear her prophecy.
Women in trouble need to stick together.
No one helps us, but we can help each other.

HELEN

I'm finally persuaded. Let us go
into the house immediately, and learn
which way the wheel will turn—   330

CHORUS

which way without delay.
Why are you hanging back? We must go now.
What are we waiting for?

HELEN

I'm terrified, that's why.
What horrors lie in wait?

CHORUS

Do not cry out before you're hurt.

HELEN

                                But what
about my husband? Does he see the light
still, or has he gone down
into the house of death, that endless night?

CHORUS

Hope for the best. What else is there to do?   340

HELEN

But if the rumor of his death proves true,
then, oh then—

CHORUS

Then what? What do you mean?

HELEN

With my own hands I'll wrap
a noose around my neck,
and then I'll plunge a sword into my throat,
make of my life a double sacrifice—
first to the triple goddess
and then to shepherd Paris, Priam's son,
a harmless herdsman once upon a time,   350
playing his simple flute to silly sheep.

CHORUS

No! You must not die.
Happiness, not distress
may come of this.

HELEN

                    O Troy,
O city done to death by an illusion!
The tears of anguish flow,
blood, tears fall like rain

for every mother who has lost a son,
for every girl whose brother
lies dead beside the river—   360
all Greece cries out, all Greece
beats her own face with her fists,
scratches her own cheeks
until the blood runs down.

Zeus had plenty of lovers
luckier than my mother.
Callisto, whom he turned into a bear,
lost, yes, her woman's shape,
but shed along with it all human care.
And Artemis snatched away   370
the daughter of Merope
from the line of dancers,
transformed her to a doe
with golden horns. And why?
Yes, she was beautiful.
I'm beautiful as well.
But what does my beauty signify?
What does it accomplish or portend?
Death for the Greeks. For Troy, an awful end.

(Exuent Helen and Chorus into the palace. Enter cautiously Menelaus,
                    dirty, skinny, wrapped in a ragged piece of
                    sailcloth, but still carrying himself with
                    some swagger.)

MENELAUS

Pelops, once victor in a chariot race   380
with Oenomaus, served the gods a feast
of his own flesh. If only he'd died then!
No such luck—he lived to sire a son,
Atreus, who wed Aerope, who bore
Agamemnon and me—a famous pair,
who sent the greatest (in all modesty

I say this) of the armies against Troy,
not by compelling them, as tyrants would—
the flower of Greece fought of its own accord.
Some of those now are numbered with the dead.   390
Others are gladly back—the ones who fled
shipwreck and brought their comrades' names back home.
But up and down the swelling seas I roam.
The span of time it took to fight the war
at Troy I've wandered, longing for the shore
of my own land—a wish the gods refuse.
To every godforsaken landing place
in Libya I've sailed, but when I near
my native coast, then hellish gales appear
to blow me backward. Fair winds never come   400
to fill my sail and let me reach my home.

And now my ship's been shattered on the stones;
my friends are lost, I'm shipwrecked here alone.
Somehow the keel was saved, and that saved me—
as well as Helen, whom I'd snatched from Troy
just as we were leaving.

                    Where am I?
The country and the people—what they're named
I haven't dared to ask. I felt ashamed
to speak to anyone, I'm such a mess.
I wanted to conceal my shabbiness.   410
For prosperous men, misfortune is far worse
than if they were unlucky from the first.
But things have reached a crisis now. I lack
food for my belly, clothing for my back.
I'm starving, naked, wrapped in shreds of sail.
Fine robes I had—the sea's devoured them all.
Meanwhile I've hidden in a cave nearby
my wife, the cause of all my misery,
and told my friends—the few who still remain—

to guard her while I came here on my own 420
to see what I could find for us to eat.
Spying this palace with its sturdy gate,
I knew the place must shelter fortunate
folk, so I entered. To my hungry crew
wealth equals hope. For what could peasants do
to help us, even if they wanted to?
(Approaches the palace and pounds on the door.)
Hey there—doorkeeper! Move a little faster.
I want to tell my troubles to your master.
(A burly woman opens the door a crack.)

DOORKEEPER
Who's that at the gate? Get out! Be off!
Hang around the courtyard like an oaf 430
pestering my masters, and you'll die!
You look Greek, and no Greeks need apply.

MENELAUS
What a splendid speech! You're too polite.
Agreed, I'll not come in. No cause to fight.

DOORKEEPER
Take yourself off. I have my orders, sir;
no Greek is allowed to enter here.

MENELAUS
Keep your hands off! Don't dare push me away.

DOORKEEPER
But since you keep ignoring what I say . . .

MENELAUS
Now go inside and tell your boss I'm here.

DOORKEEPER
You're crazy. I can't be your messenger. 440

MENELAUS
A stranger, shipwrecked—shelter's all I need.

DOORKEEPER
Then find it in some other house instead.

MENELAUS
Oh no, I'm coming in. Let go! Give way!

DOORKEEPER
Nuisances get pushed out with no delay.

MENELAUS
I wish my famous troops were here with me.
I was the general of a whole nation!

DOORKEEPER
Elsewhere. You're zero here—no reputation,
nobody, nothing.

MENELAUS
                    Gods, what a disgrace!

DOORKEEPER
Now what? Tears are running down your face.

MENELAUS
I was a prosperous man in former years.   450

DOORKEEPER
Go find your friends and let them dry your tears.

MENELAUS
What is this country? Who rules in this house?

DOORKEEPER
The house is Proteus'; Egypt is the place.

MENELAUS
  I've sailed to Egypt? Damn my dreadful fate!

DOORKEEPER
  The shining Nile is something that you hate?

MENELAUS
  It's not the Nile, it's my bad luck I curse.

DOORKEEPER
  Many have had bad luck. You're not the first.

MENELAUS
  The man you called the king—is he at home?

DOORKEEPER
  His son's king now. The sire lies in this tomb.

MENELAUS
  Where is the son, then? He's the man I seek.   460

DOORKEEPER
  He isn't home. And he loathes all that's Greek.

MENELAUS
  What is the reason for this prejudice?

DOORKEEPER
  Helen, the child of Zeus, lives in this house.

MENELAUS
  What? Run that by me one more time.

DOORKEEPER
  Tyndareus' daughter. Sparta was her home—

MENELAUS

What are you saying? She came here—from where?

DOORKEEPER

I tell you, she left Sparta and came here.

MENELAUS

I left my wife inside a cave just now.
Has she been stolen?

DOORKEEPER

                    This was long ago,
stranger, before the Greeks went off to Troy.   470
Now *you* be off. It's not a lucky day
inside the palace. Everything's upset.
Death is the only welcome you will get
should my master learn that you are here.
Myself, I like the Greeks. It was for fear
of my master that I was so rough.
(goes back inside)

MENELAUS

What is this? Have there not been enough
troubles? Now on top of my old woes
I'm hearing of a brand new wretchedness.
I brought my wife here, taking her from Troy,   480
stowed her for safety in a cave nearby.
But there's another one, with the same name,
living in this house at the same time,
and Zeus' daughter was the porter's claim.
Can it be Zeus is a common name
in Egypt? No, there's one Zeus—in the sky.
And where else in the world could Sparta be
except along Eurotas' reedy stream?
Could two men bear Tyndareus' name?
Can any place exist synonymous   490

with Sparta or with Troy? I'm at a loss.
Yet is it so astounding, after all?
The world is big; therefore, identical
names for women, cities, men should be
common.
           I won't let her frighten me,
that bitchy porter. I won't run away.
No man's so barbarous as to deny
me food, once he learns my identity.
Nowhere on earth could my name be unknown—
Menelaus, who burned Troy down!   500
I'll wait here for the master of the house.
When he appears, I'll see which path to choose.
If he is savage, I'll first hide, and then
make my way somehow to the wreck again;
but if he shows me any gentleness,
then I'll beg for help in this distress.
Of all my trials this is the worst yet,
that I, a king, must beg for food to eat
from other kings. But so it has to be.
A wise man said (although it wasn't me)   510
nothing is stronger than necessity.
(Helen and the Chorus emerge from the palace.)

CHORUS

Inside the house I heard her prophesy!
Hungry, stateless, vagabond
since he set sail from Troy,
Menelaus lives,
but still the winds pursue him
over a swelling sea
to every possible coast, seaport, shore
but that of his own country.

HELEN

Back to my seat upon the tomb. I've heard   520
omniscient Theonoe's welcome word:

my husband lives, he sees the light of day!
But he is driven all across the sea
on countless paths of suffering. Only when
it's time for all this wandering to end
will he return.
              One thing she didn't say:
will it be safe when he does come this way?
In my relief that he's all right so far,
on this detail I didn't press her more.
He and his friends are shipwrecked—and quite near   530
this place, she says.
              Oh, wherever you are,
come to me quickly! Longing and desire
for you—

(She sees Menelaus. Starts.)
              What's this? A trap? An ambush? Can
Proteus' vile son have laid some cunning plan?
Swift as a colt or Maenad, let me run
back to the tomb. How wild he looks, this man
chasing me!

MENELAUS
              You there, scuttling toward the tomb,
wait a minute! What are you running from?
The moment that I saw you I was struck
with such amazement that I couldn't speak.   540

HELEN
Women, help, we're in a trap!
This fellow's seized me and won't give me up.
He wants to hand me over to the man
whose vile advances I am running from.

MENELAUS
I'm neither villain's hireling nor thief!

HELEN
> Your clothing is uncivilized enough.

MENELAUS
> Stay here. Don't be afraid, don't sneak away.

HELEN
> I've reached the tomb, and that is where I'll stay.

MENELAUS
> Who are you? Whose is the face I see?

HELEN
> I could ask you the question you ask me.   550

MENELAUS
> How could a resemblance be so strong?

HELEN
> God has let me recognize my own—

MENELAUS
> Are you native here or are you Greek?

HELEN
> Greek. And you? Speak, speak!

MENELAUS
> The image of my Helen you seem to me.

HELEN
> And you of Menelaus. How can this be?

MENELAUS
> You've recognized him, the unhappiest
> of men.

HELEN
>   Then welcome to my loving breast
> after all these years—a wife's embrace!

MENELAUS
>   Wife? What wife? Don't touch me! Get away!   560

HELEN
>   Wife—whom my father Tyndareus gave to you.

MENELAUS
>   Hecate's phantoms must be blinding me.

HELEN
>   This is no ghostly vision you see.

MENELAUS
>   I am one person. I can't have a pair
> of wives!

HELEN
>   But what other wife is there?

MENELAUS
>   Back in the cave—the one I brought from Troy.

HELEN
>   There is no other wife. There's only me.

MENELAUS
>   My mind and eyes are blurring. Can this be?

HELEN
>   Look at me. Isn't it your wife you see?

MENELAUS
>   In body, yes. But how can I make sure?   570

HELEN

    Use your eyes. What better proof is there?

MENELAUS

    I won't deny you look enough like her—

HELEN

    You see? Eyes are the best teachers—

MENELAUS

                    No, no!

    I tell you I've another wife, not you.

HELEN

    A phantom went to Troy. It wasn't I.

MENELAUS

    A phantom fashioned so realistically?
    How and by whom?

HELEN

             Spun right out of thin air,
    the image which the gods contrived to share
    your bed.

MENELAUS

        Which gods? This strains credulity.

HELEN

    Hera made it—a substitute for me,   580
    to keep me out of Paris' clutches.

MENELAUS

              So
    you were here all this time—and in Troy too?

HELEN
> My name went everywhere; my body, no.

MENELAUS
> I've had my fill of troubles. Let me go.

HELEN
> You're leaving me, then, for an empty bed,
> an image?

MENELAUS
> Yes. You look like her—Godspeed!

HELEN
> My long-lost husband now is shunning me!

MENELAUS
> Not you—it's my own troubles that I flee.

HELEN
> Ah, who could be more miserable than I?
> My loved ones leave me, I am stranded here.   590
> When shall I see my homeland? Nevermore!
> *(Enter Messenger, another ragged Greek.)*

MESSENGER
> I've looked for you, but you've been hard to find,
> Menelaus. The friends you left behind
> sent me all through this godforsaken land—

MENELAUS
> What is it? Have barbarians robbed you?

MESSENGER
> The tale I have to tell is strange but true.

MENELAUS
    Speak out, if you have such important news.

MESSENGER
    You know that you have suffered countless woes?
    Well, all were needless!

MENELAUS
                            That's an old refrain.
    Tell me something new.

MESSENGER   ·
                            Your wife is gone!   600
    Folded into air invisibly,
    she's actually hiding in the sky.
    Her parting words were: "Men of Greece and Troy,
    all you who beside the bloody stream
    of Scamander perished through the scheme
    of Hera, you were killed because you thought
    that Paris possessed Helen. He did not!
    I've stayed here to fulfill my destiny;
    I go now to my maker in the sky.
    Poor daughter of Tyndareus—ill fame   610
    is showered on her, yet she's not to blame."
(*Sees Helen; does a double take.*)
    Daughter of Leda, how did you get here?
    I've just told how you vanished through thin air
    somehow to heaven, but I never knew
    that flying was among your talents too.
    Now please do not be mocking us again
    with claims your husband went to Troy in vain,
    in vain the allied armies suffered all their pain.

MENELAUS
    Just what she said! Oh, all of it is true—
    everything fits! Oh blessed day   620
    that gives you back to me!

HELEN

> Dear Menelaus—yes, the time was long,
> but now that you are here, the joy is strong.
>
> O friends, I have found him,
> my husband, I have flung my arms around him.
> At the end of the long black tunnel, light!

MENELAUS

> Now you are in my arms, where to begin
> the weary narrative of where we've been?

HELEN

> Oh, god, my hair stands up for happiness,
> my eyes fill. Let me throw   630
> my arms around you, it is such
> a joy to feel your touch.

MENELAUS

> Do you hear me blaming you, dear heart?
> A company of riders on white horses
> brought Zeus and Leda's child
> to me as my bride,
> who then was snatched away
> and now miraculously,
> oh, at long last, is now restored to me.

HELEN

> Good and ill fate combine   640
> to reunite us after all this time.
> May all be smoothest sailing from now on!

MENELAUS

> Amen. And let me pray for this also:
> when two lives combine,
> their happiness must be harmonious too.

HELEN

> No tears, no tears for what is finally past.
> O friends, I have him now,
> I hold him here, my husband,
> my long-awaited lord.

MENELAUS

>   And I have you.
> Tedious toil of twenty thousand suns!   650
> Time crawled, but now at last I see it whole,
> the fabric woven by the goddess—now
> I finally weep, but not for grief, for joy.

HELEN

> Who could have hoped for this? What can I say?
> I hold you in my arms; I'm drunk with glee.

MENELAUS

> And I hold you. We all thought you had gone,
> thought you spelled ruin for Troy's cursed town.

HELEN

> Oh god, you take me back to the dark day
> all this began.

MENELAUS

>   But how on earth did they
> manage it, how did it happen,   660
> how did they contrive to spirit you away?

HELEN

> A bitter question.

MENELAUS

>   It deserves to be
> answered. All things come from divinity.

HELEN

    I spit it out, the vileness I must tell.

MENELAUS

    It's sweet when troubles dwindle to a tale.
    Speak.

HELEN

          To begin with, then, I didn't float
    off to Paris' bedroom in a boat
    with madly flailing oars. Nor did I fly,
    lustful wings flapping, toward adultery.

MENELAUS

    But what fate or divinity   670
    tore you from your own home?

HELEN

                  Hermes, Zeus' son,
    brought me here to Egypt.

MENELAUS

              And who sent him?
    I'm at a loss—all this is a bad dream.

HELEN

    I wept, believe me; I am weeping still.
    It was the wife of Zeus who wished me ill.

MENELAUS

    Hera had it in for us? But why?

HELEN

    Oh, the fountain with its foaming pools,
    the bath, the running water's bright caress,
    the goddesses
    sitting in judgment on my loveliness—   680

MENELAUS

A verdict Hera used to hurt you—how?

HELEN

By cheating Aphrodite out of—

MENELAUS

Who?

HELEN

The person she had pledged to Paris. Me.

MENELAUS

Poor you!

HELEN

Poor me indeed. Helpless me, too.
She sent me here to Egypt, as you know.

MENELAUS

While fooling Paris with the ghost of you.

HELEN

But then, oh god, the suffering!
Mother, in our own house—

MENELAUS

What is this?

HELEN

I have
no mother, for a noose   690
strangled her. She
committed suicide for shame of me.

MENELAUS

Gods . . . And our daughter? How's Hermione?

HELEN

A spinster, childless . . . Who with better right
condemns what was my marriage—and was not?

MENELAUS

O Paris, you destroyed my house for me,
but all this meant destruction for you too,
and for the whole Greek army.

HELEN

And for me.
God snatched me from my home and family.
I left my house,   700
deserting bed and hearth for—what? Disgrace!

CHORUS

If henceforth Fortune shows a kindly face,
all past pain it will surely compensate.

MESSENGER

Explain, please! I've not understood it yet.
Menelaus, you have good news. Share it.

MENELAUS

Yes, old friend, it's right for you to hear it.

MESSENGER

You mean this lady wasn't at our woes
in Troy?

MENELAUS

That's right. The gods made fools of us.
A figure shaped of air—this was the bane
that I embraced.

MESSENGER

In other words, our pain   710
was suffered for a cloud?

MENELAUS

                 Exactly right.
Hera's work—and those three goddesses' spite.

MESSENGER

So this one here's your wife, you mean to say?

MENELAUS

Believe me, no one is my wife but she.

MESSENGER

Daughter, the mind of God is hard to know.
He shuffles things, he shunts them to and fro.
One suffers and another seems immune
yet ends his days in some appalling pain.
Life is uncertain—of that much we're sure.
Both you and he have had more than a fair   720
portion of trouble: rumors, you; he, spears.
Long years he strove to no avail. Today
good fortune comes to him so easily!

(pause)

Your twin brothers; your father's old gray head—
you never shamed them, then, as people said!
Ah, now it's coming back to me, how you
rode in the four-horse chariot long ago.
I waved a torch, and you stood close beside
your husband, leaving home a happy bride.

A hired man who fails to sympathize   730
with both his master's sorrows and his joys
is a wretched fellow in my eyes.
Although I am a servant, let me be
if not in fact at least in spirit free.
To be a servant is less dreadful than
working my poor fingers to the bone
toiling for strangers, all the livelong day,
nurturing some vengeful fantasy.

MENELAUS

    Old man, through many battles close to me
    you fought, you shared my burdens. Now that joy   740
    is what you share, go quickly—take the news
    to friends who wait to hear a word from us.
    Tell them stay near the coast and be alert;
    keep their eyes peeled and wait for the result
    of what will be our challenge now: can we
    manage to steal silently away
    and take the woman with us, out of here,
    safe out of reach of this barbarian power?

MESSENGER

    It shall be done, my lord.
                        But prophecy,
    I understand now, is sheer idiocy!   750
    Flames on the altar, bird calls—silliness!
    I see it's only simplemindedness
    to think that poultry benefits mankind.
    Calchas said nothing, gave us not one sign
    when so many soldiers died. Died why?
    All for a cloud! And Helenus stood by
    silent. No one knew—and so Troy fell
    all in vain. You might call it god's will.
    Then who needs prophets? When we sacrifice,
    we pray god for good fortune. Prophecy's   760
    useless, a bait for greed. Away with it!
    No lazy man through prophecy grows fat.
    True divination's in our mother wit.

CHORUS

    I must say I wholeheartedly agree
    with the old man concerning prophecy.
    First make the gods your friends, and you will find
    auspicious prophecies don't lag behind.

HELEN

> Enough of that.
>
> > Life here's been good to me.
>
> But how, poor dear, you got away from Troy—
> what do I gain by knowing? Yet we thirst   770
> to learn our loved ones' stories, even the worst
> of what they've suffered.

MENELAUS

> > It is much you ask.
>
> To tell it all would be an endless task.
> All those men lost on the passage home;
> the beacon fires lit at Nauplion;
> our stops at Crete and Libya—lengthy tour—
> and Perseus' lookout . . . You'd still wish for more
> while I would have to suffer double pain.
> All that I've been through must I live again?

HELEN

> Your answer makes more sense than my request.   780
> Answer one question and forget the rest:
> how long were you a wanderer on the sea?

MENELAUS

> In addition to ten years at Troy,
> seven of circling.

HELEN

> > Seven more years! Oh my dear . . .
>
> Well, all that's past.
>
> > But you face murder here.

MENELAUS

> What are you saying?

HELEN
                    This: that you will be
slain by the man who holds the sovereignty
here.

MENELAUS
        But why? I'm guilty of no crime.

HELEN
        Your crime was to arrive at the wrong time
        and stop our wedding.

MENELAUS
                    Someone's marrying you?   790

HELEN
        By force, by violence. What could I do?

MENELAUS
        By private force? Or with a ruler's power?

HELEN
        Being the son of Proteus, he's king here.

MENELAUS
        Aha, the portress' riddle—now it's clear!

HELEN
        You stood before barbarian gates—but where?

MENELAUS
        Here, like a beggar—and was driven away.

HELEN
        You mean you had to beg for charity?

MENELAUS
> Begging was simply what I had to do.
> It wasn't who I was.

HELEN
>   Apparently
> you know, then, of his plan to marry me.   800

MENELAUS
> I know all I need to know but this:
> whether you yielded to his vile caress.

HELEN
> To that suspicion the answer's No.
> I've kept my bed and body pure for you.

MENELAUS
> Prove it! This sounds too good to be true.

HELEN
> There at the tomb—you see a kind of seat?

MENELAUS
> I see a mattress stuffed with straw—for what?

HELEN
> This place was my asylum from that man.

MENELAUS
> No altar—how barbarian!

HELEN
> This seat worked just as well as temples can.   810

MENELAUS
> Why can't I simply take you and set sail?

HELEN

Because what would await you is cold steel,
not my embrace.

MENELAUS

Oh miserable mess!
Of all men I must be the wretchedest.

HELEN

Flee this country. Flight is no disgrace.

MENELAUS

And leave you here? I who sacked Troy for you?

HELEN

Better than let my love destroy you too.

MENELAUS

Cowardly talk—unfitting for a man
who fought at Troy.

HELEN

But do not think you can
kill the king, though that may be your plan.   820

MENELAUS

You mean he has a body made of steel?

HELEN

You'll see. The man who dares impossible
deeds is not a hero but a fool.

MENELAUS

So I stand meekly while my hands are tied?

HELEN

In this emergency what we most need
is some clever plot.

MENELAUS

     I'd rather die
in action than just wait here passively.

HELEN

 One hope does exist for you and me.

MENELAUS

 By bribes, by boldness, or by argument—
how?

HELEN

    What if the king were ignorant   830
that you had ever come here?

MENELAUS

       Nobody
has told him, and he'll never learn from me.

HELEN

 An ally, strong as gods, lives in his hall.

MENELAUS

 You mean his house conceals some oracle?

HELEN

 The house conceals his sister Theonoe.

MENELAUS

 The name's oracular. Who may she be?

HELEN

 There's nothing she does not know. She'll betray
·your presence to her brother.

MENELAUS

       Then I'll die.
There is no place to hide here.

HELEN

                                        What if we
persuaded her—implored her—

MENELAUS

                                      But to do   840
what? What is the hope you lead me to?

HELEN

That she won't tell her brother we are here.

MENELAUS

Say we persuade her. Can we disappear,
escape this place?

HELEN

                        With her help, easily.
Without her knowledge, it could never be.

MENELAUS

Woman to woman, you must talk to her.

HELEN

I'll kneel, embrace, beseech her—never fear.

MENELAUS

But what if all we ask for is denied?

HELEN

Then you will die, and I must be a bride.

MENELAUS

Traitor! He threatened violence, you said?   850

HELEN

No, for I swore an oath upon your head—

MENELAUS
That sooner than remarry you would die?

HELEN
By this same sword. Beside you I will lie.

MENELAUS
Give me your right hand. Promise me again.

HELEN
I promise you that if you should be slain
I will forsake the sunlight.

MENELAUS
                              And if you
are killed, I swear that I'll end my life too.

HELEN
How can we manage to die gloriously?

MENELAUS
Here at the tomb I'll kill first you, then me—
but not without a desperate fight for your   860
bed. Let anyone approach who dares!
I'll not besmirch the Trojan War's renown;
I'll not slink home to Greece disgraced, a clown.
I who slaughtered Thetis' famous son,
who witnessed Ajax son of Telamon
go down in blood, and Nestor's son die too—
am I not man enough to die for you?
Of course I am. For if the gods are wise,
they sprinkle dust upon the man who dies
in battle, honoring his heroic end.   870
Cowards they simply toss on barren sand.

CHORUS

> Oh gods, may Tantalus' family, once free
> of its old woes, attain prosperity!

HELEN

> Oh, misery. For now what do I see?
> We're ruined, Menelaus. She is coming,
> the prophet Theonoe! The house is booming,
> doors are flung open. Run!
>   And yet what for?
> Absent or present, she knows you are here
> and how you came. Oh miserable me!
> Escaping Troy, from far-off lands you come;   880
> yet here barbarian blades will be your doom.

(The doors open. Enter Theonoe with stately pace. She stops and turns to
her attendants.)

THEONOE

> You with the gleaming torches, go before;
> make holy all the corners of the air
> so that every breath we draw is pure.
> And if our path's been sullied by profane
> feet, use fire to make it clean again:
> wave the pine torch so that I may go in.
> Only when my tribute to the god
> is duly paid may you go back inside.

(to Helen)

> Helen, have all my prophecies come true?   890
> Here is your husband Menelaus now,
> without his ships, without the ghost of you.

(to Menelaus)

> Poor wanderer, what travails brought you here!
> And even now your path is far from clear
> whether you'll be allowed to go or stay.
> The gods are meeting on this very day;
> you are the subject of divine debate.

Hera, who formerly was full of hate
for you, now kindly wants to send you home
together with your wife, so Greece may learn   900
that Paris' bride and Aphrodite's gift
was never real at all but only myth.
But Cypris plots to wreck your voyage home,
her motive being to avoid the shame
of having won the beauty contest by
the ruse of a false Helen—trickery!
Finally the choice is up to me. I may
do as Aphrodite wants, betray
your presence to my brother and destroy you;
or else, as Hera wants me to, stand by you   910
and hide you from my brother, whose command
was to announce your presence in this land.

Since I consult self-interest when I can,
will someone please inform the king this man
is here?

HELEN *(rushes to Theonoe and kneels before her)*
                O holy virgin, on my knees
a suppliant, I humbly beg you—please,
both for my own sake and for that of my
husband—he's just arrived; now must he die?
Conceal the truth. Let not your brother know
my husband has returned to me just now,   920
back to my loving arms. I beg you, be
kind! Do not sacrifice your piety
for the sake of family loyalty;
do not for his sake do this wickedness.

Both to my joy and to my wretchedness,
Hermes bestowed me on your father to
keep me here safely for my husband, who
has come to take me back. But he must be

alive to do so! And your father—how
could he entrust a living woman to   930
a corpse?
      Consider it as heaven's will:
would not the gods, and your late sire as well,
wish to restore all stolen properly?
Of course they would. Therefore, listen to me!
Don't give in to your scoundrel of a brother.
Do not prefer him to your virtuous father.
If you, although a prophetess, a seer,
ignore your father's goodness and prefer
your brother's vice, then surely it is vile
for one who knows all holiness so well,   940
who understands what will be and what is
not to discern where simple justice lies.

I'm overwhelmed with troubles. Lift me out!
And with this kind addition to my fate:
no man alive does not loathe me today.
All over Greece they claim that I betrayed
my husband for the golden luxury
of Troy. If I could get to Greece once more,
to Sparta, everyone could see and hear
that heaven's machinations caused these ends,   950
that I am not a traitor to my friends.
At last they'll understand that I meant well.
Our daughter, languishing unmarried, will
finally find a husband, be a wife;
and I can leave this vagabondish life
for the treasures that are mine at home.

Were my husband dead, of course I'd mourn
his loss with loving tears. But now he's here,
safe and rescued, can I let them tear
him from my arms? No, virgin, I implore!   960
Do me this kindness. Be like your good sire.

There can be no more valuable praise
for good men's children than when someone says
they follow in their parents' virtuous ways.

CHORUS
Touching words. Let Menelaus now
plead his case. I want to hear him too.

MENELAUS *(to Theonoe)*
I will not plead with you on bended knee
or gush with tears. Such acts are cowardly;
they'd only bring still more ignominy
to Troy and all that happened. Though they say   970
a man may weep in a catastrophe
and still be brave, I do not choose this way,
decent though it be, toward happiness.

But if you'll aid a stranger to this place
who only wants his wife back, help me, please!
Give her back to me! If you refuse,
I've suffered many times in life before,
but you will be revealed as what you are,
an evil woman. Justice itself owes me
this—and it should touch you especially   980
that as I speak I kneel beside the tomb
of your late father.
(kneels)
                        From your bed of stone,
hear me, old man. I ask that you restore
my wife. Oh, give her back to me once more!
Zeus sent her here for you to keep for me.
Since you are dead, I know it cannot be
you'll hand her over to me personally.
But can this lady here stand meekly by
while I heap your name with infamy
that once was glorious? That is up to her.   990

194   *Helen*

Lord of the dead, I call on you! Come here.
You welcomed many bodies of men killed
for my wife's sake, slain by the sword I wield—
let that be your payment. Either give
back those corpses—bring them back to life—
or make this priestess give my wife to me,
thus equaling her father's piety.

But if you choose to keep my wife away,
I'll tell you everything she didn't say.   1000
Lady, I have sworn, you understand,
that I will fight your brother hand to hand
in mortal combat. One of us will fall.
But if he doesn't dare to fight at all
and tries to starve us in our haven here,
I have another oath: first I'll kill her,
then into my own body drive the sword
here on this tomb until it runs with blood.
And there our corpses will be sprawling, two
reproaches to your father and to you.
For no one else shall marry her—not your   1010
brother, not anyone. I'll carry her
home or down to death—away from here,
anyway!
          Oh, what a pointless threat.
I've turned so womanish my eyes are wet
with tears—I'm pitiable, not a man!
But kill me if you like. You never can
quench the ill fame that will wreck your life
unless you heed my words, return my wife—
finally unless you choose the good.

CHORUS
Maiden, both have spoken now. You should   1020
make your mind up, being fair to all.

THEONOE
Awe for the sacred: that is what I feel.
My will and instinct are identical.
My person and my father's reputation—
I would not subject these to pollution.
Nor would I do my brother any favor
that would sully both of us forever.
Inside my heart Justice has made a shrine.
It was my grandfather's; now it is mine.
Justice therefore decrees I help you now,   1030
Menelaus. Hera wants this too.
She's on your side; I cast my lot with her.
May Aphrodite too be kind, though I
lack any commerce with her, and shall try
to stay a virgin till the day I die.

For your reproaches at my father's tomb:
all that applies to me. I would be wrong
not to repay the debt. If he were now
living, he'd reunite the two of you.
Among the living and among the dead,   1040
consequences follow every deed.
Dead men lack living thoughts, yet nonetheless
they do retain a kind of consciousness
blended with deathless ether.
                          Enough of that.
As far as your request goes, I will not
betray what you have told me to another,
nor will I abet my wicked brother.
Indeed, by thwarting his impiety
I'm benefiting him, it seems to me.

You must decide the means of your escape.   1050
My promise is to stand aside and keep
silent. For you, however, prayers should come

first: that Cypris guides you safely home,
and then that Hera wishes you both well
and hopes to help you both to safety still.
May my father's spirit never be
called ungodly while there's strength in me.
(*Exit.*)

CHORUS

Relying on wrongdoing, none succeeds.
The hope of safety lies in virtuous deeds.

HELEN

We need fear no harm from this priestess now,   1060
Menelaus. But consider how
you and I can safely get away.

MENELAUS

You've lived here in this palace long enough
to be familiar with the household staff,
isn't that so?

HELEN

                    Yes. Your idea must be
some clever ruse to spirit us away.

MENELAUS

And do you think you could see your way clear
to borrowing a chariot and a pair
of horses from the stable?

HELEN

                    I think so.
But how would that be helpful? We don't know   1070
the country; this is alien terrain.

MENELAUS
You're right—that's hopeless. Wait! Here's a good plan:
suppose I sneak into the palace, hide,
and kill the king as soon as he's inside
with his own sword?

HELEN
You're reckoning without
his sister. Would she stand by and permit
her brother to be slain?

MENELAUS
So much for that.
Nor do we have a ship in which to flee;
my boat is at the bottom of the sea.

HELEN
Wait, I have a good suggestion. Could   1080
you—still alive—pass yourself off as dead?

MENELAUS
Bad omen! But if it's a useful lie,
I guess I'm ready to pretend to die.

HELEN
So that before the lawless king I'll mourn,
with women's lamentations and hair shorn.

MENELAUS
But how can such a trick do anything
to get us out of here?

HELEN
I'll ask the king
(explaining that you drowned) if I may have
permission to construct a cenotaph.

MENELAUS

Say that he grants it—we still need to sail.   1090
How can an empty monument avail?

HELEN

I'll ask him for a ferry whence we may
cast burial gifts for you into the sea.

MENELAUS

A good idea. But you understand
it comes to nothing if my tomb's on land!

HELEN

It goes against Greek custom, we will say,
on land to honor those who died at sea.

MENELAUS

Bravo! And I'll set sail with you, my dear,
in the same ship, and pack the burial gear.

HELEN

Of course you will. The members of your crew,   1100
all who survived the wreck—I'll need them too.

MENELAUS

Get me a ship at anchor, and I'll fill
her deck with swordsmen all prepared to kill.

HELEN

That part is up to you. Meanwhile, may all
favorable winds swell out our sail.

MENELAUS

They will, they will! Finally the gods allow
an end to all my troubles. Wait, though. Who
will you say informed you that I drowned?

HELEN

> You! You will tell them that you were the lone
> survivor and saw Atreus' son go down.   1110

MENELAUS

> Yes! And my being clad in shreds of sail
> also bears witness to this shipwreck tale.

HELEN

> There is a use for everything, you see.
> How quickly joy can come from misery!

MENELAUS

> Venture now into the house with you
> or sit still on the tomb—which should I do?

HELEN

> Better stay here. In case he should attack,
> you have your sword; the tomb is at your back.
> I have to go inside and cut my hair
> and change this spotless linen robe I wear   1120
> for black, and scratch my face with bloody nails.
> This is the crisis, for I see the scales
> equally balanced. I will die, I know,
> if I'm caught plotting. Otherwise, I go
> home with my husband, having saved him too.
>
> O Hera, you who share the bed of Zeus,
> have mercy, we implore you. Pity us,
> we beg, our arms outstretched toward the dome
> of heaven, where you make your deathless home
> among the stars' embroideries. And you,   1130
> Aphrodite, who won your prize through me,
> have you not tortured me sufficiently,
> lending if not my body then my name
> to barbarians?
>   Let me die at home,
> if you've determined that I have to die.

Passion, deceit, and every kind of lie,
love potions, family murders—all such stuff
is your delight. Have you not had enough?
Given a modicum of sanity,
you'd be the goddess sweetest to humanity.   1140
(Exit.)

CHORUS
Nightingale high in a tree so green,
come and sing me a song of pain,
a song for Helen and all the men
slaughtered when Greeks destroyed the town,
a song for Paris' rapid flight
and the fateful wedding night,
a song of sword and spear and shield
and heroes sent to the underworld.
Widows wailed and cut their hair
in silent houses—no men were there.   1150

Divine or not divine
or something in between:
what mortal man
after long scrutiny
of the mind of god
could undertake to see
and then come back
and somehow make it plain,
all he had understood—
with what impossible luck   1160
leaping the mortal gap?

A song for the swan who was Helen's sire,
having come to Leda with his desire.
So Helen is the child of Zeus,
yet they attack her all through Greece:
Unjust! Faithless!
Godless! Traitress!

But I can see
no clarity
anywhere among mankind.   1170
Only the mind
of god, I find,
is clear, is free.

And why, oh why do heroes try
to prove their excellence in war?
As if a spear could guard a man
from the onslaught of life's pain.
Strife will be with us forever
if blood is the criterion,
from our cities vanish never,   1180
just as it ruined Priam's town,
Helen, discord over you.
Once it still could be
cured, this malady
of hatred, violence, war—
no more, no more.
Disaster's bolt has struck;
the city walls burn black.
And why, we wonder. Why?
There is no answer. Only misery.   1190
(Enter Theoclymenus, returning from the hunt.)

THEOCLYMENUS
Tomb of my father Proteus, greetings! I
interred you by the gate, and this is why:
entering or exiting my house
I speak to you—I, Theoclymenus.
Attendants! Hounds and hunting gear—now go,
take these inside where they belong.
                                    I know
I'm far too lenient. I should execute
all wrongdoers at once, yet I do not.
And now I'm told some Greek has landed here

who's managed to escape my guards so far—   1200
either a spy or looking for a chance
to abduct Helen. Let me get my hands
on him—he dies.
                        Aha! Am I too late?
My fears borne out—the tomb, the empty seat—
Helen's been carried off, without a doubt!
Open the gates and let the horses out,
prepare the chariots! Let my bride not be
stolen without a strong response from me.

But wait—the ones I was about to chase
stand by the gate. They haven't left this place.   1210

(to Helen)

Why have you changed from the white dress you wore
into black? Why have you cut your hair?
Your cheeks are wet with tears. Why do you weep?
Do nightmares come upon you in your sleep
and terrify you? Or perhaps you've had
some word from home. If so, the news is bad.

HELEN

O king—you see I use the word at last—
I am destroyed. My life, my hopes—all lost.

THEOCLYMENUS

Where does the disaster lie? What's wrong?

HELEN

How can I say it? Menelaus is gone.   1220
He's dead.

THEOCLYMENUS

            I can't rejoice in what you say,
though I confess it does bode well for me.
How did you learn the news? Did Theonoe
tell you?

HELEN

> Both she and one who saw him die.

THEOCLYMENUS

> There's someone here then who can verify
> this fact?

HELEN

> There is. And may he go where I
> wish to go.

THEOCLYMENUS

> Who and where? I must be clear.

HELEN

> He's skulking at the tomb—right over there.

THEOCLYMENUS

> By Apollo, what a ragged sight!

HELEN

> Alas, I think my own poor husband might   1230
> look just like this man.

THEOCLYMENUS

> Where's the fellow from?
> And what might be the country he calls home?

HELEN

> Greek—an Achaean from my husband's crew.

THEOCLYMENUS

> And he reports your husband died. But how?

HELEN

> Midst the wild waves he drowned—most pitiful.

THEOCLYMENUS
> And over what wild waters did he sail?

HELEN
> He was washed up on Libya's rocky shore.

THEOCLYMENUS
> Why did this man not drown, since he was there?

HELEN
> Sometimes the nobodies have all the luck.

THEOCLYMENUS
> When he came here, where did he leave the wreck?   1240

HELEN
> Wherever he has left it, let it rot!
> The ship, I mean, but Menelaus not.

THEOCLYMENUS
> Your husband has already met his doom.
> This fellow here: in what ship did he come?

HELEN
> He says some soldiers took him on their way.

THEOCLYMENUS
> What of that ghostly thing that went to Troy
> in your place?

HELEN
> That cloudy shape, you mean?
> Dissolved in air as if it had not been.

THEOCLYMENUS
> Oh Troy and Priam, ruined all in vain!

HELEN
I had my portion of the Trojans' pain.   1250

THEOCLYMENUS
Did this man leave your husband's corpse to lie
or did he hold a funeral decently?

HELEN
Left him unburied, to my deep despair.

THEOCLYMENUS
So this is why you've cut your golden hair.

HELEN
He's dear to me. He always will be dear,
wherever he may be.

THEOCLYMENUS
                              Are you sincere,
I wonder, weeping so at this disaster?

HELEN
Would it be easy to deceive your sister?

THEOCLYMENUS
Hardly. Well then, what next? Will you stay
on the tomb?

HELEN

Oh, can't you let us be?   1260
Don't mock at me. And leave the dead alone.

THEOCLYMENUS

Yet you shunned me in favor of your own
husband.

HELEN

No more. Let the wedding preparations
begin.

THEOCLYMENUS

How fortunate I had the patience
to wait so many years! I'm happy now.

HELEN

I think we should forget the past, we two.

THEOCLYMENUS

And on what terms should our agreement be?
One good turn deserves another.

HELEN

Make
peace. Do not be angry, for my sake.

THEOCLYMENUS

There goes our quarrel—may it fly away!   1270

HELEN

If you are indeed the friend you say,
I beg you by these knees—

THEOCLYMENUS

What can it be
that as a suppliant you ask of me?

HELEN

    Permission to bury my husband, who is dead.

THEOCLYMENUS

    A burial in absentia? For a shade
    you'd hold a funeral?

HELEN

                  For those lost at sea,
    Greek custom is to honor them this way.

THEOCLYMENUS

    Describe the ritual. How does it proceed?

HELEN

    They hold a funeral with an empty shroud.

THEOCLYMENUS

    Then build a tomb wherever in this land   1280
    you wish.

HELEN

           No, you do not quite understand.
    Rituals for the drowned work differently.

THEOCLYMENUS

    How? All these Greek ways are strange to me.

HELEN

    We must set sail upon the open sea
    with all the dead man needs.

THEOCLYMENUS

              I will supply
    provisions for the dead. What do you need?

HELEN *(gesturing to Menelaus)*
> He knows, not I. Till now my luck's been good.

THEOCLYMENUS *(to Menelaus)*
> Stranger, it's welcome tidings you have brought.

MENELAUS
> Welcome? Not to me, nor to the dead.

THEOCLYMENUS
> How do you bury people lost at sea?   1290

MENELAUS
> According to what each one's wealth may be.

THEOCLYMENUS
> For her sake, say however much you need.

MENELAUS
> First, for the gods below blood must be shed.

THEOCLYMENUS
> Blood from what beast? You tell me; I'll provide.

MENELAUS
> Do so—the animal you may decide.

THEOCLYMENUS
> Custom here dictates a bull or horse.

MENELAUS
> And you'll select a perfect one, of course.

THEOCLYMENUS
> Naturally. Our herds have many such.

MENELAUS
> Next you must equip a funeral couch
> although no body lies upon the bier.   1300

THEOCLYMENUS
> Granted. What else by way of funeral gear?

MENELAUS
> Bronze panoply. He was a fighting man.

THEOCLYMENUS
> I'll supply arms worthy of Pelops' line.

MENELAUS
> And produce, the earth's fruits—bring these to me.

THEOCLYMENUS
> How will you throw all this into the sea?

MENELAUS
> A ship and rowers you must furnish me.

THEOCLYMENUS
> How far from land will this ship have to sail?

MENELAUS
> Until its wake is scarcely visible.

THEOCLYMENUS
> I'm puzzled; please explain this ritual.

MENELAUS
> We fear pollution washing with the tide   1310
> back to our shores.

THEOCLYMENUS

> I see. I will provide
a swift Phoenician ship.

MENELAUS

> This is nobly done;
I thank you on behalf of the dead man.

THEOCLYMENUS

> Are you not able to perform alone
these rites? Must Helen go?

MENELAUS

> They must be done
by mother, wife, or child of the dead man.

THEOCLYMENUS

> Burying her husband is her duty, then?

MENELAUS

> Call it an honor to the dead we owe.

THEOCLYMENUS

> I want a pious wife, so let her go.
Take from my house whatever gear you need   1320
to celebrate this ritual for the dead.
Be responsive to what she demands,
and you'll not leave my realm with empty hands.
In payment for the good news you have brought
I'll clothe and feed you, so that you need not
return to Greece in such a sorry state.

(to Helen)

> And you, poor woman—don't wear yourself out
mourning what can't be changed. It was his fate.
Your husband's dead; he can't come back to life.

MENELAUS

    Your task now is to be a loving wife   1330
    to your new husband. Let the old one go.
    Fortune has worked out for the best for you.
    And if I ever manage to get home
    to Greece, I'll put a stop to all this blame.
    No hint of scandal will besmirch your name
    as long as you're the wife you ought to be.

HELEN

    My husband never will find fault with me,
    I promise you. You'll be there; you will see.
    But now, poor traveler, will you not go
    inside and bathe and change? I'll not delay   1340
    to do you all the kindness that I may.
    You'll best serve Menelaus' memory
    by taking everything you need from me.
(Exeunt.)

CHORUS

    The Mother of Gods went rushing once
    through woods, over rivers, and out to sea,
    searching, searching frantically
    for her daughter who had been taken,
    the virgin whose name may not be spoken.
    Lions and tigers pulled her chariot;
    cymbals clashed with a noise like war   1350
    as she went to find her stolen daughter.
    Artemis, arrows in her quiver,
    and bright-eyed Athena in full armor
    swooped down like a double storm
    to help their sister. But from his throne
    Zeus looked serenely down
    and chose another doom.

Wearily wandering on and on, the mother,
trying to track the hidden thief of her daughter,
having climbed Ida's snowy peak, lay prone,   1360
grieving, exhausted, on the icy stones.
Never again, she vowed, would earth turn green,
never would harvests come
to feed each generation.
So beasts began to die—
not by sacrifice but by starvation.
No one could make an offering at the altar;
she parched, she paralyzed the bubbling water
of every spring in grief for her lost daughter.

She'd blighted every festival   1370
when finally Zeus saw he must call
the Muses and the Graces all
to soothe her burning pain
with dancing and with song.
First Aphrodite took
the cymbals and the leather drum
at whose hypnotic beat
Demeter smiled and reached out for the flute,
lulled by its throbbing note.

But Helen, Helen, Helen,   1380
what fiery monster ate
a hole in your bedroom wall,
arousing all the Mother Goddess' hate?
Did you not sacrifice?
Did you not worship her?
Ah, fawnskins, twining ivy, strands of vines,
and aromatic pines,
and tambourines that rattle in the air!
Ah, the Maenads who twirl and toss their hair
out of their eyes all night   1390
(eyes that are open, gleaming in the moonlight)

as they dance for the Mother.
But Helen, you—
you worship your own
beauty all alone,
in a vacuum.

HELEN

Friends, inside the house all's well so far.
Proteus' daughter, our co-conspirator,
out of kindness to me will not tell
her brother that my lord's alive and well   1400
and here in Egypt: no, she claims he's died
and nevermore will look upon the light.
My husband meanwhile manages beautifully.
The very arms he swore to throw away
into the sea, both shield and spear, he has
put on, as if to do the dead some grace.
But that's deceptive; he is armed for war.
He'll kill a thousand enemies or more
and set up trophies for them when we go.
I've changed his sailor's rags, as you can see,   1410
and dressed him in fresh clothes. I've washed him, too,
in river water—a bath long overdue.

No more. The man's approaching who commands
my marriage, holds my future in his hands—
or so he thinks. I'm mum. Be silent too—
one day it will be my turn to help you.

THEOCLYMENUS

The stranger gave your orders. Hurry, slaves!
Carry these offerings destined for the waves.
(to Helen)
Helen, I say this to you even though
it may offend you: stay here. Do not go.   1420
You'll honor your late husband just the same

whether you're at the funeral or at home.
I'm fearful lest a sudden surge of grief
convinces you to throw away your life.
You mourn your former lord excessively;
for love of him you'll leap into the sea.

HELEN

New husband, let me answer what you've said.
I came a virgin to my first lord's bed.
Decency requires that though he's dead,
I honor him. And yes, I loved him too—   1430
so much that with him willingly I'd die.
And yet what good would dying with him do?
No, it is better if you let me go
myself to do these burial rites. So may
the gods grant you whatever I desire,
as well as, for his help, this stranger here.
Having helped me, and Menelaus too,
you'll find in me the perfect bride for you.
I know that henceforth all things will be well.
My cup of gratitude will be quite full   1440
once you provide a ship so we can sail.

THEOCLYMENUS

Get a Sidonian ship with fifty oars;
make certain that she is equipped with rowers.

HELEN

The man who organized the funeral rite
is also the ship's captain, is he not?

THEOCLYMENUS

He is. My sailors must report to him.

HELEN

Can you announce this order one more time
so it is clear to all?

THEOCLYMENUS
                    Of course I can—
two or three times, if such is your command.

HELEN
    Blessings upon you—and on what I plan.   1450

THEOCLYMENUS
    You'll ruin your complexion, sobbing so.

HELEN
    This day will show my gratitude to you.

THEOCLYMENUS
    The dead mean nothing. All these tears are vain.

HELEN
    The dead and living both are in my mind.

THEOCLYMENUS
    You'll find that I'm a husband equally
    good as Menelaus.

HELEN
                    Certainly—
    who said you weren't? What I most need now
    is fair fortune.

THEOCLYMENUS
                As to that, you'll see
    I'll·treat you kindly if you're kind to me.

HELEN
    I need no tutoring in loyalty.   1460
    Love of my friends comes naturally to me.

THEOCLYMENUS
    Do you desire that I accompany you?

HELEN
>   Oh no, my lord. That's work for slaves to do.

THEOCLYMENUS
>   Very well. All Greek ceremonies I
>   omit, for Menelaus did not die
>   within these walls, and so my house is pure.
>   Now let the wedding presents be brought here,
>   let songs and celebrations fill the air,
>   let blessings echo through the countryside:
>   *Happy the man with Helen as his bride!*   1470
> (to Menelaus)
>   You, stranger, go; and an the sea confer
>   these offerings for the man who once was her
>   husband. Then swiftly bring my bride back here.
>   Feast at our wedding. Then you have a choice:
>   to go home or stay here in happiness.
> (Exit.)

MENELAUS
>   Zeus, you are father of the gods, and wise.
>   Look down; release us from our miseries.
>   And as in our despair we drag along,
>   a single touch from you can cheer us on.
>   Of troubles we have had enough before.   1480
>   I've often called upon the gods to hear
>   my ups and downs; but I deserve no more
>   woes! I only wish to stand up straight
>   and to move freely. Grant me merely this;
>   then all my life henceforth is happiness.
> (Exit.)

CHORUS
>   Mother of oars   the sea is your lover
>   Phoenician galley   skim swiftly over
>   the gray green breakers   wind at your back

dancing dolphins   daughter of Ocean
pull at the oars   sailors, sailors   1490
over the breakers   skimming, skimming
till Helen can touch   her land once more
by the swirling river   again can see
the temple dances   and festivals
and can embrace   Hermione
her virgin daughter   whose bridal torch
is still unlit.

Give us wings and we would fly like a flock of birds over the
          plains
leaving Libya's winter rains,
led by their commander's cry   1500
over the desert, keeping pace
with clouds that scurry through the sky,
cleaving a path through the Pleiades,
past Orion's midnight glow.
Cry aloud at the river: *Oh,*
Menelaus has fought and won!
Menelaus is coming home!

With horse-drawn chariots hurry, come,
Castor and Pollux, Tyndareus' twins,
under the stardome, heaven-dwellers,   1510
come here quickly and save your sister.
Over the ocean's salty swell
and dark blue crests of foam that spill,
come on the wings of heaven's wind
and purge the rumor from every mind,
wipe out that persistent lie
about where lovely Helen lay,
the lie that blames her for the war
although she never went to Troy—
never set foot in Apollo's towered city.   1520
(*Enter Messenger.*)

MESSENGER
>   I'm loth, O king, to meet you here. Alas,
>   you must be first to hear some dreadful news.

THEOCLYMENUS
>   What?

MESSENGER
>   You should seek some other lady's hand.
>   Helen has departed from this land.

THEOCLYMENUS
>   Has she grown wings, so swiftly to take flight,
>   or did she walk?

MESSENGER
>   She sailed, and her escort
>   was Menelaus—he who only now
>   reported Menelaus' death to you.

THEOCLYMENUS
>   Worse and worse. But wait—what transportation
>   could take them hence? It strains imagination.   1530

MESSENGER
>   Exactly that which you yourself bestowed.
>   The ship in which they sailed is being rowed
>   by your own men. And there you have the fact.

THEOCLYMENUS
>   I want to know how they devised this act!
>   How one strength could subdue so large a crew
>   I can't imagine. You were with them too?

MESSENGER
>   When Zeus' daughter left the palace here
>   and was escorted down to the sea shore

daintily pacing, cleverly she cried
in mourning for her husband—who'd not died,   1540
you understand, but walked right by her side.
Arriving at your shipyard, we picked out
a brand new fifty-oared Sidonian boat
with rowing benches. Every sailor knew—
his place: mast, benches, oars, and tiller too,
all were being manned. But in the midst
of all these tasks, some Greeks who'd watched for this
very moment now approached the shore.
They'd sailed with Menelaus before—
handsome but salt-stained, weather-beaten men.   1550
And when he saw them, Atreus' son
hailed them with a pity he put on:
"Long-suffering sailors, from what ship and how,
escaping shipwreck, do you come here now?
And can you help us bury Atreus' son
Menelaus in an empty tomb?
Chief mourner is Tyndareus' daughter here."
At this, the sailors, feigning many a tear,
picked up the offerings and approached the ship.
By now we sensed that something might be up.   1560
We whispered to each other "What a crowd!"
Yet we were quiet, knowing what you'd said.
You had commanded that we should obey
the stranger; but destruction came that way.
We stowed our baggage quickly; it was light.
Only the bull, refusing to set foot
upon the narrow gangplank, simply stood
and bellowed, rolled his eyes and arched his back.
Horns lowered, he was threatening to attack
whoever touched him. Helen's husband cried   1570
"You veterans of Troy, get him inside
the way Greeks do it; hoist his body high
on your strong shoulders, and then make him lie
under the prow"—and here he drew his sword.
"He is the sacrifice we owe the dead."

The men moved forward, heeding these commands,
and seized the bull, and raised it in their hands.
Menelaus stroked its neck, persuaded
it to be still.

           The ship was now all loaded.
Helen, having got her slender feet   1580
down the ladder, took a central seat
with Menelaus (dead, supposedly)
beside her. All the others equally
to left and right took places on the deck,
sitting in pairs, a sword beneath each cloak.
The boatswain's shout was echoed by the roar
of waves. Now we were neither near the shore
nor too far from it when our steersman said:
"Far enough? Or should we move ahead,
stranger? We obey and you command."   1590
"Far enough." And gripping in his hand
his sword, he went to sacrifice the bull.
Of the dead man he spoke no syllable,
but cut the throat and prayed: "Poseidon, you
ocean dweller, and your daughters too,
you Nereids, safely may you now convey
my wife and me to Nauplia, away
from Egypt."
           Bull's blood flowed into the sea,
auspiciously for him.
              "Tricks! Treachery!"
someone shouted. "Sail to Nauplia? Why?   1600
No, we should sail for home immediately!"

But Atreus' son, not moving from the side
of the dead bull, to his companions cried
"Flower of Greece, come on! Recall our plan:
kill every barbarian you can!"
And then our steersman to your men in turn:

"Come on, seize weapons, anything you can—
pry loose a bench, break off a piece of oar,
drench these cursed strangers' heads with gore!"

They all sprang up; each seized some stick of wood   1610
to fight with, and the deck soon ran with blood,
the Greeks being armed with swords. And Helen stood
shouting exhortations from the stem:
"Come on, you Greeks! Let these barbarians learn
what glorious warriors you were in Troy!"

Some men fell fighting; you could see them lie
there on the deck. Some kept their feet. But he,
Menelaus, wherever he could see
his men in trouble, rushed immediately,
sword in hand, to help them; so that we   1620
were finally forced to jump into the sea.
And having driven every single one
of all your men away, he turned again
toward the steersman, urging him "Sail home!
Onward to Greece!"
                    The sails were up, the wind
favorable—they left us far behind.
They're gone forever.

                    I survived somehow,
clinging to the anchor; then let go.
A fisherman pulled me struggling from the sea—
here on dry land I tell the news to you.   1630
Nothing is more useful in this life
than a shrewd sense of what not to believe.

CHORUS
    My lord, I never dreamed this man could be
    thus hiding here, unknown to you and me.

THEOCLYMENUS

Caught in a web of women's treachery!
My marriage has escaped! Could I pursue
these traitors, I might catch them even so.
But now my anger starts to fix upon
my treacherous sister. Though she saw the man,
learned Menelaus was here, did she warn me?   1640
No! So much, then, for her prophecy.
She'll never fool another man that way.

CHORUS

King, where are you rushing? Toward what
act of violence?

THEOCLYMENUS

                    Stand aside! Do not
block my path, for justice leads the way.

CHORUS

You're bent on crime. I cannot let you go—

THEOCLYMENUS

A slave would rule his master?

CHORUS

                              For the best.

THEOCLYMENUS

Release me now, or it will be the worse
for you.

CHORUS

            I can't release you. For I must—

THEOCLYMENUS

Slay my evil sister—

CHORUS

No—kind and good!   1650

THEOCLYMENUS

She who betrayed me—

CHORUS

Doing what she should:
an act of justice.

THEOCLYMENUS

gave away my bride—

CHORUS

to the right man.

THEOCLYMENUS

What is *his* right beside
mine?

CHORUS

He first received her from her father.

THEOCLYMENUS

But twisting, turning fortune brought her hither.

CHORUS

And then took her away again.

THEOCLYMENUS

You should
not judge me.

CHORUS

Since I recognize what's good,
I've every right to.

THEOCLYMENUS
                    I am not king, then,
    but subject to another?

CHORUS
                    You're king when
    you honor what is just, and only then.   1660

THEOCLYMENUS
    I think you want to die.

CHORUS
                    I do not care
    if you kill me. But while I live, beware:
    never will I let you harm your sister.
    Many a slave dies nobly for his master.
(Enter aloft the Dioscuri.)

DIOSCURI
    Your rage confuses you. Regain control,
    Lord Theoclymenus! On you we call,
    we sons of Zeus and Leda—twins, and born
    brothers of Helen, she who now is gone.
    You mourn the loss of what could never be,
    a hopeless marriage. Nor does Theonoe,   1670
    Nereus' daughter and your sister, do
    you wrong. She heeds the gods—her father too.
    Until this very hour fate ordained
    that Helen here within your halls remained.
    But when at the destruction of Troy
    she lent the gods her name, it could not be.
    She'll now be once again her husband's wife;
    she sails home to resume her married life.

    Stop threatening your sister with your sword.
    All her motivation is good.   1680

Since being deified by Zeus, we two
would have saved our sister long ago,
but our strength was no match for destiny
and for the gods who wanted this to be.
Thus much to you.
           To Helen now we say:
the wind sits in your sail, so sail away
home with your husband, while, escorting you,
we ride the breakers bareback all the way
home to Sparta. When your life is done,
your status will be changed; you'll be divine   1690
as we are, and with us will share libations
from mankind, with all sorts of celebrations;
Zeus wills it so.
           When Hermes from the sky
first reached down and stole your shape away
to keep you safe from Paris, you were placed
on an isle that seems to guard the coast
and which will be called Helen evermore,
since it received you from your native shore.
For wandering Menelaus, fate decrees
eternity on the island of the blessed.   1700
To noble persons thus the gods are good;
greater pain's suffered by the multitude.

THEOCLYMENUS

Leda and Zeus' sons, on Helen's behalf
I hereby lay aside all former strife.
Nor will I do my sister any harm.
Let Helen—the gods will it—sail for home.
You're fortunate in being kin to one
so virtuous and so wise at the same time.
Know that you both ought to take delight
in her nobility—no common trait   1710
in womankind. And now, hail and farewell!
Blessings be upon you as you sail!

CHORUS
    What is divine
    is multiform.
    What we await
    may remain incomplete.
    What seemed implausible
    god may make possible.

    And so it was
    in this case.   1720
(The end)

Electra

Translated by
Elizabeth Seydel Morgan

Just two days before I was to leave for my first visit to Greece, David Slavitt called to invite me to join the more than three dozen poets translating Greek drama for the Penn Series. "My" play would be the *Electra* of Euripides. I thought he had the wrong number. "I don't know Greek," I said; "And I know very little about that play." "You're a poet," he said. "That's what we're after." When I told him that by coincidence I would be in Mycenae the following week, he said, "Perfect. Think about my offer while you're there."

He must have known. I could say I made the decision to accept David's challenge when I walked through the Lion Gate and stood on the excavated mosaic floor of the Palace of Mycenae. I had the feeling that historic places can sometimes evoke—that I was standing in the exact posture, gazing down at the exact sunbaked September landscape, as another woman had done when this had been the floor of an outer room of the bronze-age citadel. I liked to think that woman was Electra.

I thought of the young Electra at the end of the Trojan War, aware of her mother's treachery, looking as I was now across the Argive plain toward the sea—yearning for, and dreading, her father's homecoming. I knew I wanted to know more about her and the enduring mythology of her Mycenean family. And what better way (not "having Greek") than to go line by line, word by word, attempting to comprehend not only Electra but one great dramatist's interpretation of her story.

So there in Greece, I took out my notebook and the 1912 Loeb edition of Euripides I had brought, turned to Electra's first speech—and tried to re-fashion "I . . . wail to the broad welkin for my sire." But then I didn't know what a "welkin" was. (Eventually I have Electra send her lament "for my father / into the endless skies.")

I didn't think of this as translating—I still don't—and I felt that no matter how many English versions I read, how much background reading I did, however sensitive my poetic antennae might be, I couldn't take on this project without the help of a classicist who could read Euripides' words. And there he was, guiding our Washington & Lee University group through Delphi, Epidaurus, Mycenae: Dr. Christopher Pelling, Oxford Fellow and Praelector in Classics.

When Dr. Pelling offered his assistance on the project, I had no concept of what he was willing, or had time, to do. But a year later I could say he went over every single line that I refashioned. In eighteen mailings we called "Lots" (I sent nine sections of the play to him at Oxford; he mailed them back fully annotated to Virginia), he kept me on the narrow and unflowery path of Euripides' original poetry. A Pelling note would assess some poetic metaphor I imagined or read in a translation: "lovely, but unfortunately not said by Euripides."

Thus one of the lessons the Pelling Lots taught me over time is that Euripides was more often than not a plainspoken poet. Only his choral odes are filled with fanciful imagery and figurative language; neither they nor the lyrical lamenting of the self-conscious Electra can be considered the "style" of Euripides. And bombast is found only in the words of bombastic speakers; as Shakespeare (2000 years later) puts now-famous precepts into the mouth of hypocritical Polonius, Euripides gives the callow Orestes a stream of pronouncements on judging character. But when it's time for the core Orestes to step forth, he speaks with heartbreaking simplicity: "What are we going to do? Kill our own mother?"

Euripides' unadorned diction for truth is also found in Clytemnestra's last defense, "I'm not so very glad, daughter, for every deed I've done," and Electra's stark sentence to her weeping brother after the murder: "I am to blame."

Chris Pelling filled his notes with facts, intertextual references (which sent me to Homer, Aeschylus, and Sophocles), a little Greek (which sent me first to the alphabet, then to the dictionary)—and bright spots of humor. His notes were a learning experience for me. Here is one of hundreds:

"line 265: ανδρων [andrōn] doubles as 'husbands' and 'men'. Just 'Women are friends of their men . . . '? And 'friends' is the φ word again: φιλος [philos]."

And here, an example of his Brit wit:

"line 20: [you write] 'bloomed into maidenhood': well, marriage-ability, really. The Greeks had this idea that females were born virgins (παρθενοι) [parthenoi]. But maybe they do things differently in Richmond."

Obviously, I changed line 20!

I came away from my year's association with Euripides with many new *philoi*: among them, Chris Pelling's colleagues at University College and his wife Margaret; David Kovacs, classicist and translator at University of Virginia (who e-mailed me his introduction to his new Loeb *Electra*); Elaine Terranova, poet and translator for this Penn Series, and David Slavitt, my persuasive editor whom I finally met in Philadelphia. (That phi-word again!) And I guess it isn't too odd to say that the new friend I feel closest to is Euripides himself.

Many of these new friends have books I enjoyed and learned from—as I did from the writings of Edith Hamilton, D. J. Conacher, Oliver Taplin, Bernard Knox, G. M. A. Grube, Shirley A. Barlow, Simon Goldhill, and Ann Michelini. I particularly appreciate Pelling's introducing me to an essay by his colleague Judith Mossman, and to the indispensable prose translation and notes of M. J. Cropp. And naturally I have loved reading other English translations of *Electra* in poetry—after I had given it a try myself. I am certain my final draft owes a debt to Philip Vellacott.[1]

Not only interesting people and books, but unforgettable experiences filled the year I worked on this project: in the fall of '95, seeing my first e-mail from England come across the screen; on a spring visit to Oxford, sitting in the Bodleian Library Reading Room where scholars bend over ancient manuscripts and laptop computers; at University College, hearing

1. For example, *Electra*, Greek with trans. and commentary by M. J. Cropp, intro. by Shirley A. Barlow (Warminster: Aris and Phillips, 1988); *Electra*, trans. Philip Vellacott in *Euripides: Medea and Other Plays* (London: Penguin, 1963); Shirley A. Barlow, *The Imagery of Euripides: A Study in the Dramatic Use of Pictorial Language* (London: Methuen, 1971); D. J. Conacher, *Euripidean Drama: Myth, Theme, and Structure* (Toronto: University of Toronto Press, 1967); Simon Goldhill, *Reading Greek Tragedy* (Cambridge: Cambridge University Press, 1986); G. M. A. Grube, *The Drama of Euripides* (London, 1941; reprint New York: Methuen, 1973); Ann N. Michelini, *Euripides and the Tragic Tradition* (Madison: University of Wisconsin Press, 1987); Oliver Taplin, "Opening Performances: Closing Texts?" *Quarterly Journal of Literary Criticism* 45, 2 (April 1995).

the euphony and rhythms of Euripides' Greek as Dr. Pelling read aloud; at the end of summer watching for the first time Michael Cacoyannis' stunning 1962 film, *Electra*, where Irene Pappas' expressive face and the stark, timeless Mycenean landscape almost replace some of the lost ritual drama of the masked and musical fifth-century performances; writing my first—simple—line of English from Euripides' Greek (not something I could do often, but what a thrill to watch those artful squiggles make a word, make a meaning). And then, in September, almost a year after I began, coming at last to the climax of the drama—the murder of their mother by Orestes and Electra. I am not exaggerating to say that by this point, slowly writing out each line by hand, I felt that I was there—aghast, shaken, implicated in the tragic scene.

Though I came as a stranger to the world of classicists, I am not new to poetry. I can recognize the strategies of poets translating Greek drama into my language, and I know there is no such thing as a literal verse translation. This is especially true of the Loeb edition I was using, with its Victorian metrical embroideries and "poetic" attempts to rhyme the lyric passages. (Arthur Way in the Loeb: "O father Agamemnon, thou art lying / In Hades, thou whose wife devised thou dying"; ll. 122–23.) I found that literal prose translation results in unwieldy branches of English, almost impossible to prune into verse. (Cropp's recent—and highly regarded for accuracy—prose translation has the Chorus leader say in lines 213–14: "With many troubles the Greeks and your own house can reproach Helen, the sister of your mother.") This is typical of the English thickets challenging a contemporary poet.

Eventually I came to translations of other Greek plays by modernist and contemporary poets whose work I know and admire (examples are H.D.'s *Ion*, Robert Lowell's *Oresteia*, Seamus Heany's *Philoctetes*, C. K. Williams' *Bacchae*[2]), and I saw that each poet fits ancient Greek into a structure and diction demanded by the English language and by his or her own time and particular voice. Some poets have clearly adapted the play, making it their

---

2. H. D. (Hilda Doolittle), *Ion: A Play After Euripides* (Redding Ridge, Conn.: Black Swan Books, 1986); Seamus Heaney, *The Cure at Troy: A version of Sophocles' Philoctetes* (New York: Farrar, Straus, Giroux, 1991); Robert Lowell, *The Oresteia of Aeschylus* (New York: Farrar, Straus, Giroux, 1978); C. K. Williams, *The Bacchae of Euripides* (New York: Farrar, Straus, Giroux, 1990).

version; others—as I do—have tried to give each line its original intent with their own poetic vocabulary and ear for rhythms. I was encouraged to discover that several poets are not translating directly from the Greek (Lowell credits Lattimore as his starting point), and heartened to find that many individual poems spun out of a poet's immersion in the classical period. A recent and beautiful example is Seamus Heaney's "Mycenae Lookout." [3]

Three different dramatic characterizations of *Electra*—by Aeschylus, Sophocles, and Euripides—exist today. Their three plays are based on the same story. King Agamemnon had a daughter who adored him. She grew to young adolescence in the palace of Mycenae while he was fighting the Trojan War—and while her mother Clytemnestra was having an affair with his blood rival. When her father returned in triumph, he was murdered by Clytemnestra and Aegisthus, the lover who then usurped the throne. As the years passed, Electra longed for Orestes, her younger brother, who had been living in exile since the murder, to come home and avenge their father's death. In all three plays he does so. In Aeschylus' *Libation Bearers*, Sophocles' *Electra*, and Euripides' *Electra*, Orestes returns to Mycenae, reunites with his sister, and with her encouragement kills Aegisthus and Clytemnestra. But only in Euripides is Electra present—and a participant—in the murder of their mother.

It is my guess that Euripides' unique characterization of his Electra grew out of his imagining her participation in the matricide. Every new twist Euripides brings to the old story, every reinvention of setting, plot, character, goes to creating a young woman who we can believe would and could guide the blade into her mother's neck.

ORESTES
I held my cloak in front of my eyes—
for the final sacrifice—
when I thrust my sword into her throat.

ELECTRA
Yes, and I urged you on,
placed my hand next to yours on the sword. (ll. 1210–14)

The daughter does not hide her eyes behind a cloak.

3. In Heaney, *The Spirit Level* (London: Faber and Faber, 1996).

If we grant that Euripides could have worked backward from this imagined climax, we can better understand his changes to the old story—and to Aeschylus' by-then-familiar version in *The Oresteia*. His first audience must have been surprised from the beginning, for Euripides' invention became apparent to the fifth-century theater-goer, festival-participant actually, from the minute he took his stone seat in the amphitheater. He would have been struck by the oddity of the structure depicted below him on the skene—a house of some kind, rustic, clearly not the exterior of the Mycenean palace where this tragedy was meant to unfold.

All the action of this play will take place before the farmhouse of Electra's peasant husband. Only in Euripides is Electra (which in Greek means unbedded in the sense of unmarried) married but unbedded. Early on we learn that she has been married off by Aegisthus to a poor, older farmer in the hinterlands of Argos—a humble man who believes it would dishonor the house of Agamemnon if he slept with her. We hear in the farmer's monologue that Aegisthus wanted to kill Electra, but that Clytemnestra proposed this less dire way of getting rid of her.

Then we meet Electra and hear her own assessment of her plight; we understand that for this Electra a sexless life of ugly poverty in a remote area is worse than death. For her, no existence could exacerbate her grief for her murdered father more than this one. And it was ordered by her mother and her father's murderer.

Again and again Euripides' Electra reveals to us that she blames her mother not only for taking her father away from her, but for taking away all the trappings that belong to the daughter of Agamemnon. With the new setting, new character (the farmer), and new subplot, Euripides provides an Electra with a plethora of motives for matricide.

In all his plays, Euripides is not content to give his tragic heroes external motivation; he creates psychological motivation as well. So Electra not only has a mother who has stripped her of sexual fulfillment and material luxury (while having plenty of both herself); but Electra also has a psyche—like her mother's—that longs for both. Thus Euripides fuels Electra's burning desire for vengeance for her father's murder with sexual jealousy and materialistic envy. These emotions, as revealed by her own self-pitying words, often supersede her understandable loneliness and grief.

Thus characterized, this Electra is hard to like. But she is fascinating to watch. And fascinating too is Euripides' development of the three other main characters as they play off his conception of the daughter of Agamemnon. Orestes is no longer the brave Homeric exemplar of a son's duty to avenge his father; he is the uncertain younger brother whom Electra must wheedle and shame into murder. Even the expected villainy of Aegisthus and Clytemnestra is skewed by the playwright. When we finally meet them as we move toward the climax, each is presented with some degree of surprisingly ameliorating description or dialogue—which contradicts what Electra has said of them.

In the first half of this play I felt distaste for self-pitying Electra, jejune Orestes, murderous Clytemnestra, and arrogant Aegisthus. But as the drama drew toward its climax, as I worked through its unfolding, I began to feel a certain sympathy for all four of these doomed, ignoble characters. At the very end, no optimistic pronouncement of the god could cancel my terror at the murders and pity for the brother and sister as they part, for their separate exiles, understanding what they have done.

I am convinced now that Euripides planned to jolt his audience out of its easy assumptions about these noble mythic figures by making them unlikable—and then making the question of our admiration for them the least important issue of the drama. Instead, he asks us to understand them.

Cast

PEASANT, poor but honorable Mycenean, married in name to
    Electra
ELECTRA, daughter of Agamemnon
ORESTES, son of Agamemnon
PYLADES, prince of Phocis, friend of Orestes
CHORUS OF ARGIVE WOMEN
OLD MAN, once servant to Agamemnon
MESSENGER, servant to Orestes
CLYTEMNESTRA, wife of Agamemnon
CASTOR and POLYDEUCES (the Dioscuri), sons of Zeus and
    Leda, brothers of Clytemnestra and Helen
NONSPEAKING
    Attendants

*(Dawn, a mountain farm in Mycenae. A peasant emerges from a
cottage and looks toward the plain of Argos.)*

PEASANT

Ah, old Argos . . . Once, King Agamemnon
sailed from these streams of Inachus,
his thousand galleys bound for Troy.
And when he had slain their king Priam
and sacked that glorious Ilian city, he
returned to Argos and filled its lofty shrines
with countless Barbarian treasures.
On foreign soil he triumphed. But once at home,
he fell to his treacherous wife, Clytemnestra,
killed by her guile—and Aegisthus' hand.   10
And so the scepter of Tantalus dropped:
Aegisthus, Thyestes' son, reigns with Agamemnon's
wife, Tyndareus' daughter, now his own.

And what of Orestes, the male child left
when he set sail for Troy—and Electra, the girl?
His father's old tutor stole the son away
to Phocis, gave him to Strophius to nurture,
for Orestes' death was certain at Aegisthus' hand.
But Electra lived within her father's house
until the child bloomed into a maiden   20
and many Grecian princes sought her hand.
Then Aegisthus was afraid she'd bear
a prince's son, who'd grow to seek revenge
for Agamemnon; he confined her in the house,
refusing all her suitors. But still he feared
that somehow she'd conceive a noble's child;
so he made his plan to kill her.
                    It was her mother, cruel
as she is known to be, who saved her from Aegisthus'
hand. She thought her husband's murder had excuse,
but feared her fate for taking her child's life.   30
So then Aegisthus made this plan: he put
a price on Agamemnon's exiled son:
whoever finds and kills him will win gold.
As for Electra, he gave her away—
to me, to be my wife.
                Now, I am from a long line
of Myceneans; I can't be scorned for lack
of noble blood. But I am poor, and poverty
can grind nobility to nothing. So nothing
is what he fears if I'm her husband.
A ranking husband might have stirred   40
the sleeping spirit of just vengeance
and made Aegisthus pay for Agamemnon's death.

But I can swear—Aphrodite as my witness—
that I have not dishonored her. She is a virgin.
It would be an outrage and my shame, for one
of my low state to take to bed the daughter of

a king. And I mourn for Orestes, my kinsman now
in name, if ever he gets back to Argos—
how he would feel about her wretched marriage.
To anyone who says that I'm a fool   50
not to touch the virgin I've brought home,
tell him he's the foolish one for judging
what is right by his low standards.
(Electra enters with a water jar on her head.)

ELECTRA

Out into the night, the black-winged nurse
of the golden stars, to the river-feeding spring,
to fill this jar I bear upon my head.
Not that I've sunk to doing chores of slaves,
but I'll show the gods Aegisthus' tyranny
and send my lamentation for my father
into the endless skies.
                        My own mother, Tyndareus' evil child,   60
threw me out of the house to make Aegisthus happy,
and gave Orestes' and my inheritance
to the sons they bred together.

PEASANT

Why do you work for me so hard, poor girl,
though you were raised as royalty?
You won't even stop when I tell you to.

ELECTRA

You're a friend as valuable as the gods
for not flaunting your advantage over me.
It is the best of luck when victims of fortune
find such a healer as I've found in you.   70
So I should, as long as I have strength, help
lighten your load and share your work—
even though you haven't asked me. You have
enough work in the fields; I'm the one

who should keep our house. It is good
to come in from work to an ordered home.

PEASANT

Go on, then, if that's what you think—
the springs are not really so far from our halls.
At dawn I'll drive my team to the field. No one,
though he prays to gods all night and day,   80
can make a living without labor.

(Peasant and Electra exit; Orestes and Pylades enter.)

ORESTES

Pylades, I count you first of all in loyalty
as friend and host. Alone of all my friends,
you have supported me, knowing how
Aegisthus has abused me . . . Aegisthus.
He killed my father—he and my demonic mother—
The mysteries of the god at Delphi
direct me here to Argos to pay those murderers
back with murder.
                        No one knows I'm here.
Tonight I visited my father's tomb,   90
I cut off locks of hair to offer
with my tears, then poured out on the altar
the sacrificial sheep's blood.
No despot's spy could see me in that dark.
So far I haven't gone inside their walls,
but come here to the border for two reasons:
I need a quick escape if I am recognized,
and I'm searching for my sister—a maiden,
I've been told, no longer, but married now—
to learn what's going on behind the walls   100
and gain her help in plotting my revenge.

Now Dawn's eyes open on the night;
let's leave this path and wait,
then stop some passerby—

some fieldhand or a serving woman—
who may know if my sister lives near here.

Look—there I see a slavegirl now—
see the water jar on her cropped head?—
Crouch down, Pylades. When she walks up
we may overhear her say   110
something we came here to know.
(Electra re-enters.)

ELECTRA
    Faster, I must walk faster,
    even while I'm weeping.
    I am Agamemnon's child,
    but horrible to say
    that daughter of Tyndareus,
    the vile and hated Clytemnestra,
    is my mother.
                    The people of this city
    call me "pitiful Electra."
    I hate my life, my days of toil,   120
    a life with nothing to console me.
    Father, father Agamemnon—you lie
    in the house of Hades, murdered by Aegisthus
    and the woman who shared your bed.

    Oh raise again the same lament!
    There's some relief in these wet tears.

    Faster, I must walk faster,
    even while I'm weeping.
    Where are you, Brother?
    What city did you wander to?   130
    What home—while your sister,
    left in Father's house,
    wept in grief as I do now?

Where are you! Come save me
from this anguish, this pain—
Zeus! O Zeus!—Come and avenge
the hated bloodshed of my father:
Bring those wanderer's feet to shore in Argos!

Take this pitcher from my head—
I'll meet dawn's light   140
with dark laments for my lost father.
My screams will penetrate the grave
and find you, Father, down in those
dark hallways of the dead.
I cry down to you day after day,
my cheeks blooded
by my own nails, my head
bruised by my own hands,
my hair cut off to mourn your death.
Ah, beat my head and wail   150
in grief—like the swan's
wild sound by the river banks,
its anguished trumpet call
to its beloved father, killed
in the tricky mesh of the snare,
so over you, my father,
the wild sound of your child
over the bed where you lie
cleansed by water in that last bath.
Oh cruel the edges of the axe   160
that dripped with your red blood.
Oh cruel the day you sailed from Troy
to the plot at home awaiting you.
Were you greeted by your wife
with a victor's garland?
With ribboned wreaths? Oh, no!
With a sharpened two-edged blade
all for Aegisthus' filthy love.
(*Chorus enters.*)

CHORUS
> Electra, Agamemnon's child,
> I have come to your farmhouse   170
> to tell the message from Mycenae
> brought down to us today from one
> who drinks milk on the vineless mountain:
>
> Argos proclaims three days from now
> a holy feast for Hera
> and every maiden will join
> the dance to pay her homage.

ELECTRA
> Dear friends, I cannot think
> of festivals. It is not for finery
> nor golden bracelets that my heart races.   180
> How could I lead the dance of Argive maidens,
> keeping time with grace and rhythm
> to those intricate, braided steps?
> No, not when all I do
> is cry, through the night and every day.
> Look at what was once my shining hair.
> Look at my gown in filthy rags.
> Are these fitting for a princess?
> Agamemnon's daughter?
> For the conquered Troy   190
> who remembers him in nightmares?

CHORUS
> The Goddess must not be neglected.
> Come, I'll lend you a finely woven robe
> and jewels to set its beauty shining.
> You must worship the gods;
> these tears of yours will do nothing
> to bring your enemies low,
> It is not with constant moaning
> but revering gods with prayers
> that you will win fair weather, my child.   200

ELECTRA

No god hears the prayers
of Electra in despair. No god
saw the sacrifices flaming
on my father's altars long ago.
Oh, no hope for the dead to return!
Or for the living to come back home!
My brother wanders foreign lands;
the son of a hero, landless here,
while I am barely sheltered by a cabin
among the mountain crags—outcast   210
from my father's castle, exiled to misery.
And all this time, my mother lies
in a blood-stained bed,
married to her partner in murder.

CHORUS

What troubles to Greece and to your house
Your mother's sister set in motion!
(Orestes and Pylades approach.)

ELECTRA

O friends! I'll have to end my
lamentation—for look—strange men
move from the bushes toward my house—
Quick! Run down the path,   220
I'll dash inside—they're dangerous!

ORESTES *(intercepting her)*
Wait, poor girl. Don't be afraid of me.

ELECTRA

Apollo! I beg you—I don't want to die!

ORESTES *(extending his hand)*
Apollo, may I only kill my enemies.

ELECTRA

Get away! You have no right to touch me.

ORESTES

There is no one I have more right to touch.

ELECTRA

Why, then, do you stop me armed with a sword?

ORESTES

Stay and listen, and you will soon agree.

ELECTRA

I have no choice, I am yours.

ORESTES

I've come to bring you news of your brother.   230

ELECTRA

O my friend! My friend! Is he alive?

ORESTES

He is alive. That's my good news.

ELECTRA

Bless you. These are the sweetest words.

ORESTES

His life is blessing to us both.

ELECTRA

Where is the poor man in wretched exile?

ORESTES

He's a citizen of nowhere. An outcast.

ELECTRA

Oh, no! Tell me he's not starving.

ORESTES

He has food, but an exile is helpless.

ELECTRA

What is the message you've brought to me?

ORESTES

He asks if you're alive, where and how you live.   240

ELECTRA

You can see my dry skin . . . how thin I am—

ORESTES

So wasted by grief that I could cry myself—

ELECTRA

My hair shaved off—

ORESTES

In mourning for your brother's fate, your father's death?

ELECTRA

I love no one more than those two men.

ORESTES

And doesn't your brother love you as much?

ELECTRA

His is an absent, not a present love.

ORESTES

Why do you live here so far from the city?

ELECTRA

> Stranger, I've been married off—an arranged death.

ORESTES

> To one of the Myceneans? Oh, your brother—   250

ELECTRA

> Not to a man my father hoped to give me.

ORESTES

> Tell me . . . so I can explain it to your brother.

ELECTRA

> I live a long way from Argos—in this house.

ORESTES

> But that's a cowherd's house! A poor farmer's—

ELECTRA

> Poor, yes, but he's well-born . . . and he reveres me.

ORESTES

> What can you mean, your husband reveres you?

ELECTRA

> He's never asked to share my bed.

ORESTES

> Is this some vow of chastity—or distaste for you?

ELECTRA

> He feels it would insult my royal fathers.

ORESTES

> I would think he'd celebrate with such a bride.   260

ELECTRA
    He believes the man who gave me had no right.

ORESTES
    I see. He fears Orestes' punishment someday.

ELECTRA
    That's true—but also he is simply good.

ORESTES
    Ah! He *is* a noble soul—and deserves reward.

ELECTRA
    Yes, if the one who's absent ever comes to this house.

ORESTES
    And your own mother—she allowed this?

ELECTRA
    Women are loyal to their men—not to their children.

ORESTES
    And Aegisthus—why did he crush you like this?

ELECTRA
    So my sons of a powerless father would have no power.

ORESTES
    Else you might bear sons who could avenge the wrong?   270

ELECTRA
    So he thought—may he one day know my vengeance!

ORESTES
    Does your mother's husband know you're virgin still?

ELECTRA

No, we've kept this secret from him with our silence.

ORESTES

These are trusted friends, then, listening now?

ELECTRA

True friends who'll keep our words here to themselves.

ORESTES

And if Orestes came to Argos, what help could he—

ELECTRA

What help! How can you ask? Isn't it time!

ORESTES

How could he kill his father's murderers . . . if he came?

ELECTRA

With the same daring his enemies dared.

ORESTES

Would you—could you—join him in the murder of
                your mother?   280

ELECTRA

Yes! Yes, with the very axe that killed my father!

ORESTES

Can I tell him that you're certain of your part?

ELECTRA

Once I have shed my mother's blood for Father's, I will welcome
                death.

ORESTES

Ah! if Orestes were here to listen to your words!

ELECTRA
> I wouldn't know him if I stood before him, Stranger.

ORESTES
> No wonder. You were children when you parted.

ELECTRA
> Only one friend would recognize him now.

ORESTES
> The one, men say, who rescued him from certain death?

ELECTRA
> That old man who long ago was Father's tutor.

ORESTES
> And your dead father—was he given a proper burial?   290

ELECTRA
> He is buried where his body was thrown from his house.

ORESTES
> Oh! What a story you tell!
>   See? Even a stranger's
> pain can sting the human heart to grief.
> Tell me more so that I can repeat
> this sickening history to your brother—
> he must hear it.
>   One with a trained insight feels
> this kind of sympathy—not the ill-bred or untaught.
> But for some the price of vision is to feel *too* much.

CHORUS
> Like him, I yearn to hear.
> I live so far from the city,   300
> I know nothing of its troubles.

ELECTRA

Then let me tell. I ought to share
with a friend the horror of my fate—
and my father's. And you, stranger, who woke
in me this nightmare, please tell Orestes all
my woes, for they are his.
                    Describe my ragged clothes,
this squalor dragging me into the mud, this stable
I call home—I, who was raised in a palace!
How I bend my back at the shuttle, weaving
whatever I can to cover my naked body.   310
How, as you saw, I must fetch my own water.
Tell how I have no part in the festive dance;
there is no rite for the married virgin. Tell of
shame before Castor—my kinsman and promised
husband before he was raised to the gods.

While my mother lounges on luxury's throne,
surrounded by all the spoils of Troy; girls—
enslaved by my father in Asia—wait at her feet,
their sumptuous robes flowing from clasps of gold.

Yet below that roof my father's blood, now black   320
and clotted, stains the floor.
                    His murderer
parades in Agamemnon's carriage, flaunting
in his bloodstained fist the very scepter
Father used to lead the whole Greek world.

His burial place is shamed. Agamemnon's
grave is bare of tribute, of myrtle spray;
no drink offering was ever given.
But drunk with wine, my mother's husband—
the so-called "glorious one"—leaps onto
the grave, pelts the monument with stones,   330
then he dares to taunt us both out loud:

"Oh where is your brave boy Orestes? Where's
the protector of your tomb?" So he mocks
those absent.
                    O Stranger, I beg you
on my knees, tell him to come home.
Many voices call him: these hands, my tongue,
my broken heart, my shorn head—and his own father.
His father destroyed the Trojans. How shameful
if the son, younger and better born,
could not slay one man face to face.   340

CHORUS

Look there, a man—your husband—
hurries home from work.
(Peasant enters.)

PEASANT

What's this? Who are these strangers at my door?
Why should they have come inside my gate?
Are they looking for me? It really isn't proper
for a wife to stand out talking to young men.

ELECTRA

Kind heart, don't be suspicious of me—
I'll tell the truth—these strangers bring me
news of Orestes.
                    And please, sirs, excuse his words.

PEASANT

What news? Can he be alive!   350

ELECTRA

Yes, by their account—and I believe it.

PEASANT

Ha! . . . and remembers evil done you and your father?

ELECTRA
All we have now is hope; in exile he's powerless.

PEASANT
So what word does Orestes send through them?

ELECTRA
He sent them to discover my condition.

PEASANT
They can only see part—I'm sure you told the rest.

ELECTRA
Now they know everything.

PEASANT
Well, our doors should have been opened wide
before now! Come on in—for your good news
please take what comforts my house can offer—   360
You others, take their gear inside—
Don't say no—you are friends who have come
to me from a friend. I may be poor,
but I will never behave like one ill-bred.
(*goes to rear*)

ORESTES
Gods! Is this the man who keeps the secret
of your marriage, who will not shame Orestes?

ELECTRA
It is he ... called "husband of the pitiful Electra."

ORESTES
Ah! There's just no way to judge a person's worth;
human natures are so confused among us.
I've seen a son of noble birth prove worthless,   370

fine sons grow from sickly stock; I've seen
a miser's shriveled soul in a wealthy man,
a generous heart in a starving body.
How do we tell? By wealth? That's a useless
test. By the lack of it? Poverty is too well known
for bringing out the bad in desperate men.
What about courage? Which one of us who's ever faced
the spear can swear which warrior is good?
These things must all be left to random fate.
Look at this man—a nobody in Argos, from no   380
great, respected house. Yet from such lowly
origins, he has proved a prince.

This is a lesson to those confused
by dreamed-up theories. One should judge men,
even the noblest, by the way they act each day,
by the company they keep. People like this man
run their homes and city well.
                              A fine physique on ·
a stupid man is just a statue in the marketplace.
Muscles do not make one brave in battle—
Courage comes from character we're born with.   390

And as Agamemnon's son—present or absent—
is worthy, and we are here in his name,
we accept the shelter you have offered.
                              Come, men,
enter the house.
                   I'll take a man whose heart
is in his welcome over a host who's merely rich.

Thank you for the welcome into this man's house—
even though I wish it were your brother, in good
fortune, leading us inside his fortunate halls.
He may come yet; Apollo's oracles do not fail.
Though I don't trust a future told by man.   400

CHORUS

    Oh, so much more than before, Electra,
    my heart warms with joy. Your fortune, after
    stalling so long, may arrive with happiness.
(Orestes and Pylades follow servants inside.)

ELECTRA

    How could you! You know your house is bare.
    How can you invite men so superior to you?

PEASANT

    Why, if they are gentlemen as they seem to be,
    won't they be happy with whatever I offer?

ELECTRA

    Well, you've done it. Since you have nothing,
    go look for the dear old man—outcast from the city—
    who nurtured my father. He's tending a flock   410
    by the banks of Tanaus where it forms
    the border between Argos and Sparta.
    Ask him to come to us quickly
    and bring some meat to offer the strangers—
    Oh, he'll be so happy, he'll thank the gods
    to hear the child he saved is still alive!

    We can't ask my mother for anything
    from my father's house. We would regret it
    if that wretch ever heard Orestes lives.

PEASANT

    If that's what you wish, I'll take   420
    your message to the old man. But hurry on in
    and get everything ready. When a woman tries,
    she can make a pleasant meal from very little—
    I'm sure we have enough to fill their bellies
    for this one day.
(Electra enters cottage.)

> When I think about such things,
> I understand that wealth is an advantage
> for entertaining guests, or buying cures for
> illness. But to provide our daily meal it means
> so little. For once he's full, it makes no difference
> to his stomach if a man is rich or poor.   430

(Peasant exits.)

CHORUS

> Oh famous ships propelled to Troy
> by myriad rhythmic oars,
> circled by Nereids, dancing in foam
> beside the dark blue prows,
> led by the dolphin, tumbling
> to spellbinding music,
> carrying Achilles, swift-footed son
> of Thetis, with Agamemnon,
> to the shore of Troy
> where Simois meets the sea.   440

> The Nereids swam from
> the cliffs of Euboea
> bearing arms for a hero
> forged in gold by Hephaestus,
> scouring Pelion and glens of Mount Ossa,
> scanning from peaks
> of the mountain nymphs' home
> for a sign of Achilles, the son of Thetis,
> the son of the sea whom the centaur nurtured,
> raised to be swiftest of all of the mortals   450
> and the light of the Greeks in the Atreids' war.

> A traveler from Ilium,
> in the harbor at Nauplia, told
> me, Achilles, of your famous shield:
> how it was blazoned and graven all round

with the powerful images
to terrify Trojans—
fashioned in gold on the rim of the buckler:
throat-cutting Perseus flying over the sea,
clutching the Gorgon-head dripping with blood,   460
while Maia's son Hermes, god of the pastures
and Zeus' own herald, speeds at his side.

On the shield's center
the rounded Sun blazing, his chariot
drawn by his winged coursers,
where stars dance in darkness—
Pleiades, Hyades, shining their news
into Hector's shocked eyes, turn him to flight;
and molded in beaten gold of the helmet
the sphinxes clutch victims   470
trapped by their song, while the fire-
breathing lioness, on the curve of the cuirass,
claws out of the way of Pegasus' hooves.

And the sword of Achilles! What warhorses
galloped before the black whirlwind!—

You killed the commander, Tyndareus' daughter,
who led heroes—like this—that we won't see again.
It was deception, your adultery that killed him
and the gods in the heavens
will send death back to you.   480
I see it, shall see it, your lifeblood spilling
when the blade has laid open your throat.
(*Old Man enters.*)

OLD MAN
    Where is my lady, my young mistress?
    Daughter of Agamemnon whom once I raised?

It's a hard trial for this wrinkled old man
to make the steep climb to her house—
but for one I love, I'll drag and push
these crooked legs, my age-bent back.
(Electra and an attendant enter from the house.)
Daughter!—I see you now at your door.
I have come. I've brought you a lamb   490
from my flocks, a suckling I took from the ewe,
and garlands, and cheese fresh from the press,
and this aged and precious gift of Dionysus—
a little drop—it will make a delightful cup
when poured with this weaker wine.
Now someone take these to the guests inside,
while on my raveled sleeve I wipe
away the tears that blur my eyes.

ELECTRA

Why are your eyes filled with tears, old father?
I hope my sufferings haven't reminded you   500
of old troubles after all of this time.
Or do you cry for Orestes in wretched exile
and for my father whom you held long ago
in your arms? All for nothing for you and your friends—

OLD MAN

For nothing.
                  It was this last grief I couldn't bear:
on my way here, I turned my steps to his tomb,
where I was alone. I knelt down and wept.
I poured a libation from the wineskin I brought
your guests; I dressed the tomb with myrtle boughs.
And then I saw it—a black ewe on the altar,   510
just slain, its poured blood still red.
And nearby, severed locks of golden hair.
I wondered, daughter, what kind of man had dared
come near the tomb. Surely he was no Argive.
There's a chance your brother's here in secret
to pay this honor to his father's poor grave.

Look at a lock of hair; place it by your own.
Is its color not the same as yours?
Those who share a father's blood
show many similarities.   520

ELECTRA

Sir, your words aren't worthy of your wisdom.
To say my fearless brother might return
in secret because he feared Aegisthus!
And besides, how could locks of hair be matched
when one is from a nobleman, trained as an athlete,
and the other is a woman's, often combed. It's not
possible! And though they may have no relation,
many people can have hair whose color is the same.

OLD MAN

The print of a foot is there, my child;
go see if it matches with your own.   530

ELECTRA

How is a footprint made in stony ground?
And even if a print is there, a brother's
foot will never match a sister's. A man's
is always larger than a woman's.

OLD MAN

Maybe a piece of weaving from your own loom
will reveal him to you if he returns—
I wrapped him when I stole him away from death.

ELECTRA

You know that when Orestes fled
I was a child. Even if I wove a robe
how could it still be worn today—   540
unless clothes grow as bodies do.

. . . .
. . . .

OLD MAN

But where are the strangers? I want to see them
and ask them about your brother.

ELECTRA

Here they come now, hurrying from the house.
(Orestes and Pylades enter.)

OLD MAN

They are nobles, but may not be gentlemen.
Many who are nobly born don't act as if they are.
Anyway—I'll greet the strangers warmly.

ORESTES

Greetings, old sir!
                    What friend of yours,
Electra, owns this relic of a man?

ELECTRA

This is the man who raised and loved my father.   550

ORESTES

What! The man who stole your brother away?

ELECTRA

The one who saved his life—if he still lives.

ORESTES

Why is he gazing at me—as one examines the stamp
on a new silver coin? Do I look like someone?

ELECTRA

Maybe he's happy to see one who grew up with Orestes.

ORESTES

Yes, his best friend—but why does he circle me like this?

ELECTRA

    I'm wondering at that myself, Stranger.

OLD MAN

    O Daughter! Lady Electra! Pray to the gods!

ELECTRA

    For what? For things we have—or have not?

OLD MAN

    To grasp this precious treasure a god reveals.   560

ELECTRA

    Old sir, I'm praying—but what do you mean?

OLD MAN

    Look at him, now, child—at your most beloved.

ELECTRA

    I am looking—but I'm afraid you've lost your mind.

OLD MAN

    Lost my mind! I, who look at your brother—there!

ELECTRA

    What can you mean by these incredible words?

OLD MAN

    I see Orestes here, the son of Agamemnon.

ELECTRA

    How can I believe you! What sign do you see?

OLD MAN

    The scar there on his brow—where he was cut in a fall,
    chasing a fawn with you in his father's courtyard.

ELECTRA

What! Can you—yes, I see it, the scar!   570

OLD MAN

Then why are you slow to embrace the one you love?

ELECTRA

I'm not, not now, old sir—these signs of yours—
my heart is certain!
You're here at last—
against all hope—Oh, let me hold you!

ORESTES

In my arms at last!

ELECTRA

I never expected—

ORESTES

I never dared hope—

ELECTRA

You really . . . are he?

ORESTES

Yes, yes, your one champion—
if I can snare the prey I'm after. And I am certain
I shall. We can no longer believe in the gods
if wrongdoing triumphs over right.

CHORUS

You've come, you've come, hesitant dawn,   580
suddenly shining across the sky,
lifting the long-gone exile to light,
after the dark and lonely years
forbidden his father's home.

The beacon of victory, O my friend,
God is bringing us victory!
Lift up your hands, lift up
your voice in prayer to the gods
that fortune will shield your brother
as he sets foot within his city.   590

ORESTES *(breaking off long embrace with Electra)*
Enough . . . we have to end this happiness,
but I will hold you in my arms again.

Now you, old sir, it's good you've come. I need
advice to plan revenge on Father's murderer—
and on my mother, his adulterous partner.
Do I have any friends still here in Argos?
Or, like my fortune, are they all lost?
Who would be on my side? Should I go by
night or day? How can I approach my enemies?

OLD MAN
Ah, son, you're friendless in misfortune.   600
It is always rare to find that treasure,
a friend who'll share bad times as well as good.
Your friends have given up on you, since
you long left them without hope. I tell you,
all you have is luck and your own hand
to retake your father's palace and his city.

ORESTES
But what do I do now to win this goal?

OLD MAN
Kill Aegisthus and your mother.

ORESTES
That's what I came here for. How shall I do it?

OLD MAN

You'll never get inside the walls.   610

ORESTES

He's surrounded by armed guards?

OLD MAN

Always. He's afraid of you. I hear he hardly sleeps.

ORESTES

So. What then, old sir? Advise me.

OLD MAN

Listen: an idea has come to me just now.

ORESTES

A plan, I hope—I'm eager to follow.

OLD MAN

As I struggled up here, I saw Aegisthus.

ORESTES

Welcome news! You saw him—where?

OLD MAN

Near these fields, where he pastures his horses.

ORESTES

What was he doing? . . . My despair is turning to hope.

OLD MAN

It seemed he was preparing a feast for the Nymphs.   620

ORESTES

To bless a newborn? A birthing?

OLD MAN
I know nothing except he was planning a sacrifice.

ORESTES
Was he with many guards? Or alone with slaves?

OLD MAN
Household slaves, no one from Argos . . .

ORESTES
No one, then, who will recognize me?

OLD MAN
All slaves, who've never seen your face.

ORESTES
Who would—if I win—come over to my side?

OLD MAN
Luckily, that's the usual way with slaves.

ORESTES
How, then, can I approach him?

OLD MAN
At the hour of sacrifice, walk right by him.   630

ORESTES
I assume his lands border the highway . . .

OLD MAN
Yes, he'll see you—and invite you to the feast.

ORESTES
A guest he will regret, gods willing.

OLD MAN

At that point you decide—be guided as the dice fall.

ORESTES

Good advice. And my mother? Where is she?

OLD MAN

In Argos. She'll come later to the feast.

ORESTES

Why didn't my mother travel with her husband?

OLD MAN

She stayed behind; she fears the heckling crowds.

ORESTES

Of course. She knows men still condemn her.

OLD MAN

It's always so—everyone hates an unholy woman.   640

ORESTES

How shall I kill them both together?

ELECTRA *(breaking in)*

I will take care of my mother's murder.

ORESTES

And Fortune will take care of his.

ELECTRA

And this one man can help the two of us.

OLD MAN

I will. What is your plan for your mother's death?

ELECTRA

> Go, old sir, tell Clytemnestra this:
> Electra is the mother of a son.

OLD MAN

> Born some time ago? Or recently?

ELECTRA

> Within the purifying time, within ten days.

OLD MAN

> How can this news end in your mother's death?   650

ELECTRA

> When she hears I've been through labor, she will come.

OLD MAN

> But why? Do you believe she still could care for you?

ELECTRA

> Yes. She'll even shed tears—for my son's low birth.

OLD MAN

> Maybe—but please get back to your plan.

ELECTRA

> Once she comes here, it's certain: she will perish.

OLD MAN

> Aye . . . and she will come, to this very door.

ELECTRA

> And isn't the path from here to Hades short?

OLD MAN

> Oh, to see this happen; then I could die happy!

ELECTRA
> But first old sir, you must be this man's guide.

OLD MAN
> To where Aegisthus plans his sacrifice?   660

ELECTRA
> Then meet my mother, give her the news I told you.

OLD MAN
> It will be as if the words came from your lips.

ELECTRA *(to Orestes)*
> On to your work. It is your lot to go first in murder.

ORESTES
> I'm ready to go, if I have someone to guide me.

OLD MAN
> And I'm more than willing to show you the way.
> *(Orestes, Old Man, and Electra assume attitudes of prayer.)*

ORESTES
> Zeus, god of my father, slayer of my foes—

ELECTRA
> Have pity on us: we've suffered pitiable wrongs!

OLD MAN
> Yea, have pity for those descended from you.

ELECTRA
> Help us, Hera, O Queen of Mycenae's altars!

ORESTES
> Grant us victory if our claims are just.   670

OLD MAN

Grant them just vengeance for their father.

ORESTES

O Father, sent by evil murder beneath this earth—

ELECTRA

O Earth, Queen, I press my hands to you—

OLD MAN

Help them, help these beloved children.

ORESTES

Come! Bring all your allies slain in battle—

ELECTRA

All those whose spears joined yours to vanquish Troy—

OLD MAN

All who despise polluters of the sacred!

ORESTES

Do you hear, you who suffered horror at my mother's hands?

OLD MAN

Your father hears it all, I know. But time is pressing—

ELECTRA

And there's something I must say: 680
Aegisthus has to die. For if you are thrown and fall
in death, I too shall fall—I could no longer live.
I'll drive a two-edged sword into my heart.

Now I'm going in to get things ready.
If the news I hear from you is good
this house will sing with joy. But if you die,
believe me, it will be a different story.

ORESTES
     I understand.

ELECTRA
     So, in this action you must play the man.
     (She turns to Chorus as Orestes, Pylades, and Old Man exit.)
     And you women: raise a cry like a beacon   690
     to signal the outcome. I will keep steady watch
     holding the sword in my hands, ready to hear.
     For if I'm defeated I will never allow
     my hated enemy to violate my body.
     (Electra re-enters cottage.)

CHORUS
     The old story's still told
     in the mountains of Argos
     of the meadow-lord, Pan—
     how he breathed the sweet tune
     through his well-crafted reeds,
     enchanting the lamb from its mother,   700
     led off the lamb whose fleece was pure gold.

     From the platform of stone
     the herald called out:
     "To the Square! To the Square, Mycenaeans!
     Behold this wondrous portent
     of a reign that is blessed!"
     They praised the Atreids with dance and song.

     All over Argos, the gleaming streets
     reflected the sacrificial flames
     from altar-braziers of beaten gold;   710
     everywhere flute notes, serving the muse,
     wove in the air with ravishing songs—
     Then a harsh sudden voice
     made claim to the lamb:

In secret seduction Thyestes had lain
with Atreus' own dear wife,
snared her heart and sped her
and the horned marvel off to his halls.
To the gathered people he cried out
his House now held the gold-fleeced lamb.   720

Then, then, Zeus stopped
the stars in their tracks,
set them off backward—
reversed the sun
so that sunset was dawn-gleam
and western lands burned;
clouds swollen with water
drove northward and now
Ammon's dry city withers away
bereft of the sweet rain of Zeus.   730

Or so it is told.
But I find it hard to believe
that the golden sun would turn
and change its burning place
to make man suffer, to chasten mankind
for a mortal's crime.
Unless the tale is for teaching
us awe and respect for the gods.
But you, sister of two famous brothers,
no lesson held back your murdering hand.   740

Oh, Oh! Friends—
did you hear—? Did I imagine—?
A rumble like the thunder of Zeus?
Listen! Now—like a swelling storm—
Princess, come out of the house! Electra!
(Electra enters.)

ELECTRA

Friends, what happened! What is the outcome?

CHORUS

I only know I hear a cry of death.

ELECTRA

Yes, I hear . . . from far off . . . I hear!

CHORUS

A far distant cry—but clear.

ELECTRA

But is it from Argives—or from those I love?   750

CHORUS

I cannot tell, the sounds are so confused.

ELECTRA

Your answer means my end. Why wait?

CHORUS

Stay, stay until you know your fate for sure.

ELECTRA

No—it's over! Where could his messengers be?

CHORUS

They will come. Kings are not easily slain.
(Messenger enters.)

MESSENGER

Victory! O women of Mycenae, victory!
My friends—Orestes has triumphed!
Agamemnon's murderer, Aegisthus—lies on
the ground! Praise and thank the Gods.

ELECTRA

>Who are you? Can you prove this news?   760

MESSENGER

>Look at me—don't you know your brother's man?

ELECTRA

>Dear friend, fear made me slow to recognize
>your face. But now indeed I know you.
>Say it again: my father's murderer is dead.

MESSENGER

>Dead. I am glad to say it twice for you.

ELECTRA

>Gods! Justice, seeing all, has come at last!
>How did he do it, what means did he use
>to kill Thyestes' son? You must tell me!

MESSENGER

>Soon after we walked from your house we turned
>into the two-tracked road the chariots use.   770
>Then soon we came upon Mycenae's well-known
>king, strolling in his watered garden,
>picking scented myrtle sprays to bind his hair.
>He saw us, hailed us: "Strangers, who are you
>and where are you from? What is your country?"
>Orestes answered, "Thessalians, traveling
>to Alpheus' streams, to offer sacrifice to Zeus."
>When Aegisthus heard this, he replied.
>"Then be my guests here at this feast;
>join me in sacrifice unto the Nymphs.   780
>You can rise at dawn and not lose time.
>Come now, let me show you to the house."
>Then he took our hands and led us in,
>repeating, "You must not say no to me."
>Once inside his doors he spoke to servants

"Let one bring water quickly so our guests
can come before the altar with cleansed hands."
But Orestes spoke: "We have just purified
ourselves in your clear stream, O King.
If strangers may join your citizens, we   790
won't refuse; we are ready for the sacrifice."
All of us could overhear these words.

Then the tyrant's guards—his slaves—
put aside their spears and set their hands to work.
Some brought the bowl for sacrificial blood,
some brought baskets, others lit the fire or set
the caldrons on the hearth; noise rang through the house.
Then your mother's lover took the barley
and strewed it on the altar, praying loudly,
"Nymphs of the Rocks, allow me and my wife at home,   800
Tyndareus' daughter, to sacrifice to you often,
blessed as we are now, our enemies still cursed."
He meant, of course, you and Orestes—who prayed
the reverse in silence, to gain his rightful place
in his ancestral halls.
                          Next Aegisthus took
the straight blade from the basket, cut the forelock
from the calf and with his right hand cast it on pure flame.
When servants heaved the calf to shoulder-height,
he slit its throat. Then he addressed your brother:
"In our land we've heard you men from Thessaly   810
take great pride in deftly butchering a bull
as well as breaking horses. Choose a knife, my guest,
and prove the boast of the Thessalians true."
Orestes grasped a well-wrought Dorian blade
and casting off his handsome cloak, he motioned for Pylades
to come forward, the servants to stand back. He seized
the calf's foot, bared white flesh, and in one arm's
sweep he flayed the carcass faster than a runner
laps a mile. Then he laid its belly open.

Aegisthus grasped the sacred parts and gazed   820
upon them. He saw the liver had no lobe;
the gallbladder and artery portended peril
to anyone regarding them. He scowled.
Your brother asked him,"What's the matter?
What upset you?"
                "I fear a stranger's guile;
Of all the enemies of my house, the one
I hate the most is Agamemnon's son."
Orestes spoke: "But you're the king! You cannot fear a
fugitive's tricks! Come now, let us share the
feast of sacrifice—someone bring a Phthian cleaver,   830
better than this Doric knife for smashing bone."
That done, he split the breast. Aegisthus grasped
the entrails, bent over for a closer look—
and then your brother raised up on his toes and
crashed the blade down on his back and crushed
the linking spine-bones. His body shuddered,
writhed; he cried out in hard and agonizing death.

Immediately the servants grabbed their spears,
formed a troop against the two. Pylades and
Orestes faced them unafraid, brandishing their   840
weapons. Orestes cried, "I have not come to Argos
as an enemy to the city or to my own servants;
but I have wrought vengeance on my father's slayer.
I am the ill-fated Orestes. Do not kill me,
you who served my father!"
                When they heard his words
they lowered their spears. One ancient servant
gasped in recognition; then with shouts of joy
they quickly set a crown of leaves upon his brow.

Now he comes to show you—not the Gorgon's head—
but Aegisthus, the one you hate. Blood for blood: 850
the slain man repaid his borrowed life.
(Messenger exits.)

CHORUS

> Come dance, beloved friend, come dance!
> With nimble fawnlike feet
> leap lightly to the sky in joy!
> Your brother's won a victor's crown
> far greater than Olympia's!
> Come match my steps
> with your triumphant song!

ELECTRA

> O light, O glorious chariot of the Sun!
> O Earth—and Night that filled my gaze before!   860
> Now my eyes are free to open wide—
> Aegisthus is dead! Father's killer is dead!
> Let me go in the house and bring out what I can—
> whatever adornments I still may have—
> to crown my conquering brother's head.

CHORUS

> Go make a crown for the victor's head
> while we step to the dance that the Muses adore—
> Now, destroying those who rule unjustly,
> our own dear kings of old
> will be just masters of our land—   870
> Rejoice with the flute!
> Shout out the joy of our hearts!

(Orestes and Pylades enter.)

ELECTRA

> O glorious champion! Orestes! Son
> of the father crowned in triumph in the war
> with Troy! Accept this wreath to circle your hair.
> You've come home, having raced no idle
> furlong, a man who has slain our enemy
> Aegisthus, murderer of your father and mine.

And you, Pylades, his comrade in arms,
raised by a righteous man—take from my hand   880
this other wreath—for from this contest you
have gained an equal share.

                                May I see you prosper always.

ORESTES

First give credit to the gods, Electra,—
they shaped this day's outcome—then praise me.
I was the instrument of gods and Fortune.
I come having killed Aegisthus, not in word,
but in fact. And for proof—if any one needs
it—I have brought his body here.
If you want to, cast him out for animals
to eat. Or impale him on a stake for birds—   890
the children of the air—to tear apart.
Now he's your slave, who used to be your master.

ELECTRA

I am ashamed—but I feel I have to speak.

ORESTES

Of what? Speak—you're no longer a prisoner of fear.

ELECTRA

I'm ashamed of censure for insulting the dead.

ORESTES

There's not one man who would blame you for that.

ELECTRA

Our people are hard to please—quick to condemn—

ORESTES

Speak, sister. Say whatever you want to.
There was no truce made with this enemy.

ELECTRA *(to Aegisthus' corpse)*
> Then I will.

> > > Where shall I begin my bitter charges?   900
> Where end? Which indictment make the midpoint?
> Every day at dawn I've practiced what I'd say,
> how I'd revile you to your face, if an end
> came to my longtime terror, and I stood
> before you. Now I do. And now I'll pay
> with words just what I owed you when you lived.

> You ruined my life. Though we had never wronged you,
> you robbed us both of our beloved father.
> You vilely wed my mother, killed her lord,
> the chief of Hellas' armies—you, who never looked   910
> on Troy!
> > > You were so stupid you could dream
> that in my mother you had found a loyal wife—
> even as you fouled my father's bed!
> Men know if you seduce your neighbor's wife,
> that when you have to take her for your own,
> you'd be a fool to think that she'll be true
> when she's betrayed one husband.
> > > > > > Your life
> was miserable, though it appeared to be blessed.
> You knew your marriage was a sacrilege;
> She knew that she had wed a villain.   920
> Sinners both, you shared each other's lot:
> she assumed your evil, you took on hers.
> In Argos they all called you "Clytemnestra's
> husband"; no one ever said "Aegisthus' wife."
> How shameful when the woman, not the man,
> controls the home! And I hate to hear a son
> called by his mother's, not his father's name
> by people in the city. For when a man is married
> to a higher-ranking woman, he is not
> important; all attention goes to her.   930

And you were so deluded, blind with pride,
you thought that wealth alone had made you great.
But money doesn't keep you company long;
a man's possessions go, his nature stays.
A noble nature lasts to lift life's burdens—
but money made by trafficking with knaves
blooms a moment, then flies far away.

As for your way with women—a maiden
should not know the words to tell—so I'll
say a riddle clearly: outrages were committed   940
by a man with pretty looks and royal halls.
Give me a husband not girlish but manly,
whose sons choose service to the god of war;
the fair-faced only shine at dances.

Perish, then, still blind to all the crimes
you're punished for, now that time has found you out.
Let no felon dream—though he starts out well
in his race with Justice—that he'll outrun her
to the finish when he rounds the end of life.

CHORUS
What he did was terrible; terrible   950
is his payment to you both. Mighty Justice!

ELECTRA
Now men, you must carry the corpse inside
and hide it in the dark. When my mother comes
she must not see the dead before her . . . sacrifice.
(Pylades and servants take the body into the house.)

ORESTES
Wait—we must speak now of another subject—

ELECTRA
Do you see our allies coming from Mycenae?

ORESTES
No. I see the mother who gave me birth.

ELECTRA
Ha! She parades nicely into our net.
Look at the pomp of her carriage and clothes!

ORESTES
What are we going to do? Kill our own mother?   960

ELECTRA
What! Has pity seized you at the sight of her?

ORESTES
Oh, Gods.
She nurtured me, gave birth to me—how can I kill her?

ELECTRA
Just as she killed my father—and yours!

ORESTES
O Phoebus—your command was cruel, unwise.

ELECTRA
If Apollo is ignorant, who can be wise?

ORESTES
To kill my own mother? A command against nature!

ELECTRA
Can you be wronged for avenging your father?

ORESTES
I've done right so far, but I'll be charged with a mother's murder.

ELECTRA
Yet more guilty if you don't defend your father.   970

ORESTES

But won't I have to pay a price for Mother's blood?

ELECTRA

If you fail to avenge Father—you will pay him!

ORESTES

Cannot a demon of destruction feign the voice of God?

ELECTRA

A voice from Delphi's holy seat? I do not think so!

ORESTES

I cannot . . . completely . . . believe this oracle to be right.

ELECTRA

Is your manhood turning coward now?

ORESTES

But how . . . ? Will I set the same trap for her?

ELECTRA

Yes—the way she lured and killed her husband with Aegisthus.

ORESTES

I will go in. A horror, this act will be—
a horror—but I will begin. If this is the will   980
of the God, so be it—sweet deed most bitter!
*(Enters hut. Clytemnestra enters in chariot, with attendants, captive
                        maids of Troy.)*

CHORUS

My lady, Queen of Argos,
daughter of Tyndareus,
sister of two noble sons of Zeus—
bright heroes placed among the stars
to shine the storm-tossed sailor

safely home.
Greetings! For your great wealth
and prosperity I revere you as a god.
Your good fortune   990
calls for reverent care, O Queen.

CLYTEMNESTRA

Step down from your wagon, Trojan women,
take my hand and help me from my chariot.
As the gods were given spoils of Troy
to adorn their temples, I have these prizes, too,
to compensate for my lost daughter. Poor
exchange—though fine possessions for my house.

ELECTRA

May not I then—a slave as well—outcast
from my father's halls, living in this wretched
place—may I, Mother, take a hand so blessed?   1000

CLYTEMNESTRA

I have these slaves to help . . . don't trouble yourself.

ELECTRA

Why not? you made me a captive, too, threw me out,
took me, my home—am I not the same
as these sad, fatherless girls?

CLYTEMNESTRA

That is the result of your father's plots
against those who deserved his deepest devotion.
I will speak—though when a woman's name
is tarnished, her tongue is bitter;
I think that unjust. Let people hear
the truth; if I deserve to be abhorred, then   1010
hatred is just. But if I don't, why hate me?
Tyndareus did not give me to your father
to be slain. Not I, nor the children I bore.

Yet, he took my child to Aulis where the fleet
was bound—lured by the lie that she would wed
Achilles. There he held her stretched above the altar
and slit open Iphigenia's soft white throat.

Had he been trying to cure our city's capture,
or winning favor for his House to save
his other children—slaying one in place of many—   1020
then he might be forgiven.
                              But for that slut Helen's
treachery, left unpunished by her foolish husband,
for that alone he killed my child.

Even for this wrong, no matter how severely wronged
I was, I did not rage, nor would I have killed
my husband. But he brought home that god-crazed girl,
installed her in our bed and tried to keep
two brides together underneath one roof!
Women are weaker—I'll agree—
so when an erring husband slights   1030
his own true bride, the wife will imitate
his course and find herself another love.
Then the beam of scandal lights on us—
while no one blames the man who showed the way.
Suppose that Menelaus had been stolen
from his home—should I have killed Orestes
to save my sister's husband? How would your
father have taken that? Should he who killed
my child be spared when he would have murdered
me had I so much as touched his son?
                              I killed him.   1040
I took the only way and turned to those
who were his enemies. For what friend
of your father would have joined me in his murder?

Speak, say whatever you want. Try your best
to prove your father's death was not deserved.

CHORUS LEADER

There's some justice in your words—shameful justice.
A woman with good sense defers to her
husband in every way. Anyone who disagrees
is not worth my consideration.

ELECTRA

Keep in mind Mother, what you just said: 1050
that I may state my case with total freedom.

CLYTEMNESTRA

I'll say it again; I do not take it back.

ELECTRA

Yes, Mother, but will you listen now—and punish later?

CLYTEMNESTRA

Not at all—say whatever pleases you.

ELECTRA

Then I will speak—and I will start with this:
O Mother, if only you had a purer heart!
Your beauty has most justly won you praise,
yours and Helen's. Such sisters in the skin are you!
Both immoral women unworthy of Castor:
she, abducted from home and loving it;   1060
you, murderer of the noblest son of Greece.
You pretend you killed your husband
for a daughter's sake, but no one knows you
as I do.
            You, who long before your daughter's death,
and soon after your husband left the house,
stood at your mirror sleeking your bright hair.
The name of a woman should be blotted out
who primps when her husband is far from home!
What is her need to wear makeup in public
unless she's up to some immoral act?   1070

I know of all Greek women only you
were glad when Troy appeared to triumph—
and scowled when it seemed her fortunes turned.
For you did not want Agamemnon home from Troy.
Yet you had every reason to be faithful—
your husband was not inferior to Aegisthus;
all of Hellas chose him as commander.
And when your sister Helen fell in sin,
you could have won high praise for being good—
for sinners make the virtuous stand out. 1080
Granted, as you say, my father killed your child,
but how did I wrong you? How did my brother?
How is it, after murdering your husband, you did
not give us our ancestral home—but purchased
man and marriage with our property?
And why isn't this husband exiled for exiling
your son? Killed for dealing living death to me?
Twice what my sister suffered!
                      Yes, if murder
must be met with murder to requite it,
I, with Orestes, must kill you to avenge our father. 1090
For if your defense is just, then ours is also just.

CLYTEMNESTRA

Child, it's been your nature to adore your father.
It's always this way: some children are closer
to their father, some love their mother more.
I forgive you—for to tell the truth, I'm not
so very glad, daughter, for every deed I've done.

Oh, my own devising made me miserable;
my fury at my husband was too great.

ELECTRA

Too late to regret what you cannot cure.
My father is dead. But what about your son? 1100
Why not bring my wandering brother home?

I'm afraid. I'm concerned about myself, not him.
Men say his wrath is great for his father's death.

CLYTEMNESTRA

ELECTRA

And why do you let Aegisthus treat me harshly?

CLYTEMNESTRA

That is his temperament. You, too, are stubborn.

ELECTRA

Out of my grief—but I will get over my anger.

CLYTEMNESTRA

Really? Then he will cease his persecution.

ELECTRA

Living in my house has made him arrogant.

CLYTEMNESTRA

See there? You're stirring up the flames again.

ELECTRA

I'll be silent. I fear him as I fear him.   1110

CLYTEMNESTRA

Enough on that. Why did you summon me here?

ELECTRA

I think you've heard I've given birth—
I wanted you to make the sacrifice,
the tenth-night offering. The ritual is strange
to me, as this is my first child.

CLYTEMNESTRA

That's the job of the woman who was your midwife.

ELECTRA

I had no help. I delivered my baby alone.

CLYTEMNESTRA

Your house is so far from friends and neighbors?

ELECTRA

No one wants poor people for their friends.

CLYTEMNESTRA

And you, even when the pain of birth is over,   1120
you can't wash and put on something nice?

I will go in and make the sacrifice
for your child's completed term. That favor
done, I'll ride to the field where my husband
sacrifices to the Nymphs.
                Come, servants, lead
my horses to the feed stalls. As soon as you think
I have finished this sacrifice to the gods,
come for me—for I must give this favor to my husband.
(Slaves exit.)

ELECTRA

Go on inside my humble house . . .
(watches her mother proceed toward cottage)
                      Be careful!
The sooty walls might smear your gown   1130
as you prepare the sacrifice the gods expect.
(Clytemnestra enters the cottage.)
The basket is ready, the knife is whetted
which killed the bull you will fall down beside.
You will lie beside him, too, in Hades—as you slept
with him in life. This favor I will give you,
as you give your life in payment for my father's.
(Electra follows into the cottage.)

CHORUS

    Vengeance for evil! The winds of fortune
    that lashed the house have turned!
    Before it was my ruler, falling
    as he was bathed. The very rooftop shrieked,   1140
    The capstones screamed, as he cried out
    "Woman, wicked woman, why will you kill me
    when I have come at last, after ten seed-times,
    to the homeland I love."
    . . . .
    . . . .
    The tide of justice surges back
    to judge the faithless wife.
    Her luckless husband home at last
    to the lofty Cyclopean towers,
    she held in her hands the keen-edged axe
    and met him with his murder.   1150
    Oh, wretched husband—whatever wrongs
    produced this vicious woman,
    ruthless as a lioness stalking mountain
    thickets, she finished off her prey.

CLYTEMNESTRA *(within)*

    Oh, children—Gods!—don't kill your mother!

CHORUS

    Did you hear that scream from the house?

CLYTEMNESTRA *(within)*

    No! Not me, me!

CHORUS *(shrieking, severally)*

    I cry out, too! . . . Her own children overwhelm her!
(chanting)

God dispenses justice when its time comes.
Your suffering is great; great was the evil   1160
you did your lord.

(*Orestes, Electra, Pylades emerge from the house. The bodies of Aegisthus
and Clytemnestra are displayed in front of
the doorway.*)

CHORUS LEADER
They come, come now from the house,
splattered with their mother's red blood, . . .
with trophies of the grievous sacrifice.
There is no family, nor ever has been,
more full of griefs than the line of Tantalus.

ORESTES
O Earth!
O Zeus whose eyes see everything
men do—behold the horror
of this sight! These bleeding bodies   1170
side by side on the ground, struck
down by my own hand for wrongs they did me.

Now my tears begin . . .

ELECTRA
And, oh, I weep with you, brother. I am to blame.
My fury burned against the one who gave me birth.
I am her daughter. This is my mother!

CHORUS
You were their mother.
                    Grievous,
more than grievous, the horror of your fate,
your suffering at your children's hands,
but you paid justly for their father's murder.   1180

ORESTES

> Apollo, the justice you directed
> was not clear to me—but all too clear
> is the agony you exacted, granting me
> a murderer's lot, exiled from all of Greece.
> What city am I to turn to?
> What friend, what righteous person
> will look me in the eye—after
> I have killed my mother?

ELECTRA

> Oh, weep for me! Where will I find refuge?
> Where will I be allowed to join a dance, a wedding?   1190
> What man would ever take me as his bride?

CHORUS

> Turn, your windblown thoughts
> turn back. Now, your mind is right,
> my friend. It was unholy when
> you pushed your brother to perform
> a dreadful wrong against his will.

ORESTES

> Did you see how—dying—she clung
> to my tunic and pulled her gown aside
> to bare her breast? O God!—her legs folding—
> like a birthing—I was grasping her hair—   1200

CHORUS

> I understand your anguish.
> To hear the death cries
> of the mother who gave you life!

ORESTES

> She stretched her hand to my cheek
> and screamed, "My son! I beg you . . ."

And while she was still clinging to me,
my sword fell from my hand.

CHORUS

Poor, miserable woman. How could you bear
to look on your mother gasping her last breath?

ORESTES

I held my cloak in front of my eyes—   1210
for the final sacrifice—
when I thrust my sword into her throat.

ELECTRA

Yes, and I urged you on,
placed my hand next to yours on the sword.
I have done the unspeakable.

ORESTES

Take this robe to cover her arms and legs;
try to close her wounds . . .
The children you bore became your murderers.

ELECTRA

Now, loved one who was not loved,
I shroud you with this robe.   1220
The end—so may it be—of the great evils of the House.
(The Dioscuri fly into view above the stage.)

CHORUS

Look! Up over the rooftop!
Spirits are shining. Or have gods
stepped down from the heavens?
No mortal could walk on air.
What brings these beings here
before the eyes of men?
(The gods alight on the roof of the building.)

CASTOR

> Hear us, Son of Agamemnon. I am Castor,
> this is Polydeuces. We are twin sons of Zeus,
> the brothers of your mother. We made   1230
> the storm-whipped waters safe again to sail
> and came in haste to Argos when we saw
> you kill your mother and our sister.
> Her punishment is just, but what you did is wrong.
> As for Phoebus, Phoebus . . . he is my lord; I remain
> silent. He is wise, though his command to you
> was not wise. What is done, you must accept
> and now enact what Zeus and Fate ordain.
>
> Give Electra to Pylades as his wife.
> Then you must leave Argos. You are forbidden,   1240
> as your mother's murderer, to set foot in this city.
> The dreaded, hound-eyed goddesses of Fate
> will stalk your wanderings and drive you mad.
>
> Get to Athens. Embrace the awesome image
> of Athena, and she will save you from the
> serpent-writhing Furies. They cannot touch you
> when she holds her Gorgon shield above your head.
>
> There is a Hill of Ares, where first the gods
> convened to judge by vote a case of murder,
> when savage Ares killed the Sea-lord's son,   1250
> in wrath at him who'd raped his daughter.
> Ever since, this court of justice is revered,
> its decisions trusted in the eyes of gods.
> You too will there stand trial for murder,
> and when your judges cast a tying ballot,
> you will be saved from death. For Apollo,
> who ordered you to kill your mother, will accept
> the blame. And from now on the law will be
> that equal votes will free the man accused.

The thwarted Furies will be devastated.   1260
They'll sink into a cleft beside the Hill—
a sacred place, an oracle, thereafter.
Then you will travel to Arcadia.
By Alpheus' streams close to the shrine of Zeus,
you will found a city and give to it your name.
Thus I tell your destiny.
                                    This corpse of Aegisthus
will be buried by the Argives.
                                    As for your mother,
Menelaus, just arrived at Nauplia long after
conquering Troy, will bury her. And Helen,
her long sojourn in Egypt over, will assist him.   1270
For Helen never went to Troy;
Zeus dispatched a double of her there
to foment strife and bloodshed among men.
So. Let Pylades take his virgin wife
out of Achaea to his home in Phocis, and take
with them this farmer called your brother-in-law;
make him there a wealthy man.
                                    Now you must set out
to cross the narrow neck at Corinth, headed
to that blessed hill in Cecrops' city, Athens.
When your appointed penance is completed   1280
your pain will cease, your happiness begin.

ORESTES

O children of Zeus! Are we
permitted to talk with gods?

CASTOR

Yes—you are not defiled by this murder.

ELECTRA

May I also speak, Tyndareus' sons?

CASTOR

You, too: for I hold Apollo responsible
for the blood spilled here.

CHORUS

Why is it that as gods, and brothers
of this murdered woman, you did not shield
her house from the powers of vengeance?   1290

CASTOR

Necessity led to what Fate decreed.
And the unwise order of Apollo.

ELECTRA

But what word from Apollo, what oracle
proclaimed that I must be my mother's killer?

CASTOR

You shared the deed, as you share the destiny.
One ancestral curse passed down
has ravaged both of you.

ORESTES

O my sister, to have seen you at last
and then be torn from your love so soon!
To leave you, be left by you . . .   1300

CASTOR

She will have a husband and a home.
She only suffers the pain
of leaving the Argives' city.

ELECTRA

What grief is greater than looking back
at the border of your homeland?

ORESTES

And I must not only leave my father's
home, but be tried by a foreign code
for the murder of my mother.

CASTOR

Don't be afraid. You will fare well
in Athena's sacred city. Have courage.   1310

ELECTRA

Oh hold me close to your breast,
my dearest brother.
The curse of our mother's blood
severs us from each other and our father's home.

ORESTES

Come to me, oh, hold me. Keen a lament
as if I were dead and this my grave.

CASTOR

Ah, ah. Your pitiful cry
can break the heart of a god.
For I, and all the immortals, can feel
compassion for human misery.   1320

ORESTES

I shall never see you again.

ELECTRA

Nor shall I come within the light of your eyes.

ORESTES

These are our last words to each other.

ELECTRA

Ah, my city—goodbye!
And farewell to you, my countrywomen.

ORESTES

Most loyal sister . . . are you leaving so soon?

ELECTRA

I go . . . these tears burning my eyes.

ORESTES

Then, Pylades, farewell.
Take Electra to be your wife.

CASTOR

These shall go to be married. But you—   1330
run—the hounds are near—flee to Athens.
With their dreaded tracking they'll pursue you,
these charred-skinned demons; their serpent-wrapped
and writhing arms will bear you mortal agony.
We must speed now to seas off Sicily,
to protect the ships in danger there.
But know that as we fly down paths of air,
we never rescue those defiled by evil
but only those who honor righteousness
and hold as precious what is godly.   1340
It is only these we save from suffering.
So let none of you do wrong by choice
or sail on ships with men who are corrupt.
I, a god, declare this to all mortals.

(The Dioscuri ascend.)

CHORUS

Farewell. The mortal life that does fare well,
that never meets misfortune,
is a life most truly blessed.

Cyclops

Translated by
Palmer Bovie

Translator's Preface

The satyr play formed the fourth unit of the poet's tetralogy offered in the dramatic festival of Athens in the fifth century B.C. Its normal features were a story derived from mythology or epic poetry embellished by a chorus of satyrs. Euripides chose for his *Cyclops*, our only surviving complete example of this form of drama, the sensational episode from the Ninth Book of Homer's *Odyssey*: the blinding of the Cyclopean one-eyed giant Polyphemus. The chorus consists of a band of young satyrs and their elderly leader Silenus, whose very presence instills a somewhat bright and radiant glow after the dire solemnity and brooding atmosphere of the preceding tragic trilogy.

Silenus' opening soliloquy rehearses the background story of how he and his youthful followers have fallen prey to the giant and become enslaved as his servants and shepherds. They cannot play their usual roles as limber, lascivious woodland spirits, faun-like demigods under the protection of Bacchus (Dionysus). Silenus longs for the support of Bacchus, whose tutor and first guardian he was. Shipwrecked and abandoned, his companions are no longer free, happy creatures of nature, guided by their sage elder, Bacchus' friend and favorite. When Odysseus and his crew land here and clamber up to the Cyclops' den unwittingly, in search of food and water to replenish their supplies, they become trapped in the same predicament. The Cyclops returns from his hunting expedition and fastens on the newcomers as the fare for his cannibal feasting.

Before the Cyclops herds Odysseus and his men into his ghastly cavern, Odysseus engages him in a spirited argument against the brutal slaughter. Odysseus argues eloquently for the principles of moral law, justice, common hospitality, and respect for the gods. The Cyclops argues in favor of personal advantage and private pleasure, calling the framework of social justice a fraudulent invention devised by the weak as a protection against the strong. As regards piety toward the gods, Polyphemus insists that the only god worth worshiping is wealth, that material advantage, not Zeus, reigns supreme. The terms of this debate, quite unlike anything in Homer's account, seem to reflect Euripides' interest in the bold challenge to conventional moral principles launched by the Sophist orators of the fifth century and their doctrines of moral relativity.

It is small wonder that the Cyclops is labeled "godless" throughout the play or that Odysseus' devout prayers to Athena and Zeus inspire him with a "heaven-sent thought." "Something godlike came to me."

Athena's olive tree and Dionysus' powerful infusions become instrumental in Odysseus' strategy for escape. The truth is realized a bit too late, since two of Odysseus' men have already been sacrificed to the giant's bestial tastes, and Odysseus is now bent on revenge as well as survival, eager to exact a wild justice for the unholy crime. The climate in Euripides' play has become markedly different from the resourceful ruses for getting out alive in Homer's narrative. Euripides' scenario pitches and tosses in a sea of violence and revenge like the climate of traditional tragedies.

But this is a satyr play, not a horror show. Odysseus' heroic struggle is accompanied by voices from the chorus often sounding lively and undaunted. Silenus, also, bibulous and unsteady of purpose at times, can attract Polyphemus' attention and distract him at strategic points. The young satyrs chant their refrains, seeming blithely unaware of the predicament while nevertheless commenting on it. In Euripides' melodious verse we hear them caroling their startling chorales. They avoid *pain,* thereby defying the fundamental current of tragedy proper. They shrink comically from helping Odysseus wield the fatal olive limb: "Somehow or other I've just sprained my ankle just standing here." "The wind just blew a huge handful of dust into my eye. Oh, shoot! Or maybe it was soot." They might be capable of offering a song, a magic charm to make that heavy olive limb lift itself unaided. Timid, frivolous, too sensitive, they are somehow fun to have around. Silenus himself is a congenial character to meet. He is vivacious and helpful, willing to deal with the threat of impending doom. He can come up with a good line of talk when the pressure is on. These devotees of Dionysus create the feeling that rescue is not out of the question. They adorn the scene and outclass the creature who fails to see (!) that nature and humankind are animated by the spirit of the divine.

Shelley's (1802) translation of the *Cyclops* employs firmly fashioned blank verse for the dialogue and narrative content. The choral passages are cadenced in bell-like rhymed stanzas. Arthur Way's solution (1924) was to translate the entire text in rhymed verse, a bit of wizardry marred only by lapsing occasionally into Glaswegian dialect. David Kovacs' 1994 version is in clear and compelling prose, ably reinforced by an interesting and informative introductory discussion of the play and its setting. Richard Seaford's 1984 edition of the Greek text offers an invaluable scholarly introduction to the play and its problems.

My verse translation is based on an iambic pentameter rhythm, with a variation of line lengths in units of two and three measures. For the choruses I follow Shelley's lead in turning to rhyme and stanza patterns. I have taken broad liberties with Euripides' fifth-century diction—while adhering as closely as possible to the meaning of the text—in favor of modern usage and contemporary speech. My main aim in making this new verse translation has been to reintroduce the energetic style and sharp-edged wit of Euripides' buoyant satyr play.

Cast

SILENUS, elderly satyr, formerly the attendant of Bacchus, now
  enslaved as the servant of Cyclops
CYCLOPS, the one-eyed giant Polyphemus
ODYSSEUS, famous Greek warrior-hero, king of Ithaca
CHORUS OF SATYRS, young companions of Silenus
NONSPEAKING
  Men of Odysseus' crew

(In front of the Cyclops' cave at the foot of Mt. Etna in Sicily)

SILENUS

  Ho, Bromio! Oh, my aching Bacchus!
  It's your fault I'm working now,
  in my old age, just as hard as I
  had to when I was . . . well, jung
  and easily freudened. Remember: I stood
  right by you when you were made mad
  by Hera and forced to run off and leave
  the mountain nymphs' sheltering arms.
  Or recall how I stood strong beside you,
  shouldering the battle fury, your right-   10
  hand-man against the Earthborn men.
  And how I brought down Enceladus,
  winged him in the center of his omphalos
  with a toss of my spear, a loss to his boss
  and to himself. This is not a dream,
  is it? No, by Zeus! I remember now:
  I showed the victor's spoils, stripped
  from the stricken general, to Bacchus.
  Teach those Earthbornies to attack us!
  But see me in this mess,   20
  cast up in such distress

on the slopes of Ole Etna.
Just because I set sail
in an effort to prevail
over the Tyrrhenian pirates.
Helped by Hera's guile,
they stole you into exile.
And I, with all my might,
and some troops, took flight,
in pursuit of your rescue   30
on our tiller-wielding quest to
slice through froth and foam,
to bring you home, master,
me at the helm. But disaster,
in the form of furious east winds,
drove us out of our path and our minds
near Cape Malea, dashing us
and our hopes, crashing us
into these rocks right here under good Ole Etna,
among these lonely caverns and dismal dens   40
where the children of the Ocean's good ole god,
Poseidon, dwell. They cause him such embarrassment
at having sired this foul form of harassment,
a gang of Cyclopean cannibals, he grows hoarse,
frothing, foaming at the mouth, fuming with remorse.

We were seized and made his slaves by one of these,
the famously feasting cannibal Polyphemus,
infamous brute . . . but at least we weren't eaten,
just beaten into submission and set on our mission
of feeding his flocks of sheep and goats: a far cry   50
from our custom of cavorting over rocks and rills
in ecstatic honor of Bacchus.
My young band of satyrs, along with their helpers
and sidekicks, take charge of the ungodly Cyclops'
four-footed charges browsing out there on the rim

of these cliffs.
And my job? Fill the troughs here, clean the cave,
serve dinner to this nauseating sinner, gulping
down humans for his horrible hors d'oeuvres.
Time now to scrape the floor with this rake   60
I've got in my hand, make sure my boss,
when he comes back, as well as his flocks,
find a nice clean cannibal's cave awaiting them.

Now I see my young lads and their helpers
coaxing their head-bobbing herds in this direction.
What's up, boys? The fancy tapping rhythm
of your prancing feet sounds like the same sort of beat
you used to hit when you circled Althaea's home
in Bacchus' train, at the touch of the harp's bright strings.
*(The Chorus of young satyrs and their helpers enter driving an assorted
flock of sheep and goats.)*

LEADER OF THE CHORUS
    Breed of noble parents,   70
    why drift away from me
    and make for the rocks?
    Here there's a softening breeze
    and fresh water from the brook
    near the cave, cascading down
    into the drinking trough.
    And your kiddies are baa for you.
    Psst . . . come munch over here,
    on the crunchy moist grass,
    and don't make me throw stones   80
    at you; as for you, old ram: I'll ram
    you one if you don't head this way;
    I'll slam you into the fold
    of your hungry head-shepherd,
    one ferocious Cyclops.

Let loose your bursting bags, open up those bulging teats
to your thirsty kiddies, left alone and pent up all day long.
It's high time you said goodbye to the succulent slopes
of Etna in favor of the sucklings waiting at home for you.
Here we hold no revels   90
in honor of Bromius.
No dancing, no whirling lines
of Bacchantes arching their backs
for Bacchus. No throbbing drums,
no wine gushing and sparkling at its source.
Here I am not found joining in
with the nymphs of Nysa
to chant in song, "Oh Bacchus,
Come back to us!" Nor am I
voicing in song a hymn to the queen of love,   100
Aphrodite, while I race across the grass
in fair pursuit of her, and in the company
of the fair-footed Bacchantes.
Ah Bacchus, you lack us! For where
are you now, oh my friend,
with your long golden locks streaming
as you roam alone and unseen?
While I your humble servant,
kow-tow to a one-eyed Cyclops,
as his slave, now a wandering stranger   110
flimsily clad in a tattered goatskin,
severed from you and your love.

SILENUS
Quiet! And tell the lads to rush the flock
in under the shelter of the cavern's rocky roof.

CHORUS LEADER *(to herders)*
Off with you; get them under cover. But, father,
Why this sudden hurry?

SILENUS

    I see a Greek ship down there
    bobbing at the shore. And the men
    are climbing up this way toward the cave . . .
(Odysseus appears, with his crew, carrying baskets for food supplies and
jars for water.)

ODYSSEUS

    Tell us, friends, is there a spring nearby   120
    where we can draw water to quench our thirst?
    Is there someone about who's willing to sell
    food to sailors in dire need? We're starved.
(pauses)
    Well . . . look here, won't you?
    We appear to have stumbled across a city
    dedicated to Bacchus. I see a band of his satyrs
    over there by the cave. Let me speak to the old one:
    Hello, and hail to Bacchus' back-up, there, in the backdrop.

SILENUS

    And hail to . . . but who are you? Your name, please,
    and your native land, of course.   130

ODYSSEUS

    Mi chiamo
    Odysseus of Ithaca, King of Cephallenia.

SILENUS

    You're *him*? The one they call the Talker, sharpest
    and slyest of the sons of Sisyphus?

ODYSSEUS

    Don't hiss at me so insultingly: I'm simply myself.

SILENUS

    Where have you come from, sailing to Sicily?

ODYSSEUS

>I beseech you, squelch the sibilants. I took off
>originally from Ilium and the troubles at Troy.

SILENUS

>But why this route? You knew your own way home.

ODYSSEUS

>Storm winds wafted me here against my will.   140

SILENUS

>For the lava volcanos! This is exactly the fix
>I'm in!

ODYSSEUS

>You too were wafted here against your will?

SILENUS

>Just as I was chasing the pirates who had kidnapped
>Our lord and master, Bromius.

ODYSSEUS

>But who owns this land? Who lives here?

SILENUS

>This is Etna, Sicily's highest mountain.

ODYSSEUS

>But where are the city walls and battlements?

SILENUS

>Nowhere, that's where: you won't find any men here.

ODYSSEUS

>But who owns the land, some nature preserve?

SILENUS

    The Cyclopses (doesn't sound quite right in the plural):   150
    They use these caves, not houses, for their shelter.

ODYSSEUS

    Who obeys whom? What's the political structure? Democracy?

SILENUS

    Hardly. Nobody's in charge. They're nomads roaming
    Around on their own. Nobody obeys nobody WHATSOEVER.
(From this remark Odysseus gets an idea he will make use of later.)

ODYSSEUS

    They grow grain, then, and reap it by Demeter?

SILENUS

    NO: they live on milk and cheese, and lamb chops
    and the occasional . . .

ODYSSEUS

                    drink, a taste of Old Bromius.
    Fresh from the vine?

SILENUS

                 Not a drop. I tell you, boy,
    There's not a drop of joy living here in this land.

ODYSSEUS

    They respect strangers and offer them a warm welcome?   160

SILENUS

    Strangers, they say, are their daintiest dish.

ODYSSEUS

    They enjoy killing men and gobbling them down?

SILENUS

    Nobody's ever docked here without being cooked.

ODYSSEUS

    Where's Cyclops now? In his house?

SILENUS

    No, he's out with his dogs
    Hunting wild animals, 'way up on Ole Etna.

ODYSSEUS

    Do you have some idea of what we can do
    To get out of here?

SILENUS

                Not a clue, but I'll do
    anything I can to help you out.

ODYSSEUS

                     Well, sell us some food,
    we're in need.

SILENUS

            As I said we only have meat . . .   170

ODYSSEUS

    which will stave off the pangs . . .

SILENUS

                   and cheese, well curdled
    with fig juice: and buckets of cow's milk.

ODYSSEUS

    Bring it out: the buyer should see the goods.

SILENUS
And how much gold are you giving in exchange?

ODYSSEUS
No gold: I'm offering the drink of Dionysus.

SILENUS
What words you speak! I've been waiting to hear them.

ODYSSEUS
And this shipment comes from Maron, Bacchus' own son.

SILENUS
Not the little Maron I once held in these very arms?

ODYSSEUS
It's Bacchus' best, and from his own best boy.

SILENUS
Down at the ship, I suppose; you don't happen to . . .   180

ODYSSEUS *(showing Silenus a corner of a goatskin bag)*
Look at this little container.

SILENUS
                              Oh, hemlock—there's hardly
enough in there to wet a man's whistle.

ODYSSEUS *(showing him the whole wineskin)*
Look again:
Twice as much in there as you can take.

SILENUS
Way to go: down, drowning in drink.

ODYSSEUS
A taste: straight from the goatskin's mouth?

SILENUS
  Good thought: may put me in the mood for more.

ODYSSEUS
  And look: here's a cup dangling from the wineskin.

SILENUS
  Just let it flow; it just may revive my memory.

ODYSSEUS *(pours)*
  Have some.   190

SILENUS *(sniffing)*
  What an aroma!

ODYSSEUS
                You caught a glimpse?

SILENUS
  No: a whiff.

ODYSSEUS
              Go right ahead: take a taste;
  don't just *say* you like it.

SILENUS *(drinks)*
  Lord, Bacchus is inspiring me
  to kick up my heels and dance.

ODYSSEUS
  Wet your whistle exquisitely?

SILENUS
                          Sure went down,
  right down to my fingertips.

ODYSSEUS

                              Then, of course, you know
I'm planning to pay for the provisions you're offering.

SILENUS

Never mind money; just let that flask loose.

ODYSSEUS

Trot out the lambs and the cheese.

SILENUS

                              I'll do it, and no thought   200
taken of my master. One draught of that drink will see me
go wild and offer in exchange, all the flocks of all
The Cyclopses; then I'd fling myself into the sea
from Lover's Leap after I'm good and drunk and have unfurled
my wrinkled brow. If a man doesn't start feeling happy
when he's drinking, be must be crazy. When you're good
              and drunk
your member will rise to the occasion, you can put your best
hand forward to practice the breast stroke; and you can toy
with the teasing tangles of Neaera's well-kempt tresses.
You dance all your troubles away. So what's keeping me   210
from paying up for my share of this powerful potion?
Here's mud in the middle of your eye, you muddleheaded
              Cyclops.
(*Silenus exits into the cave. The leader of the satyrs speaks.*)

CHORUS LEADER

Listen, Odysseus: we'd like some words with you.

ODYSSEUS

Speak up: we're meeting here as friends.

CHORUS LEADER

Did you really, actually take Troy,
and take back the fabulous Helen?

ODYSSEUS
>Not only that: we des-troyed Priam and his clan.

LEADER
>But back to Helen: did each and every one of you
>Take her, and I mean *take*, and take turns having her?
>I mean, she's got a mean reputation. Just look at what a look   220
>at a man wearing fancy pants and a golden chain
>did to get her heartbeat pounding! Up to the point
>where she up and left her fine little husband,
>Menelaus!
>>Aren't women the living end?
>They never should have been born into this world,
>under any circumstances, except those especially reserved
>for me!

(Silenus returns from the cave, bringing provisions.)

SILENUS
>>Here you are, folks, food for feasting.
>The young lambs of the baaing sheep are bowing down
>to king Odysseus, offering curdled cheeses, and plenty of them.
>Take off, then, and take them off with you,   230
>as soon as you trade me a draught of the joyful juice.

CHORUS LEADER
>Ow! Here comes the Cyclops. What can we do?

ODYSSEUS *(to Silenus)*
>I'll have to ask you, old fellow: where
>can we run? Looks like we're undone.

SILENUS
>Go into the cave and hide somewhere in the rock.

ODYSSEUS
>Risky advice that, running right into his net.

SILENUS

> It's not so dangerous: There are many ways in and out
> through those rocky apertures.

ODYSSEUS

> Aperture, capture me? Oh, no! If I run away
> from a single man, I who fought off *ranks*   240
> of Phrygians, kept them at bay with my shield—all Troy
> will shudder and moan. No. No. If we do have to die,
> then let us die a distinguished death; and then,
> if we survive, our great reputation lives on.
> *(Silenus steps back into the cave as the Cyclops lumbers into view. He*
> *does not notice Odysseus and his crew at first,*
> *but turns on the satyrs angrily.)*

CYCLOPS

> Let's have some light here: brandish the torch!
> And just zackly
> What's all this goofing off going on? Prancing, dancing!
> Breaking your backs for Bacchus! There's no Dionysus
> fancying up these premises: no sounding brass,
> no tinkling cymbals, no pulse of throbbing drums.   250
> And my new lambs in the cave: at the spigot, are they,
> nuzzling their maas? Our quota of good goat's milk
> oozed out in the osier baskets, squeezed out for cheese?
> Answer up: it doesn't behoove you to be gazing down
> at your hooves, I mean shoes, whatever . . . Look up!
> And speak up, or one of you'll soon be awash with tears,
> and trembling under the battering blows from my club.

CHORUS LEADER

> Ah, so! I mean, see; looky here at me bending backward,
> scanning the sky. Things are looking up—I can see all the way
> to Zeus; stare at the stars; focus my eye on Orion.   260

CYCLOPS
> I was wondering . . . is breakfast ready?

CHORUS LEADER
> Laid on; clear your throat.

CYCLOPS
> Bowls brimming with milk?

CHORUS LEADER
>   You can drain a whole barrelful,
> if you so desire.

CYCLOPS
>   That would be sheep's milk, or cow's,
> or maybe a mixture of both?

CHORUS LEADER
>   Whatever proportions you prefer
> for your potions. Just don't gulp *me* down along with it.

CYCLOPS
> Nope, you dope; you'd be kicking up your heels
> or hooves . . . whatever, in my gut and murdering me.
> *(Cyclops sees Odysseus and company.)*
> What's this bunch standing so aloof
> over there by the sheep pens? Has a band of pirates   270
> or a gang of den-robbers washed up on our shores?
> *(Silenus enters from the cave, bruised and bandaged up as if from*
>   *a beating.)*
> . . . and I see
> my lambs tied up with twists of withies, and there,
> some cheese presses lying around empty, and here's Silenus,
> Old Baldy, with his head bulging with bruises.

SILENUS
> Lordy, lordy,
> the trouble I've seen! Witness my splitting
> headache; I've just been pounded to pieces.

CYCLOPS
> Who by? Who's been bashing your dome, bonehead?

SILENUS
> This gang right here: I wouldn't let them loot you, I wouldn't.   280

CYCLOPS
> But didn't they know that I was a god, and born of a god?

SILENUS
> I told them that, but they kept right on doing
> your undoing, sampling your cheese, tying up lambs
> to tow away. They threatened to lash you to a frame
> of gigantic stocks: rip out your guts at the navel;
> and slice your back in strips with a flicking whip.
> Then, they said, they'd tie you hand and foot
> and stow you in their ship's bottom: sell you off
> to some building contractor as an upheaver of stones;
> or perhaps they'd plan to put you to work in a mill,   290
> grinding around and around.

CYCLOPS
>   So that's what they said, is it?
> Well, hone my cleavers; build up a good big fire and light it.
> They'll all be dying NOW . . . THEY'LL FILL MY
>   GAPING YAP—
> as I draw them hot from the blazing coals. Don't wait
> for carvers to slice the meat either, just toss big pieces
> into the simmering pot and let them stew in their juice.
> By now I've had enough forest-ranging food as fare

to last me a good long time, gorging on gorgeous
feasts of lions and tempting tidbits of ibex.
My next menu must feature the missing taste of human flesh.   300

SILENUS

Yes, mister master mouth. A welcome change, too,
from the same fare day after day. So few wayfarers
have landed on the shore below our cave recently.

ODYSSEUS

Sir Cyclops, may I ask, on behalf of the new arrivals,
a chance to speak? Coming up from our ship we were only
approaching this cave, perfectly willing to pay
for our provender. And then, in exchange for some wine,
just a slug or two for himself, he sold
the lambs to us and trussed them up. It was all
free market negotiation, nobody beat anybody   310
to bits. He made up that story when he got caught
in the act of selling your goods behind your back.

SILENUS

I did? Why don't you go to hell?

ODYSSEUS

                                                  I'm more than willing
to go if I'm telling a lie right now.

SILENUS

                                          O master, sir Cyclops
of the all-seeing eye, I swear by your father Poseidon,
by those stalwarts, Triton and Nereus, by fair Calypso,
by the waves themselves, both their troughs and their crests,
by the shuls—or is it shoals?—of fin-flaunting fish . . .
Well, better let me take that oath again, good lord
and master, clever big Cyclopsie Popsie, I'm not one   320
to sell your goods to strangers; before I'd do that
I'd let the young lads of mine go to wrack and ruin.

CHORUS LEADER
> Ruin yourself, that's what you're doing! I saw you
> with my own eyes selling these goods to our visitors.
> If I'm lying, let my father burn to a crisp,
> but don't visit ruin on our visitors.

CYCLOPS
> *You* can't be saying
> the sooth: it's *him* I trust for the truth. He must
> be a juster justice than Rhadamanthus. I do have, though,
> a few questions to ask these characters, like: where is it
> you're sailing from, and what is your native land?   330
> What city were you brought up in?

ODYSSEUS
> We were born Ithacans—
> and the winds blew us 'way off course: We were on our way
> home after toppling the topless towers of Troy.

CYCLOPS
> You mean, you're the ones who called in at old Ilium,
> beside the Scamander, hoping to grab back Helen,
> the wench who'd eloped with the interloper?

ODYSSEUS
> That's us, all right.
> And I'm here to tell you: it was one big heap of work,
> landing her.

CYCLOPS
> A shameful piece of strategy on your part,
> sailing away to Phrygia's land, just to get your hands
> on one eluctable woman.

ODYSSEUS
> Or maybe . . . deductible . . .   340
> if you chalk it up to the gods and don't blame men.

But do let me beg of you, O distinguished offspring
of the First Sea Lord, speaking now as free man,
we implore: don't kill your friends just because they've stumbled
on your cave; don't look on us as food to scarf right down
in your jaws. For surely that would constitute a feast
of sacrilegious dimensions. You must realize:
It is we who kept your father Poseidon securely placed
in his temples throughout his retreats in all Greece.
We've kept his havens clear of ungodly pirates   350
on Taenarus' serene shore. His holy shrine
on Malea's heights is safe. And the precious vein
of silver on Sunium's rocky eminence still stands
untouched, Athena's own precinct. We kept intact
his harbor refuge at Geraestos, for we shrank in horror
at the thought of the dire disgrace to the land of Hellas
it would meet at the hands of Phrygians. You too have a share
in these harvests: right here at the base of old Etna,
beneath the mountain's fire-emblazoned crater,
you have your dwelling. It is the usual procedure   360
among all fellow-mortals—ah, but now I see clearly
that you don't want me to pursue this line of argument—
Still: let me press the point that among the human nations
the customary practice is to welcome castaways,
give them better clothes than those they washed up in,
and offer hospitality: NOT for these defenseless derelicts
to be transformed into food to fill your bellying gut
and jaws, to be barbarously roasted on oxen spits.
Consider: Priam's land has already drunk the blood
of myriads, skewered with the spear and so depriving   370
Hellas of its own. It has widowed wives
and stolen away the sons of gray-haired fathers,
left mothers alone and forlorn. If you now roast
and gobble down the few survivors, a meal
that will return to take revenge on you,
where can we hope to find justice, good sir Cyclops?
Let us reason together, sir Cyclops: why not suppress

your famous appetite and choose piety
over a satiety of evil?
Euripides makes this plain   380
when he says:
"Ill-gotten gains, for many, change to pains."

SILENUS

  I advise you, Cy: Eat this man's meat complete.
  Don't leave a scrap behind. And gobble right down
  his long curly tongue, if you'd like to be
  as smart as he is at the art of conjuring up
  persuasive speech and the quick and clever riposte.

CYCLOPS

  Wealth, manikin, is the one and only god
  wise people worship. So why have you advanced
  your fine argument? Never mind the promontories   390
  where my father takes up residence. As for Zeus himself,
  I don't tremble at his thunder. I can't see, stranger,
  that Zeus is all that much more powerful a deity
  than I myself am. When it all adds up, if he rains
  down from above, I'm perfectly cozy, tucked away
  in my cavern in the rocks, having my dinner
  of fresh veal cutlets, or perhaps some venison,
  and filling my the well of my belly with lavish ladlings
  from my tub of milk. When he thunders I easily match him
  with my eructations from this resounding echo chamber.   400
  If winter wind howls down from northern Thrace,
  driving the snow before it, I warm my body
  in animal skins and light a roaring fire.
  Why should I care about snow? Of course, it's the earth's *duty*—
  and she has no choice—to produce the good green grass
  that fattens up my flock. I don't sacrifice
  my animals to anyone but myself, their one
  and only god, myself with my big belly,
  not to those other gods. In the wise man's view,

the god of gods is this: to eat and drink   410
your fill from day to day without remorse.
But politicians, who map out bewildering laws,
are worth nothing at all: messing up men's lives
by making them nervous. So, I won't keep
myself from doing me a good turn by consuming you.
But let me extend to you the stranger's gift—
and thereby clear myself of any blame—
I'm offering a good, hot fire: the cauldron over there
will be a-bubble with salt water well supplied
from my father's own element; it will be ready to boil   420
your chops and choice cuts in a savory stew.
So straggle on inside and form a circle
around the altar that makes me feel at home in
the temple of my god, my huge abdomen.

(He motions Odysseus' men and Silenus into the cave following them in,
with Odysseus bringing up the rear.)

ODYSSEUS
Whoa! Woe is me! I survived perils at sea
and the hard going at Troy, and now I've wrecked
my ship on this senseless beast's headland,
this godless moron with a whim of iron. Oh, Athena,
Heaven's queen, please come to my rescue; help me
now in these present troubles, so very much worse   430
than my heavy trials at Troy. And you too, Zeus,
the god protector of strangers, will you in your dwelling
among the starry ranks above look down and see
the fix I'm in? For if you don't regard ˙
my troubled state, surely you cannot be
yourself as Zeus, the god of gods: you must be nothing.

(Odysseus follows the others into the cave.)

CHORUS LEADER
Open wide your yawning maw, Cyclops
and give fangs for a dinner fresh off the fire:
strangers' limbs, all you could ever desire.

Boiled? Grilled? Both?   440
Don't be loath to tear right into your meal:
rip the flesh and chew it into big bite sizes,
at ease on your shaggy goatskin coat.
And don't leave off eating for my sake;
it's your boat you're in, so row it
right on all alone.
This is some cave! It should excavate itself
until empty!
And these are some burnt offerings
Cyclops is proffering on the altars   450
of Ole Mount Etna, while splurging his joy
in gorging on the flesh of perfect strangers.

What a rogue and monstrous beast!
To sacrifice his own house guests
at his own hearth and home,
visitors at his mercy in his own surroundings.
Astounding! Devastating, nauseating,
to sink his own stinking teeth
in the flesh of humans,
consuming crisp chunks   460
of torn and sliced hunks, hot off the fire.
(*Odysseus returns from the cave, horrified.*)

ODYSSEUS

O Zeus, what can I say
after the sights I have seen
inside that cavern?
Things that defy belief,
more like the fantasy tales
people peddle than anything they do.

CHORUS LEADER

What news are you bringing us, Odysseus?
Has the bestial Cyclops been feasting
on your good companions?   470

ODYSSEUS
> That he has been. Picked out a particular pair
> whose flesh was firm, filled out, and well toned,
> and held them in his hands to weigh and size up.

CHORUS LEADER
> And you, poor fellow, how did it go with you?

ODYSSEUS
> After we'd gone into his rockbound retreat
> over there, he got a huge fire going well
> on his ample hearth, piling on stacks of oaks
> from lofty trees, enough to make three wagonloads.
> Then he laid out his pine-bough couch alongside
> the hearth. When he'd milked his cows, he poured the juice   480
> into a five-gallon bowl. At his side he had a container
> fashioned of ivy wood, vast and deep. After that,
> he got his bronze pot boiling on the fire,
> and laid some spits beside him on the ground.
> They were cut from hawthorn branches, the points
> being well hardened in the fire, the shafts well trimmed
> by the ax. Then he set out a row of bowls
> to catch the blood as it spurted from the cuts.
> So then this chef de résistance had his utensils
> all ready, and he snatched up two members of my crew   490
> and cut the throat of one, right above the open mouth
> of the boiling bronze pot; he grabbed the other
> by his Achilles tendon and slammed him up against
> the sharp edge of a projecting rock, bashing in
> his brains. His eager cleaver beavered out the flesh
> in strips, to be laid out on the grill: the limbs
> he threw into a huge kettle to seethe and steam.
> I was weeping, and came up close to help—
> but the others, like frightened birds, cringed in crannies
> among the rocks, pale from their lack of blood.   500

Soon after, when this glutton had stuffed himself
full of my good companions' flesh, and stretched out
flat on his back, snorting and rumbling, an idea
came suddenly into my head. I filled a cup
with our Maronian wine and offered a taste of it
to Old Psychlo. "Psychlo, old boy," I said,
"headstrong son of Poseidon, see how this drink,
so ambrosial, stems from the vines of Hellas,
distilled by the young Dionysus, who likes us."
Bloated with his savage meal, he drank it right off,   510
gesturing his gratitude with his left hand, and said:
"O best of my guests, what a truly delicious drink
you've given me to round out this fabulous feast!"
When I saw how pleased he was I offered another
cup of wine, knowing well how totally fuddled
he would become, and the price he would have to pay
for imbibing. As he started singing I plied him
with cup after cup filled to the brim, getting him
well warmed up with wine.
                So now he's in there, singing
'way out of tune, while my good companions are wailing   520
in a minor key, and I've slipped out quietly,
hoping to save myself and all of you if you
want it. You do want, do you,
or do you not, to get out from under the thumb
of this antisocial savage, and resume living
among nubile Naiads in the handsome halls
of the good god, Bacchus? Silenus, in the cave,
says to go ahead with the plan but by now
he's so groggy from sopping up liquor he can't think
straight, or even crooked. The cup has caught him up   530
like a bird's wings stuck with lime in a snare.
He's really confused. But you lads are young, and
strong, so save yourselves, with help
from me, and get back, all of you, into the realm
of Dionysus, so different from the Cyclops' cave.

CHORUS LEADER

Noble friend, would we could see the day
we escape in flight from this godless hulk, the Cyclops!
We've gone a long time without siphoning off any pleasure
from the cask or sampling a gourmet dinner meal.

ODYSSEUS

Well then, hear the plan I've formed to pry you loose   540
from his savage grip and free you from that slavery.

CHORUS LEADER

Yes: tell me how you'll do it. My ears could hear
no sweeter music plucked from the azor than word
of the death of the Cyclops.

ODYSSEUS

He's riding high,
buoyed up by the bouncy joy juice of joyful Bacchus.
He wants to go partying with his fellow Cyclopedians.

CHORUS LEADER

I get it: you plan to grab him all of a sudden,
alone in the gorse, and do him in; or, maybe,
you'll shove him off a cliff.

ODYSSEUS

No, no. My plan
is much more sophisticated.

LEADER

Well, what is it?   550
We've heard, often enough, how subtle you are.

ODYSSEUS

I intend to persuade him *not* to go partying.
I'll say he shouldn't share his drink with comrades,

but keep it for himself and his long happy life.
When he drops off to a sleep influenced by Bacchus
I'll cut a sharp point into the end of an olive limb
I saw in the cave, and set fire to this point.
When I see it's caught the flame and held it steady
I'll lift this glowing torch and ram it down
right in the middle of the Cyclops' circled eye   560
and dissolve his sight into a dew of sizzling steam.
Then, just as you take a double thong to rotate
an auger when you drill a hole in a beam
when fitting out ships' timbers, I'll make the torch
spin in the Cyclops' eye and scorch the socket.

CHORUS LEADER
Oh, joy! I'm thrilled to hear of this invention.

ODYSSEUS
And when that's done I'll take you all aboard
my ship: you and those who want to go with you,
and old Silenus. You'll be stowed away
in the hold of my black ship with its double bank   570
of oars. You will be carried well away from this land.

CHORUS LEADER
And should I lend a hand with the burning brand
that blinds, as if I were making a libation
of the blood I shared in offering to the gods?

ODYSSEUS
Not only should, but *have* to. That greenwood brand
is huge and heavy; I'll need help holding it.

CHORUS LEADER
I'll lift a hundred wagonloads with ease
if it will gouge out this Cyclopedian eye,
as doomed to die as a nest of nasty wasps.

ODYSSEUS

Well, quiet! And now that you know my entire plan,   580
when I call on you be ready to obey
the master planner. I'm hardly the sort of man
to save myself and abandon all my friends
inside the cave. I sneaked out quite neatly
by squeezing through a tunnel in the rock.
But, no! sail off and leave my good companions,
who sailed here with me? Just to save myself
would be an act of most cruel injustice.

SEMICHORUS I

Who volunteers, now, to be the first,
and who seconds the motion,   590
to wrap his hands around
the handle of the brand
and jam it into Cyclops' eye
and so put out the light?

SEMICHORUS II

Tune it down! Here comes the sot
out of his rock-walled plot,
his homeground, yodeling
some off-key mountain music,
modeling himself on some flatfoot circus clown
as he lurches forward into the air   600
where he'll soon find grounds for crying.

SEMICHORUS I

Ah, how happy it is, after all,
to play the Bacchanal
among fountains of wine
pouring from clusters of grapes
newly distilled. How thrilled he is
stretched out at ease, his arm draped around
a good friend. A lovely girl lolls by him

on the couch, his hair shines
with fragrant essence of balsam,   610
as he calls out "Unlock the door of love
for me, you pretty thing: you have the key!"
*(The Cyclops enters, lurching out from the cave in a drunken stagger and
bellowing out a song.)*

CYCLOPS

How "Wein weib and gesangsten" I am, how full
of the finest winest and the bestest of feastest.
My hold is packed full like a merchant freighter's,
right up to the top tier of my stomach.
This grassy deck is teasing me pleasingly
to find some brother Cyclopses and invite
them out to revel. Meanwhile, you devil,
(points to one of the young satyrs)
fetch me that wineskin 'fore I tan your hideskin.   620

SEMICHORUS II

Ah! The lord issues from his mansion
bestowing his soft-focus glance on all.
(chanting)
"Someone loves somebody!"
There is the grasp of an ardent bride
waiting for you, and for your brow
a wreath of flame-colored flowers.
(Odysseus returns with the wineskin flask, followed by Silenus, tottering.)

ODYSSEUS

Listen up, Psychlo. I'm an expert, trained
in the liquid arts of Bacchus you've experienced.

CYCLOPS

Bacchus smack us! Some kind of a god, is he?

ODYSSEUS

The greatest god at giving men true pleasure.   630

CYCLOPS

He sure slurps up a nice burp: I can still taste it.

ODYSSEUS

There's no god quite like him: *he is harmless.*

CYCLOPS

How does a god like living in a wineskin?

ODYSSEUS

Wherever you put him down, he's perfectly happy.

CYCLOPS

Leather wraps don't really suit the gods.

ODYSSEUS

But he gives pleasure: does the leather chafe you?

CYCLOPS

Don't like the wineskin: but the drink has a fine spin.

ODYSSEUS

So . . . stay put, Psychlo; drink and feel happy.

CYCLOPS

Not share it with my Cyclops other chappies?

ODYSSEUS

Keep it to yourself; then you live like a lord.   640

CYCLOPS

If I give it to my friends, I'll be their friend.

ODYSSEUS

But throwing a party could end up in a lot of blows
and name-calling, and punching outs, and fights.

CYCLOPS
> I may be reeling under the impact of drink,
> but I still think nobody has the right
> to take a swing at me.

ODYSSEUS
> Then don't go out on a spree.
> Stay put at home when you're good and tight. Right?

CYCLOPS
> You're well lit up, but you still hesitate
> to go out and celebrate? Ridiculous.   650

ODYSSEUS
> The wise man stays home when soused: meticulous.

CYCLOPS
> And so, Silenus . . . what's to do? You would stay?

SILENUS
> I would. Why let others crash in on our drink?

CYCLOPS
> Not to mention that the grass is soft and bouncy,
> with its spreading clumps of colorful field flowers.

SILENUS *(sits down on the grass)*
> Drinking outside in the sun's caressing warmth
> is awfully nice. So, just let that mighty frame
> of a rib cage of yours go loose on the horizontal.

CYCLOPS *(sinks down to a sitting position)*
> All right, there! But why put the bowl behind me?

SILENUS
> So nobody walking by us can knock it over.   660

CYCLOPS

Oh no! You just want to slip a sip on the sly.
(*turns to Odysseus*)
So tell me, stranger, what name can I use now
to call you by?

ODYSSEUS

"Nobody." N. O. BODY.
And what nice favor have you got stored up for me?

CYCLOPS

After I've eaten up all your companions,
I'll save you for the last thing on the menu.

SILENUS

What an honor for your guest, to be last and best!

CYCLOPS (*turns on Silenus*)

Hey, what's that smooching? Sneaking in a drink?

SILENUS

No, it kissed me, I'm so darned handsome.   670

CYCLOPS

I'll let you feel it if you smack your lips
on it when it's not smacking its on yours.

SILENUS

The wine loves to kiss me, I'm so very pretty.

CYCLOPS

I'll take some, then: a good cupful of wine.

SILENUS (*bends over the bowl*)

I'll just test the balance of the blend.

CYCLOPS
Damn you! Hand it over here right now.

SILENUS
By Zeus, no, not until I see your brow
well crowned with a wreath, and satisfy my thirst first.

CYCLOPS
You nasty kidnapper cupbeareroff!

SILENUS
Not at all: what you ought to be saying, instead,   680
is, "How sweet this wine is!" And don't *nuzzle* it:
Here, let me wipe your schnozz; then you can down
a good clean drink, a decent looking draught.

CYCLOPS *(swipes his hand across his mouth)*
See? The beard, the lips, mustache—all dry.

SILENUS
Now lean back on your elbow sophisticatedly;
drain the cup deep the way you see me doing . . .
or rather, *can't* see me, with my face dipping so deep
into the cup.
(takes a long swig)

CYCLOPS *(sits up again)*
Hey, knock it off, don't knock it back like that!

SILENUS *(wipes his mouth contentedly)*
Ah! That was really A-Number-One in the draft!   690

CYCLOPS *(to Odysseus)*
Here, stranger: you be my wine steward instead of him. Just
                    catch this cup.

ODYSSEUS
> Watch it latch onto me.
> My hand draws out the best flavor it contains.

CYCLOPS
> Well . . . fill me in, then.

ODYSSEUS
> Don't talk, then, or you'll miss out
> on that flavor.

CYCLOPS
> But with such a sweet mouthful
> you have to talk.

ODYSSEUS
> Drain it right off, don't leave a drop. The rule is,
> never give in until the wine gives out.   700

CYCLOPS
> Damned smart piece of wood, that vine, the way
> it shapes the grape.

ODYSSEUS
> Now pour full flagons five
> Down your throat, to quench your belly's thirst,
> and the waves will lull your eyes to a sweet deep sleep.

CYCLOPS *(burying his head in the bowl)*
> Full flagons five my featherbed lies,
> as I come up for air—de bon air—or, the way
> Aeschylus once phrased it fragmentarily:
> "Dropping from his temple heights did Uranus
> bestow his kiss on Earth." And in my mind's eye I see   710
> Zeus ensconced on his throne . . . or is dis Zeus, or is

dis Odysseus? Somehow I can't see straight
and my speech ith slightly jumbled, but I can say
(to Odysseus)
I'm sure not kissing you, Odysseu, not when this
thing here
(points to Silenus)
            can serve as a replacement
for all those fetching Graces, with their beautiful faces,
my mind's eye sees swirling around my head. Instead,
I'll have this chubby chum be my Ganymede.
I actually enjoy the boys more than the girls.

SILENUS *(stunned)*
    You mean I'm meant to be the reproducer   720
    of Ganymede, favorite of Zeus the Seducer?

CYCLOPS *(tucks Silenus underneath his arm)*
    Yep, it's that Ganymede, the kid I nap from Troy.

SILENUS
    Help me, lads! It looks like I'm done for,
    not to mention about to be done to . . . the unmentionable.

LEADER
    Turning your back on your lover, when he's drunk?

SILENUS
    On my knees. Oh this wine is bitter lees!
(Cyclops reels back into the cave, carrying Silenus.)

ODYSSEUS *(to satyrs)*
    Steady now, you sturdy sons of Bacchus!
    Action! The cave man there will soon be drifting
    toward sleep, all the while bringing up great gobbets
    of the fiendish feast he downed. That olive pole   730
    inside the den is vomiting its smoke and flame.

That's why we got it ready, to cauterize his eye
out of sight. So, be steady. Act like men.

CHORUS LEADER
    You'll see my soul is a rock: it won't roll,
    But get on inside that big louse's big house
    before my father meets some unmanageable disaster.
    We're all lined up out here to lend our help,

ODYSSEUS *(prayerfully)*
    Hephaestus, lord of Etna, put out the light
    in your bad neighbor's eye! And do away
    with him for once and all. May Sleep, child   740
    of dark black Night, descend with all its might
    on this beast so detested by the gods.
    Don't let him wreck Odysseus and his crew
    after their heroic victories at Troy
    and make them victims of this inhuman being
    devoid of all respect for men or gods.
    Should that occur, we could only think of Chance
    as the goddess over-ruling the will of heaven
(He re-enters the cave.)

CHORUS *(chanting)*
    The vise will squeeze his throat
    who feasts upon his guests.   750
    This fire will soon digest
    his eyesight.
    The huge limb of the olive tree,
    its tip dipped in the embers,
    is ready for its act of dismembrance.
    So: gather strength, one and all
    to bring about his fall.
    Uproot the frantic Cyclopean's eye
    And make him regret his drinking.

As for me . . . I've been thinking 760
how marvelous it would be
for me to leave this solitary strand,
this godforsaken Cyclopean land,
and trade it for the blissful realm
of Bromius, my ivy-crowned king!
Of this fate will I sing?

ODYSSEUS *(slipping out of the cave)*
Shut your traps, you miserable mutts!
Not a peep more out of you birds. QUIET!
Don't breathe, or wink, don't even clear your throats.
We don't want to wake up the beast, 770
at least, not until the sight
in Cyclops' eye can no longer see the light,
and has expyred.

LEADER
We're still. Hush! Our jaws close only on air.

ODYSSEUS
So, all right, then. File in and wrap your hands
stoutly around the stake with its red hot tip.
That way each one of us will stand an equal chance
at the honor of giving the coup de disgrace.

FIRST SATYR
Not me! I'm much too far from the door, over here.
I'd never reach his eye or apply the fire. 780

SECOND SATYR
I've just now had this bad cramp in my leg.

THIRD SATYR
Hey, me too! Somehow or other I've sprained my ankle
just standing here.

ODYSSEUS

You sprained it standing still?

FOURTH SATYR

The wind just blew a huge handful of dust
into my eye. Oh, shoot! Or maybe it was soot.

ODYSSEUS

You pigeon-livered . . . or maybe you lack the gall
to make oppression bitter . . . you quitters!

LEADER

A solemn thought about my spinal column,
unwillingness to have my teeth smashed out,   790
are forms of cowardice? I do know, though,
a song by Orpheus, an incantation
so absolutely terrific that hearing it
the stake will snap to attention by itself,
stomp over to his skull, and whomp down on
that beast's eyeball and set it all ablaze.

ODYSSEUS

I knew all along what you'd be like when it came
to action, but luckily I brought my crew along,
so I'll use them. That's surely the best thing to do,
and in fact the only help I have to turn to.   800
As for you, if you haven't the nerve; maybe some verve
will serve the purpose if you'll chant a nice chorale
to bolster our morale, and cheer us on
with a burst of battle song.

CHORUS LEADER

To that I say okay. Let some lowdown hit man
from Iraq, or another hard place,
do the dirty work; and as for bolster,
Cyclops' eye can sizzle in its holster.

CHORUS *(chanting)*
    Heave ho, my hearties, and get your backs in it.
    Hustle in and make a true try now;   810
    singe away this man-devourer's eyebrow.
    Scorch him, baste him,
    Mount Etna's shepherd.
    Twirl the baton: paste him—
    socket to him 'round and 'round.
    But watch your crotch:
    he may be so worked up
    he'll grope or even clutch you.

CYCLOPS *(from inside the cave)*
    Omoi! They've put out my bright light,
    turned into solid anthracite.   820

CHORUS LEADER
    For you, that song is odious, Cyclopius,
    but to my ears it's most melodious. Can I hear
    it once again? Encore! I implore you.

CYCLOPS *(from inside)*
    That twist, that pain again!
    You've surely done me in!
    But you won't get away with it,
    or even get away. I'll pen
    you in my den: take my stand
    at the door and keep you in.
*(stumbles forward to the entrance and stretches out his arms on
                    either side)*

CHORUS LEADER
    But Cyclops, why are you howling so loud?   830

CYCLOPS
    I'm done for!

CHORUS LEADER
> You're sure no sight for sore eyes.

CYCLOPS
> I'm such a sad sack!

CHORUS LEADER
> Got drunk, did you and fell down
> right on your face, in the bite of the anthracite?

CYCLOPS
> No, not that. It was Nobody
> done me in.

CHORUS LEADER
> Nobody? Well, you're all right, then,

CYCLOPS
> Nobody is making me blind.

CHORUS LEADER
> Then you can't be all that blind, can you?   840

CYCLOPS
> I'm as blind as you, can't you see?

CHORUS LEADER
> Could you please explain just how nobody
> could even have made you blind?

CYCLOPS
> You're making fun of me. But tell me now,
> where is Nobody?

CHORUS LEADER
> Him? He's Nowhere.

CYCLOPS
>So it can penetrate your brain, I tell you:
>the *stranger* is the one who brought me down.
>That awful offal, he threw me down the brink
>by forcing me to drink.   850

CHORUS LEADER
>Wine is a heavyweight,
>hard to wrestle with.

CYCLOPS
>But tell me: have they all escaped
>or are they still inside?
>*(Odysseus and his men gradually slip out, past the Cyclops.)*

CHORUS LEADER
>They're out here all in a row, keeping quiet and huddling
>against the rockside for protection.

CYCLOPS
>Which side, did you say?

CHORUS LEADER
>Over there, on your right.

CYCLOPS
>Right over there? Where?

CHORUS LEADER
>Flat up against the overhanging rock.   860
>Got 'em?

CYCLOPS *(lunging, bashes his head against the rock)*
>Wow! Ouch! I've gouged a hole in my head
>by banging into this rock.

CHORUS LEADER
And they've gotten out of your grasp?

CYCLOPS
This was the right way, wasn't it? You said
over here to the right. But I can't feel them.

CHORUS LEADER
No, no: that's not the way.

CYCLOPS
Well, what way is it, then?

CHORUS LEADER
The only one left, over there to the left, thataway.

CYCLOPS
You're making fun of me in my dire lemma.   870

CHORUS LEADER
They got away. But Nobody himself is there
standing up in front of you.

CYCLOPS
Where are you, worst creature on earth?

ODYSSEUS
It's odd. I see you don't know my new name
applied to me in view of my odyssey.

CYCLOPS
Say what? You've changed your name for a new one?

ODYSSEUS
Sure, the true one, the one my father gave me.
Thought you'd go unpunished for your sacrilegious

dinner, did you, when you were doomed to pay
the price for sin? A fine hero I'd be   880
to have set fire to Troy and then stand by
and watch my comrades being killed by you.

CYCLOPS

Ai, ai! The old prophetic saying comes to pass
predicting that you would put out my eye
on your way home from Troy.
But there's another part to it:
you'll suffer for having had the heart to do it,
by being tossed about for years and years
on stormy empty seas.

ODYSSEUS

A fig for your forebodings! I've played my role   890
In my part of your prophecy. What's left for me
is to get my ship off the beach and onto the water,
head for Sicilian seas and my fatherland.

CYCLOPS

You won't make it. I'll tear a piece of this rock
loose from the cliff and bash you all to pieces,
you, your ship, and your crew. From the upper ledge,
after I've climbed up through this passage in the rock,
I'll have a launching site,
even without my own sight.

CHORUS LEADER

And us? We'll sail off with Odysseus   900
and spend our lives in service to lord Bacchus,
our good king Dionysus.
(All exit: Cyclops is left behind, stumbling and groping among the rocks.)

Pronouncing Glossary of Names

Stressed syllables are marked. The descriptions below are based primarily on the Oxford Classical Dictionary.

Achaeans (a-kee'-ans). Race of warlike bronze-age people who, with the Ionians, came into Greece from the north in the second millennium B.C. Achaea and Achaeans are often used as synonyms for Greece and the Greeks.

Achelous (a-kel'-oh-us). God of the river of the same name in Epirus.

Achilles (a-kil'-eez). Son of Peleus and Thetis, the best of the Greek warriors at Troy, and hero of the *Iliad*.

Adrastus (a-dras'-tus). King of Argos, one of the Seven against Thebes.

Aeacus (ee'-a-cus). King of the island of Oeopia, where, after a plague destroyed all his subjects, Zeus repopulated the kingdom by turning ants into human beings.

Aegeus (ee-jee'-us). Son of Pandion and king of Athens. Father of Theseus by Aethra.

Aegialeus (eye-jee-al'-ee-us). Son of Adrastus, one of the Seven against Thebes.

Aegisthus (ee-gis'-thus). Son of Thyestes, therefore a cousin of Agamemnon and Menelaus. Clytemnestra's lover.

Aerope (ee'-rop-ay). Mother of Agamemnon and Menelaus, wife of Pleisthenes or in some versions of Atreus. In the latter, committed adultery with her brother-in-law Thyestes. The twins she bore were served to Atreus as food.

Aethra (ee'-thra). Daugher of king Pittheus of Troezen, wife of Aegeus, mother of Theseus.

Aetolia (ee-tol'-i-a). Country in the middle of Greece of which Tydeus was king.

Agamemnon (ag-a-mem'-non). King of Mycenae, husband of Clytemnestra, and brother of Menelaus, king of Sparta. They were sons of Pleisthenes the son of Atreus (or, in some versions, they were themselves sons of Atreus).

Agenor (a-jee′-nor). King of Phoenicia, father of Cadmus.

Ajax (ay′-jaks). Son of Telamon king of Salamis, brother of Teucer. One of the great warriors at Troy.

Alcestis (al-ses′-tis). Wife of Admetus.

Alpheus (al′-fee-us). River in the Peloponnese.

Althaea (al-thee′-a). Mother of Meleager.

Amazons (a′-ma-zonz). Tribe of female warriors. Their name, a-mazon, has been interpreted as meaning "without breasts," and they were said to cut off a breast to improve their aim as archers.

Ammon (am′-on). Chief Egyptian deity, associated with Thebes.

Amphiaraus (am-fee-ar′-i-us). One of the Seven against Thebes.

Amphion (am′-fee-on). Son of Zeus and Antiope; with his brother Zethus founder of Thebes.

Aphrodite (af-ro-dye′tee). Latin Venus. Goddess of love.

Apollo (a-pol′ow). God of music, healing, and prophecy. Son of Zeus and Leto, twin brother of Artemis.

Arachneus (a-rak-nee′-us). Hill in Argolis near Mycenae.

Arcadia (ar-kay′-dee-a). Province in the Peloponnese.

Archelaus (ar-kel-ow′-us). King of Macedonia, patron of Euripides.

Ares (air′-ez). Latin Mars. God of war.

Argo (ar′-go). Jason's ship. His companions on his quest for the Golden Fleece were called the Argonauts.

Argos (ar′-gos). Strictly speaking, an ancient city, the capital of Argolis in the Peloponnese. But all the inhabitants of the Peloponnese, and even all the Greeks, are called Argives.

Aristaeus (a-ris-tay′-us). Son of Apollo and the nymph Cyrene. He married Autonoë; their son was Actaeon the famous hunter.

Artemis (ar′-te-mis). Latin Diana. Virgin goddess of hunting, prophecy, and childbirth. Daughter of Zeus and Leto, elder twin sister of Apollo.

Asclepius (as-klep′-i-us). God of medicine.

Asopus (a-so′-us). River in Thessaly.

Astyanax (as-tee′-a-naks). Young son of Hector and Andromache, killed at the fall of Troy. His name means "defender of the citadel."

Atalanta (a-ta-lan'-ta). Virgin huntress, companion of Artemis. Promised to marry someone who could defeat her in a footrace; mother of Parthenopaeus.

Até (ah'-taye). The personification of moral blindness, daughter of Strife and sister of Lawlessness. She presides over (and can be a designation for) the act of someone, often in a state of Hubris; what follows is Nemesis.

Athena (a-thee'-na). Latin Minerva. Goddess of wisdom and patroness of Athens.

Atlas (at'-las). Titan, son of Iapetus and brother of Prometheus. Traditionally held the world on his shoulders.

Atreus (ay'-tree-us). Son of Pelops, father of Agamemnon and Menelaus, brother of Thyestes, whom he caused to eat the flesh of his own sons. (Or in some versions, he was the father of Pleisthenes and grandfather of Agamemnon and Menelaus.)

Aulis (owl'-is). Port in Boeotia where the Greek fleet gathered. The site of the sacrifice of Iphigenia.

Autonoë (au-ton'-oh-ee). Daughter of Cadmus who married Aristaeus, by whom she had Actaeon.

Axius (ax'-ee-us). River in Macedonia.

Bacchantes (bak-kan'-teez). Also called Bacchae, the priestesses of Bacchus.

Bacchus (bak'-us). God of wine and drinking, son of Zeus and Semele. The Bacchanalia were his festivals.

Bactria (bak'-tree-a). Country of Asia, now part of Iran.

Boeotia (bee-oh'-sha). District in eastern Greece.

Bromius (bro'-mi-us). Name for Dionysus, meaning "the tumultuous one."

Cadmus (kad'-mus). Son of Agenor and sister of Europa. He established the country called Boeotia and founded the city of Thebes, which he populated with men (Spartoi) who sprang from the teeth of a dragon he had killed. He married Harmonia, and introduced the alphabet into Greece.

Calchas (kal'-kus). Soothsayer who accompanied the Greeks, and who told Agamemnon at Aulis that he must sacrifice his daughter Iphigenia.

Callisto (kal-lis'-to). Attendant of Artemis, seduced by Zeus and turned into a bear by Hera.

Calypso (kal-lip'-so). Nymph, daughter of Atlas. Rescued Odysseus when shipwrecked.

Capaneus (ka-pa-nay'-us). One of the Seven against Thebes.

Cassandra (ka-san'-dra). Daughter of Priam and Hecuba who was loved by Apollo. He gave her the gift of clairvoyance, but ruined the gift by wetting her lips with his tongue so that no one would ever believe her predictions.

Castor (kas'-tor). Son of Leda, brother of Pollux. The two are called the Dioscuri.

Cecrops (see'-crops). Legendary founder of Athens.

Centaurs (sen'-taurz). Creatures who were half human and half horse; lived in Thessaly.

Cephallenia (ke-fal-en'-i-a). Island in the Ionian Sea.

Cephalus (ke'-fal-us). Famous hunter, husband of Procris daughter of Erechtheus.

Cephisus (ke'-fis-us). River on the Plain of Athens.

Charon (shar'-on). Ferryman of dead souls across the river Styx to Hades.

Chryseïs (cri-say'-us). Daughter of Chryses. She was taken by Agamemnon as his prize and then, after Apollo visited a plague on the Greeks, was returned to her father.

Chryses (kry'-sees). Priest of Apollo and father of Chryseïs.

Cithaeron (ki-thy'-ron). Mountain in Boeotia sacred to Zeus and the Muses.

Clytemnestra (kly-tem-nes'-tra). Daughter of Leda, sister of Helen, wife of Agamemnon, mistress of Aegisthus, and mother of Iphigenia, Orestes, and Electra.

Cocytus (ko-kee'-tus). River in Hades.

Colchis (kol'-kis). Country of Asia on the Black Sea, the birthplace of Medea.

Corinth (kor'-inth). City of Greece on the Isthmus of Corinth.

Corybantes (kor-i-ban'-teez). Priests of Cybele who were required to mutilate themselves in order to be admitted to the service of the goddess.

Corycus (kor'-i-kus). Mountain in Asia Minor, now called Curco.

Creon (kray'-on). Brother of Jocasta and king of Thebes after the death of Polynices and Eteocles.

Cronus (kro'-nus). Latin Saturn.Titan, son of Heaven (Uranus) and Earth (Gaia). He married his sister Rhea; their children included Demeter, Hades, Hera, Hestia, Poseidon, and Zeus, who overthrew him.

Curetes (kur-ay'-teez). A people of Crete, also called Corybantes, who danced enthusiastically. According to Ovid, they were produced from rain.

Cybele (sib'-e-le). Daughter of Heaven and Earth, wife of Cronus. Her priests were the Corybantes.

Cyclopes (sy-klop'-eez). Race of giants who had one eye in the middle of their foreheads. Polyphemus was chief among them.

Cypris (kip'-ris). Name for Aphrodite.

Cynossema (sin-o-sem'-a). Literally "dog's tomb," Thracian headland where Hecuba was changed to a dog and buried.

Danaus (dan'-a-us). Son of Belus and Anchinoë and co-ruler of Egypt with his brother Aegyptus. He came to the Peloponnese, where either he usurped Gelanor's throne in Argos or, some say, Gelanor resigned the crown to him voluntarily.

Deiphobus (de-i-foh'-bus). Son of Priam and Hecuba. According to later authors, he married Helen after the death of Paris.

Delos (del'-os). One of the Cyclades north of Naxos, island where Leto gave birth to Apollo and Artemis.

Delphi (del'-fye). Town on the southwest side of Mount Parnassus where the Pythia gave oracular messages inspired by Apollo.

Demeter (de-meet'-er). Latin Ceres. Earth-mother goddess of grains and harvests. Her daughter was Persephone.

Diomedes (di-o-meed'-eez). Son of Tydeus, one of the bravest of the Greeks at the Trojan War.

Dionysus (di-o-nee'-sus). Another name for Bacchus. The Dionysia was the wine festival in the god's honor.

Dioscuri (dee-o-skur'-eye). The twins Castor and Pollux. Served as divine messengers.

Dirce (dir'-see). Second wife of Lycus, king of Thebes. He married her after divorcing Antiope. After the divorce, Antiope became pregnant by Zeus, and Dirce, suspecting Lycus was the father, imprisoned and tormented Antiope, who nonetheless escaped and bore Amphion and Zethus on Mount Cithaeron.

Echion (ek'-i-on). One of the men who sprang from the dragon's teeth Cadmus sowed. Father of Pentheus by Agave.

Eido. Name for Theonoe.

Electra (e-lek'-tra). Daughter of Agamemnon and Clytemnestra, sister of Orestes.

Eleusis (e-loo'-sis). City in Attica sacred to Demeter and Persephone. Site of their cult's celebrations.

Enceladus (en-sel'-a-dus). The most powerful of the giants who conspired against Zeus.

Engia (en-gee'-a). Gulf of the Aegean Sea near Sunium.

Epidaurus (e-pi-daw'-us). City in Argolis famous for its shrine to Asclepius.

Erechtheus (e-rek'-thee-us). Son of Pandion and sixth king of Athens.

Eridanus (e-ri-day'-nus). The River Po.

Erinyes (er-in'-yeez). The Furies, the spirits of divine vengeance, who later became the Eumenides.

Eros (air'-os). Latin Cupid. God of love.

Erythrae (e-rith'-ree). Town in Ionia opposite Chios.

Eteocles (e-tee'-o-cleez). Son of Oedipus and Jocasta, brother of Polynices.

Eteoclus (e-tee-oh'-clus). Son of Iphis, one of the Seven against Thebes.

Etna (et'-na). Volcano in Sicily.

Euboea (you-bee'-a). The long island that stretches from the Gulf of Pagasae to Andros, the chief cities of which were Chalcis and Eretria.

Eumenides (you-men'-i-deez). The name for the Erinyes in their benevolent aspect.

Eurotas (eu-roh'-tus). River near Sparta that the Spartans worshiped as a powerful god.

Evadne (ev-ad'-nee). Daughter of Iphis of Argos, wife of Capaneus.

Furies. See Erinyes and Eumenides.

Gaia (guy'-a). Ancient personification of the earth.

Ganymede (gan'-ee-meed). Brother of Priam and cupbearer of Zeus.

Geraestos (ger-eye'-stos). Port in Euboea.

Geryon (ger'-yon). Monster with three bodies and three heads, killed by Heracles.

Glauce (glow'-kay). Wife of Jason after he divorced Medea.

Gorgons. Three monstrous sisters with golden wings and hair entwined with serpents. Medusa, the only mortal one, is the best known.

Graces. Three goddesses, Aglaea (Radiance), Euphrosyne (Joy), and Thalia (Flowering), who dispensed charm, grace, and beauty.

Hades (hay'-deez). Latin Pluto. The world of the dead, or the god who ruled it.

Harmonia (har-mon-ee′-a). Daughter of Ares and Aphrodite, married Cadmus. Sometimes called Hermione.

Hecate (he′-ka-te or hek′-at). Goddess who presided over magic and witchcraft. Often conflated with Persephone and Artemis.

Hector (hek′-tor). Son of Priam and Hecuba, and the chief warrior of Troy. He married Andromache.

Hecuba (hek′-you-ba). Wife of Priam, mother of Hector, Paris, Helenus, Polydorus, Cassandra, Polyxena, and a number of other children.

Helen (hel′-en). Daughter of Leda, sister of Clytemnestra, wife of Menelaus, taken by Paris to Troy.

Helenus (hel′-en-us). Son of Priam and Hecuba, a soothsayer. He married Andromache, widow of his brother Hector.

Helios (heel′-i-os). Sun god, often conflated with Apollo.

Hellas (hel′-as). Name originally applied to a territory and a small tribe in southern Thessaly, it later came to include all Greeks.

Hephaestus (hef-fes′-tus). Latin Vulcan. God of fire and smithing.

Hera (her′-a). Latin Juno. Wife and sister of Zeus, and queen of heaven.

Heracles (her′-a-kleez). Latin Hercules. Son of Zeus by Alcmena. He was tormented by Hera and made to perform many arduous labors.

Hermes (her′-meez). Latin Mercury. Son of Zeus and Maia. He was the messenger god and patron of messengers and merchants.

Hermione (her-my′-o-nee). Daughter of Menelaus and Helen. She was married to Neoptolemus but had no children by him. Eventually she married Orestes and had a son Tisamenus.

Hippolytus (hip-pol′-i-tus). Son of Theseus, with whom his stepmother Phaedra falls in love.

Hippomedon (hip-pom′-e-don). One of the Seven against Thebes.

Hubris (hoo′-bris). Overweening pride.

Hysiae (his′-ee-eye). Town in Boeotia.

Ida (eye′-da). Mountain near Troy; more properly, the whole ridge of mountains that are the source of the Simois, Scamander, Aesopus, and other rivers.

Ilium (il′-i-um) or Ilion. Name for Troy.

Inachus (in′-ak-us). Founder of Argos, father of Io.

Io (eye′-o). Daughter of Inachus. Loved by Zeus and turned by him into a white cow to conceal his adultery from Hera.

Iole (eye′-o-lay). Daughter of king Eurytus who was loved by Heracles.

Iphigenia (if-i-jen-eye'-a). Daughter of Agamemnon and Clytemnestra whom he sacrificed at Aulis.

Iphis (if'-is). King of Argos and adviser to Polynices.

Ismenus (iz-may'-nus). River near Thebes.

Itys (it'-is). Son of Tereus, king of Thrace, and Procne. He was killed by his mother and served up as meat for his father. He was changed into a pheasant, his mother into a swallow, and his father into an owl.

Jason (jay'-son). Captain of the Argo whose life Medea saved and whom he married and then divorced.

Kore (kor'-e). Greek word for "maiden," often used as a name for Persephone.

Laconia. District of southern Greece of which Sparta was the capital.

Laertes (lay-air'-tees). Father of Odysseus.

Lapiths (la'-piths). Tribe of Thessaly who fought the Centaurs.

Leda (lee'-da). Wife of king Tyndareus of Sparta, mother of Helen, Clytemnestra, Castor, and Pollux.

Lemnos (lem'-nos). Island in the Aegean Sea sacred to Hephaestus, now called Stalimine.

Leto (lee'-to). Titaness, daughter of Coeus and Phoebe, loved by Zeus to whom she bore Apollo and Artemis.

Loxias (lok'-see-us). Name for Apollo.

Lydia (lid'-i-a). Kingdom of Asia Minor.

Maenads (mee'-nads). The Bacchantes.

Maia (mye'-a). One of the Pleiades, mother of Hermes by Zeus.

Malea (ma-lee'-a). Promontory of the island of Lesbos.

Maron (ma'-ron). African priest of Apollo.

Medea (me-dee'-a). Daughter of Aeetes king of Colchis, wife of Jason.

Media (mee'-dee-a). Country in Asia north of Persia.

Medusa (me-doo'-sa). Youngest of the three Gorgons, and the only mortal one. Killed by Perseus.

Meleager (mel-ee-ay'-ger). Son of Oeneus and Althaea, brother of Tydeus. His life, the Fates said, would last as long as a burning log. Althaea preserved the log, but when Meleager killed her two brothers she threw it back onto a fire. As soon as it burned, Meleager died.

Menelaus (me-ne-lay'-us). King of Sparta, son of Atreus, brother of Agamemnon, husband of Helen.

Merope (mer'-o-pay). Wife of king Polybus of Corinth and foster mother to Oedipus.

Moirae (moy'-rye). The three Fates, Clotho, Lachesis, and Atropos.

Molossia (mo-los'-i-a). Country which Molossus ruled, famous for its dogs.

Molossus (mo-los'-us). Son of Neoptolemus and Andromache.

Mycenae (my-see'-nee). Town in the Peloponnese where Agamemnon ruled.

Naiads (nye'-ads). Freshwater nymphs.

Nauplia (now'-pli-a). City in the Peloponnese.

Neaera (nee-eye'-ra). Conventional name for a woman of low reputation, a sort of "Bubbles" or "Trixie."

Neoptolemus (nee-op-tol'-e-mus). Also known as Pyrrhus. Son of Achilles, king of Epiru. He claimed Andromache as his prize after the fall of Troy.

Nereus (nee'-re-us). God of the sea who married Doris and with her had fifty daughters called the Nereids, who included Thetis and Psamathe.

Nestor (nes'-tor). Son of Neleus and Chloris, companion of Menelaus.

Niké (nee'-kay). Goddess of victory and therefore of sneakers.

Nysa (nis'-a). Region on the coast of Euboea famous for its vines.

Odysseus (o-dis'-yus). Latin Ulysses. King of Ithaca and one of the Greek heroes of the Trojan war. His domestic situation with faithful Penelope awaiting his return is often contrasted with Agamemnon's difficulties.

Oechalia (ee-kay'-li-a). Region and town in the Peloponnese of which Eurytus was king. It was destroyed by Heracles.

Oecles (ee'-kleez). Father of Amphiaraus.

Oedipus (ed'-i-pus). Son of Laius and Jocasta; husband of Jocasta, father of Antigone, Ismene, Polynices, and Eteocles.

Oenomaus (ee-no-mow'-us). King of Pisa (the area around Olympia), father of Hippodamia, whom he promised to whoever could escape with her in a chariot. Pelops did so by trickery.

Olympus (o-lim'-pus). Mountain of Thessaly so tall that the Greeks believed it touched the heavens; it was therefore the home of the Olympian gods.

Orestes (or-es'-teez). Son of Agamemnon and Clytemnestra, brother of Electra.

Orion (or-eye'-on). In the star myth, a giant hunter who pursued the Pleiades and was in love with Eos (the Dawn). He was slain by Artemis and transformed into the constellation.

Orpheus (or'-fee-us). Son of Apollo and a Muse (some say Calliope), who was so gifted with the lyre that even rivers stopped to listen to him.

Ossa (os'-a). Mountain in Thessaly.

Pallas (pal'-us). Name for Athena.

Pan. God of shepherds and hunters. He had horns and goat feet and invented the syrinx or reed flute.

Pandion (pan-dee'-on). Son of Erichton and king of Athens. He was the father of Philomela, Procne, Erectheus, Butes, and Aegeus.

Paphos (pa'-fos). City in Cyprus where Aphrodite rose from the sea; now Bafo.

Paralus (par-al'-us). Athenian general.

Paris (pair'-is). Son of Priam and Hecuba who abducted Helen from Sparta.

Parthenopaeus (par-then-o-pye'-us). One of the Seven against Thebes.

Pegasus (peg'-a-sus). Winged horse that arose from the blood of Medusa.

Peleus (pee-ly'-us). King of Thessaly who married Thetis. Achilles was their son.

Pelias (pee'-li-as). Son of Poseidon and Tyro and king of Iolcus. He murdered Aeson, his half-brother.

Pelion (pee'-li-on). Mountain in Thessaly.

Peloponnese (pel-o-po-nees'). The large peninsula of southern mainland Greece.

Pelops (pel'-ops). Son of Tantalus, who cut him up and served him to the Phrygian gods.

Pentheus (pen'-thee-us). Son of Echion and Agave, king of Thebes who refused to acknowledge the divinity of Bacchus.

Persephone (per-sef'-o-nee). Latin Proserpine. Daughter of Demeter and queen of Hades.

Perseus (per'-see-us). Son of Zeus and Danaë, ancestor of Heracles. Killed the Gorgon Medusa.

Phaedra (fed'-ra). Daughter of Minos and Pasiphaë of Crete, wife of Theseus, stepmother of Hippolytus.

Phaethon (fay'-e-thon). Son of Apollo and driver of his chariot. Killed by Zeus.

Pharos (fa'-ros). Small island in the bay of Alexandria. It had a lighthouse that was one of the seven wonders of the world.

Pharsalia (far-sayl'-ya). Plain in Thessaly.

Pharsalus (far-sayl'-us). City in the Pharsalian plain.

Phocis (foh'-kis). District of Greece next to Boeotia on the Gulf of Corinth.

Phocus (foh'-kus). Son of Aeacus and Psamanthe, killed by Telamon.

Phoebus (fee'-bus). Name for Apollo.

Phorbas (for'-bas). General of the Athenian cavalry.

Phrygia (fri'-jee-a). Country in Asia Minor in which Troy was the most prominent city.

Phthia (fthy'-a). Birthplace of Achilles in Thessaly near Mt. Othrys.

Pieria (pe-eer'-ya). Part of Thessaly in which there was a spring the Muses frequented. They are therefore sometimes called Pierean.

Pillars of Heracles. Promontories at the east end of the Strait of Gibralter connecting the Atlantic and Mediterranean.

Pittheus (pith'-e-us). King of Troezen in Argolis. Father of Aethra and grandfather of Theseus.

Pleiades (plee'-a-des). Daughters of Atlas, of whom Maia was one.

Plutus (plu'-tus). Son of Ceres and god of riches. He is blind (because indiscriminate) and lame (because he comes slowly and gradually), but he has wings with which to fly away.

Pollux (pol'-ux). Twin brother of Castor, also called Polydeuces. See Dioscuri.

Polydeuces (pol-ee-doo'seez). Alternate name for Pollux.

Polydorus (po-li-dor'-us). Youngest son of Priam and Hecuba, killed by his brother-in-law Polymestor.

Polymestor (po-li-mes'-tor). King of the Thracian peninsula who married Ilione, Priam's eldest daughter, and to whose care Priam and Hecuba entrusted Polydorus and a great treasure.

Polynices (po-lee-nye'-seez). Son of Oedipus and Jocasta, brother of Eteocles.

Polyphemus (po-lee-fee'-mus). Chief of the Cyclopes.

Polyxena (po-lix-ee'-na). Daughter of Priam and Hecuba. After the war she was sacrificed to Achilles' shade in a symbolic marriage.

Pontus (pon'-tus). The Black Sea, and by extension the region around it.

Poseidon (po-sye'-don). Latin Neptune. God of the sea, brother of Demeter, Hades, Hera, Hestia, and Zeus.

Priam (pry'-am). King of Troy.

Proteus (pro'-tee-us). Sea god and king of Egypt, father of Theoclymenus.

Psamathe (sa-ma'-the) (or Psamanthe). Nereid, wife of Proteus, mother of
    Theoclymenus.

Psychlo. Name coined by Palmer Bovie, combination of "Cyclo" (Cyclops)
    and "Psycho." Odysseus was fooling around.

Pylades (pye'-la-dees). Son of Strophius, companion and cousin of Orestes.

Pythia (pith'-i-a). Generic name for the woman who served and spoke for
    the Delphic Oracle.

Rhadamanthus (ra-da-man'-thus). One of the judges in Hades.

Rhea (ree'-a). Titaness, wife of Cronus and mother of Zeus and his brothers
    and sisters.

Salamis (sal'-a-mis). Island in the Saronic Gulf off Eleusis.

Sardis (sar'-dis). Town at the foot of Mount Tmolus, capital of Lydia.

Saronic Gulf. The indentation of the sea opposite the Gulf of Corinth, with
    the Isthmus of Corinth between them.

Scamander (ska-man'-der). River near Troy.

Semele (sem'-e-le). Daughter of Cadmus and Harmonia, and, by Zeus, the
    mother of Bacchus.

Sepias (sep'i-as). Cape in Thessaly.

Sidon (sye'-don). Town in Syria on the Mediterranean coast.

Silenus (si-lee'-nus). Demigod attendant of Bacchus, much given to drink.

Sinis (si'-nis). Son of Poseidon who waylaid travelers at the Isthmus of
    Corinth, killing them by tying them to bent pine trees. He was
    killed by Theseus on his way from Troezen to Athens.

Sirens (sye'-renz). Enchantresses who lived on an island near Scylla and
    Charybdis.

Sisyphus (sis'-i-fus). Sufferer in Hades condemned to roll a huge stone up
    a mountain, a task repeated endlessly.

Skyros (sky'-ros). Island off Euboea.

Sparta (spar'-ta). Greek city-state in the Peloponnese.

Strophius (stro'-fee-us). King of Phocis, brother-in-law of Agamemnon,
    and father of Pylades.

Sunium (soo'-ni-um). High promontory of Attica.

Taenarus (tye'-nar-us). Promontory of Laconia, southernmost point of the
    European continent. Now Matapan.

Tanaus. River in Thessaly.

Tantalus (tan'-ta-lus). King of Phrygia, son of Zeus, father of Pelops and Niobe.

Telamon (tel'-a-mon). King of Salamis and comrade of Heracles, father of Ajax and Teucer.

Teucer (too'-ser). Son of Telamon, half-brother of Ajax.

Thebes (theebz). City in Boeotia.

Themis (them'-is). Daughter of Uranus and Gaia who married Zeus and was the mother of Dike (justice), Irene (peace), Eunomia (good order), the Horae (the hours), and the Moirae (the fates).

Theoclymenus (thee-o-klim'-e-nus). Argive soothsayer, son of Proteus and Psamathe, who predicted the return of Odysseus.

Theonoe (thee-oh'-no-ee). Prophetess, daughter of Proteus and Psamathe, sister of Theoclymenus.

Therapnae (ther-ap'-nee). City in Laconia near Sparta.

Theseus (thee'-see-us). Son of Aegeus and Aethra and king of Athens.

Thessaly (thes'-a-lee). Territory to the north of Greece proper.

Thestia (thes'-ti-a). Town in Aetolia.

Thetis (thee'-tis). Nereid, wife of Peleus, mother of Achilles.

Thrace (thrays). Area encompassing most of the world north of the Black Sea.

Thyestes (thy-es'-teez). Brother of Atreus, father of Aegisthus.

Tiresias (ti-rees'-i-us). Great prophet of Thebes who was turned into a woman and then back to a man. He was blinded by Athena because he caught sight of her bathing.

Tmolus (tmo'-lus). King of Lydia, or the mountain on which he is buried.

Triton (try'-ton). Fish-tailed sea-creature, often portrayed as blowing a conch.

Troezen (tree'-zen). Town in Argolis in the Peloponnese.

Tydeus (tid'-ee-us). One of the Seven against Thebes.

Tyndareus (tin-dar'-i-us). King of Laconia and husband of Leda.

Tyrrhenians (tye-reen'-i-anz). Etruscans, inhabitants of Italy.

Uranus (you'-ra-nus). Ancient personification of the sky, produced by and then consort of Gaia, overcome by his son Cronus.

Zeus (zoos). Latin Jupiter. Son of the Titans Cronus and Rhea, brother of Demeter, Hades, Hera (whom he married), Hestia, and Poseidon. After he overthrew Cronus he became the chief Greek god.

About the Translators

PALMER BOVIE, Professor Emeritus of Classics, Rutgers University, has published many translations of the classics, including works of Virgil, Horace, Cicero, Martial, Plautus, and Lucretius. Educated at the Lawrenceville School and Princeton University, he received his Ph.D. from Columbia University and has taught at Columbia, Princeton, Indiana University, and the American Academy in Rome. With David R. Slavitt, he served as co-editor of the Complete Roman Drama in Translation Series, in which several of his own translations appeared.

RACHEL HADAS is the author of eleven books, *including The Double Legacy, Other Worlds Than This: Translations* (from Latin, French, and modern Greek poetry), the *Starting from Troy*, in addition to many essays and reviews in journals and edited volumes. She has translated into English the poetry of Baudelaire, Seneca, Karyotakis, Rimbaud, Tibullus, Valéry, and Xenos, and published her own poetry in dozens of magazines and journals. She has been awarded the Sharp Family Foundation Award, the Ingram Merrill Foundation Award in Poetry (twice), the Literature Award of the American Academy and Institute of Arts and Letters, and a Guggenheim Fellowship, among other honors. She earned her undergraduate degree in classics from Radcliffe College, her M.A. in poetry from the Johns Hopkins University, and her Ph.D. in comparative literature from Princeton University. Rachel Hadas has taught at Columbia University and at Princeton University and is currently Professor of English at Rutgers University.

RICHARD MOORE is the author of six books of poetry, most recently *The Mouse Whole: An Epic* and *Bottom Is Back*. He has taught at Boston University, Brandeis University, and the New England Conservatory of Music. His poetry has been published in the *American Scholar, Atlantic*

Monthly, Classical Outlook, Georgia Review, Harper's Magazine, New Yorker, Wall Street Journal, and elsewhere, and his essays on a scientific, mathematical, musical, and literary subjects frequently appear in distinguished journals. He has received fellowships from the Bread Loaf Writer's Conference and the Djerassi Foundation. His translation of the *Captivi* of Plautus appeared in the Complete Roman Drama in Translation series.

ELIZABETH SEYDEL MORGAN, a graduate of Hollins College, holds an M.F.A. in creative writing from Virginia Commonwealth University. Her work has appeared in numerous periodicals—including *Poetry, Southern Review, Georgia Review, Iowa Review, Prairie Schooner,* and *Shenandoah*—and in her three books, *Parties, The Governor of Desire,* and *On Long Mountain.* In 1993 her screenplay *Queen Esther* won the Governor's Screenwriting Competition awarded at the Virginia Film Festival in Charlottesville. She studied with Helen Vendler at Harvard University on a National Endowment for the Humanities fellowship.

JOHN FREDERICK NIMS received his M.A. from the University of Notre Dame and his Ph.D. in comparative literature from the University of Chicago. He has taught poetry at Notre Dame, the University of Toronto, the University of Illinois, Harvard University, Williams College, and the University of Florida; for more than ten years he was on the staff of the Bread Loaf Writer's Conference. He is the author of eight books of poetry, among them *The Iron Pastoral, Knowledge of the Evening* (a National Book Award nominee), and *The Kiss: A Jambalaya*—books that have brought him awards from the National Foundation of Arts and Humanities, the American Academy of Arts and Letters, and Brandeis University. In 1982 he was awarded the Fellowship of the American Academy of Poets, and, in 1991, the Aiken Taylor Award for Modern American Poetry. He has been the Phi Beta Kappa poet at the College of William and Mary and at Harvard University. His books of translations include *Sappho to Valéry: Poems in Translation* and *The Poems of St. John of the Cross.*